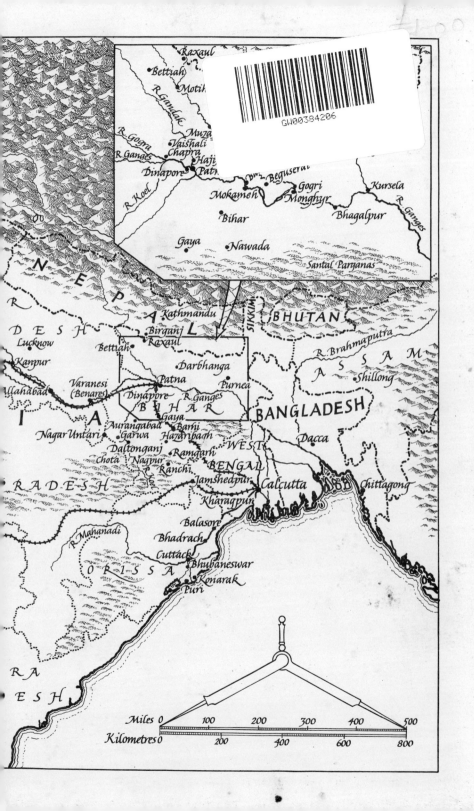

A Perception of India

A Perception of India

Richard Terrell

' . . . there is no clear truth except the present
Which alters as we grasp it, . . . '

CHRISTOPHER FRY
The Dark is Light Enough

Michael Russell

© Richard Terrell 1984

First published in Great Britain 1984
by Michael Russell (Publishing) Ltd
The Chantry, Wilton, Salisbury, Wiltshire

Printed and bound in Great Britain

This book has been published with subsidy
from the Arts Council of Great Britain

Map drawn by Denys R. Baker

*To the many persons in India
without whose kindness, hospitality,
patience and, above all, friendship
the contents of this book could not
have been assembled*

Contents

Acknowledgements

In the dedication and elsewhere in this book I have expressed my indebtedness to the many people who, wittingly or otherwise, have helped me with its contents. For its physical production, however, I want especially to thank the Hon. Mrs Diana and Fred Uhlman of Hampstead, London. When, after my return from India in December 1980, I mentioned to them that perhaps the most elusive requirements of anybody who attempts to write a book are silence and solitude, they at once offered to let me use a delightful little room in their house and a corner of their garden, secluded and sundrenched as it was on many days in spring and summer. For the greater part of the following year I was thus enabled to elaborate this minor perception of the great subcontinent.

Then, when I happened to mention to Mr and Mrs Jock Mackenzie, of Mortlake, that I had little confidence in the stamina of my portable typewriter, they lent me a quite enormous electric machine and arranged for their driver to deliver and install it for me on the other side of London. To them go very special thanks for that kindness. Incidentally, to readers

And there is Jo, my companion in these labours. Her patience with so much talk of a distant land, and her faith in the outcome, require of me far more than words of gratitude can convey.

R. T.

Introduction

My personal images of India somewhat resemble manifestations of Vishnu, the principle in the religion of the Hindus which seems to connote living existence in the interim between creation and dissolution. As in other great spiritual principles of the religion, it is envisaged in particular phases of living. In my own awareness I can distinguish five more or less distinct such images or phases. The first is a hazy awareness of historical origins when the unique and enduring structure of Indian society was formed, the foundations of caste, of the Hindu vision of the universe and of man's place in it, were established. This shadowy image develops into the documented history of India from the Mauryan empire down to the Moghuls and to the beginnings of the British Raj. All this belongs to books, museums, archaeology, temples, mosques, infinitely elaborate mythology, sculpture, paintings and very complex ritual. Its importance lies in the endurance of so much of it in modern India. The persistence of what seems an indestructible society, whatever doom may be predicted for it by the living, is perhaps the dominant feature of India today.

My second image is that of the British Raj, vivid, strong, rigid, Roman, pragmatic, limited in its vision and vast in the scale of its achievement, still unfolding into the India of tomorrow. The time span of the British Raj is long by Western standards but short by Indian ones. It is accepted by Indians as a heritage whose most significant features do not dissolve. The very consciousness of educated Indians, including all those who consider themselves to be revolutionaries, is conditioned by India's association with the British manifestations of the West. There are in India cultural forces that isolate her from the rest of the world, seeking to preserve values whose persistence was conditioned by the topographical isolation of the subcontinent itself. Strong though such forces are, they cannot eternally sustain an identity subject to implacable erosion. The British link remains, I believe, a stronger influence upon India than any internal withdrawal from the wider world.

The remaining images are personal. The third is an awareness of India as it was in my father's decade as Chief Justice of Bihar and Orissa between 1928 and 1938, when he died at the early age of fifty-seven. I was never in India myself during that period, but my notions of it then are suffused throughout by emanations from his strong, dominant personality, from his many letters to my younger self. This third manifestation is more than life-sized.

For the fourth image I did not discover India for myself until the spring of 1943 when, as a young officer in a troopship, I arrived in Bombay with the first of the two divisions of the Royal West African Frontier Force. During some months of training in the Western Ghats near Nasik I saw something of deeply rural Maharashtra. I then experienced wide vistas of the landscape of the Deccan in a very slow train journey across the country to Calcutta. I saw a great deal of the Assam hill tracts and the Arakan during a campaign and, in June 1944, went to Delhi where I worked at a military staff post for about eighteen months. During my last three months in India I had the extraordinary luck of becoming the guest of the princely state of Bhavnager for a short period. Apart from the experience itself, the visit to Kathiawar enabled me to see some of the wonderful landscape of Rajputana, as it was then called. I had several spells of work in Calcutta and, during weeks of leave, was able to visit Simla and Mussoorie and also Murree, now in Pakistan. During the first phase of training in the Western Ghats, I once had a few days of leave in Bombay, and stayed in the city again before returning to Britain in December 1945 for demobilisation.

My fifth and last image belongs to the autumn of 1980 when I spent sixty-eight days in India, most of them in Bihar and Orissa, my father's provinces, now states of the Indian Union. I was only able to visit the country again because the Arts Council of Great Britain provided a grant to meet the cost. The award was made on the strength of a book I wrote about my father,* but the contents of this book are not a sequel to the other. The only connection with the other book is provided by the names of places that I chose to visit in Bihar and Orissa, all of which were

---

* *The Chief Justice: A Portrait from the Raj*, Michael Russell, 1979.

mentioned by my father, either orally or in his letters. The Arts Council is in no way responsible for anything I have written about India, and imposed no conditions whatever upon me, apart from expressing my willingness to accept the award.

This book differs from the writings of journalists, novelists and television men whose adventures have done much in recent years to reawaken Western interest in India. Apart from Delhi, Old and New, and Bombay, Mussoorie and Patna, most of the places I visited were beyond the horizons of virtually all foreign visitors to the subcontinent. I must have been one of the very few foreigners to visit the great plain of Bihar between the Ganges and the Himalayas. In hundreds of miles of travel by road, apart from a party of young Russians in Patna itself, I saw only two other foreigners, two Frenchmen on the staff of the French diplomatic mission in Calcutta who were visiting one of the famous pillars of Ashoka, just north of the Ganges. I saw no foreigners in the hills of Chota Nagpur in south-west Bihar, and none in Orissa.

In talk with Indians, whose kindness to me is unforgettable, I found everywhere great openness of mind. People did not express opinions to me with the reserve of those who fear possible consequences of utterance. I was given forthright answers to sensitive questions, so much so that I often felt that my host was exaggerating. This liberal expression of views or convictions about policy, belief or the trend of events in their own country, though intrinsically of great value, was sometimes problematical, especially when different men, questioned separately, gave me contradictory answers to the same questions – even on seemingly quite concrete issues. If I wanted to know why the electric lights went out as I was about to take a spoonful of soup in total darkness, informants would furnish varied explanations – a go slow, lack of spare parts at the power station, inefficient management, excess of demand over supply or revolutionary zeal of one kind or another, or a mixture of causes whose relative importance could only be surmised.

I was not able to talk with people who knew no English, and this is important in Bihar, where the use of English is more restricted than in most other parts of India. Fluency in English is restricted to certain kinds of people, including senior officers in the armed forces, in the all-union public services, certain academics, the judiciary and at high levels in the private sector of the economy. Educated people are, broadly, of two kinds – those whose education has used English as the means of instruction as well as an object of mastery, and those whose higher education is sometimes known as 'Sanskritised', implying traditional learning in Indian classics, or in the living languages of the various states or regions. Such people, whilst literate, frequently know little or no English, and there is a certain concentration of persons with poor English in the political life of the country, the English speakers holding the strong positions in the unifying public services of the country as a whole. I did meet a few men, usually academics, whose education was both wide and deep enough to comprise both kinds of training. The language difficulty does not affect what I believe to be the truth of my impressions, but it did affect the kinds of truth which concerned me.

Language is of immense importance when we consider the cultural isolation of India in the world, which is very real. For none of her major languages, Hindi, Bengali, Mahratti, Gujarati, Kannada, Tamil, or Malayalam, say, is spoken by more than a few persons outside India. Many significant words, including those expressing belief or indicating ritual, moral and social attitudes, cannot, I believe, be translated accurately into English or any of the world's major languages. Had I been fluent in Hindi, for example, and ignorant of English, my images of India, my whole experience as a visitor, would have been different. Language limits the horizons of Indians and limits those of all visitors to India. There can be no glossing of this.

It was often in the evenings or at weekends that people were able to meet me, invite me to their houses for meals and talk. I was thus often alone in the heat of the day in a hotel in Patna or in a circuit house on tour (the circuit house is a building used by officials or others whilst travelling, in the absence of hotels in most centres). In such spells of solitude I was able to write up my diary, the records of my experience. I avoided all books by non-Indians and managed to read several by Indian writers, both on history and current questions and, in modern literature, novels and a little poetry. English in contemporary Indian writing is used in two ways: either by authors who express themselves directly in English, or by those who write in Indian languages and are later translated into English. A university lecturer in Indian modern literature urged me to concentrate on the work of the latter, for he felt that those who write in Indian languages are more deeply and personally aware of the changing forces in Indian society. I think he dismissed too readily Indian writers who write initially in English. I was much moved by the work of some of them, but appreciate that their authors could not possibly have written about Indian village life so convincingly as those who have written in the language of the village itself.

From this introduction the reader will expect a book about talk, argument and opinion in India. He will find more than that, however, for none of those things could be encountered without travel itself, the sensory experience of an immense landscape, of the people within it and all the happenings of movement.

I

Bombay

I had taken an overnight flight. Now, in the mysteries of dawn, we were flying over the south-western edges of the Persian Gulf. In the rocky, desolate scene there was no sign of life. Ahead of us, stretching far away somewhere to the right, must lie the great form of India. I reflected that, in the distant past, before Islam, Arabs in their dhows had settled along the coast of Malabar far to the south, down to the right of us. This desert below, hundreds of miles of burning barrenness, grit and rock, must have formed a virtually impenetrable land barrier between Arabia and India. Only far, far to the north of it had successive waves of human movement into India been possible. And even there, by the gateway of the Khyber Pass, over many centuries, only small forces of migrants could penetrate India within any period of decades, not because of military opposition but of the difficulties of movement and supply. Perhaps in the centuries of India's history, the most significant geo-cultural factor has been the relative smallness of each successive inward movement, whether by land or sea, in relation to the size of the country and the numbers of people already there. Small additions of new people, whatever power their dynasties might achieve, could not, at any period in recorded history, fundamentally transform the nature of the people, their social structure, ways of belief and living. It seems to me that it is largely for this reason that the Indians are one of the very few great peoples whose world has never turned its back upon its own past, thus presenting an enduring identity to the rest of mankind. In the language of arithmetic, it is as though India knows addition, multiplication but little of subtraction or division.

Sunlight soon intervened, slanting from the east. Blue rippling sea, a mountainous land of upthrusting volcanic rock, red and ochre, long eroded into downward gashes devoid of life – unless a small rectangular shape upon a ledge could perhaps be a village, or a vestige of one. White banks of fleecy clouds swept the sky in huge parallel arcs from west to south-east, dazzling, drifting gently to the north-east, towards India and the sun. I saw a ship heading westwards, loaded with containers, a lifeless modernity, like an empty block of municipal flats at sea, a little curve of surf at the bows.

Soon I was gazing eastwards in expectancy of India – the long line of forested hills, the Western Ghats in which I had lived for months during the war years, but it was long before any trace of them was visible. Land to the north and east could be seen, sandy wastes of an estuary, barren, windswept coastlands, grey waterways separating areas of dark vegetation, flat land of mixed cultivation and hamlets, a few palms, paddy fields, fawn cattle, a power station, gardens, rectangular buildings, factories, lines of hutments, the outer suburbs of a city, roads and telegraph poles, traffic, pylons, embankments above water, colour flashing in sunlight between monsoon clouds, the reds of saris, lighter reds of village roof tiles.

The aircraft circled over Bombay for a long time, waiting for a signal to land, and gradually, in that curving movement, I could recognise repeatedly, the same coastal scenes, rocks, beaches, waterways and buildings. Seen from the air the long flat area of the island of Bombay, its varying, curving stretches of sea and canal, bridges, seems wide and rural, that of the city itself small. Beyond, to the north, stands a great hill, forested, crossed by a road and, to the east and south, a hazy outline of the Ghats.

The airport is not grand, but shabby, brown and makeshift; its earlier buildings were destroyed by fire. The procedures for passengers have much in common with those in banks, railway stations and government offices of most kinds in India. The tasks of officials, clerical or uniformed, are broken down, split into fragments of responsibility smaller than those of such people in the rest of the world, so that one passes slowly from desk to desk, each with its own queue: one man examines a ticket, another looks at currency, another at passports, another considers security – no man can do more than one part of any operation. The primary concern of authority seems to be to provide as many jobs as possible for as many representatives of different castes, faiths, grades as the available funds will allow. They do their jobs, smiling or sullen, but with a deftness of repetition. One emerges at last, patient, chastened, prepared, into the crowd beyond the gates, into sunlight and sweat, the din of cars, awareness of touts, raggedness and small coin.

I was expecting to be met and was delighted when my young Indian friend Ananda stepped forward to greet me, glistening spectacles, thick hair, hand outstretched – taller, heavier than myself. In a moment I was beside him in his car.

I had met Ananda when he was visiting London as the managing director of an Indian publishing company. He was to be my host for a few days in Bombay before I went on to Delhi and elsewhere. He took me into the city and to his flat in a fine block near the Malabar Hill, a promontory at the northern limit of the city. The road from the airport passes through a vast area of poverty occupied by 'scheduled castes', formerly known as untouchables, in shanties of squalor almost inconceivable to a Westerner who has never visited the tropical world. Virtually all tropical cities are fringed by a kind of poverty which, in the colder zones, cannot persist for more than very short spells for climatic reasons alone. The distinction of such poverty in India is that it is conditioned by caste, rooted in the ancient history of the world's most powerful and enduring human arrangement, Hindu society. Here, in a fast-moving car, the stink of excrement and the beauty of children at play, grace and the pain of exhaustion are felt and glimpsed together.

Bombay is one of the few great cities of the world whose skyline of dominant forms is wholly and suddenly presented to the eyes. Other cities conceal a multiplicity of forms, each obscuring the rest in a pattern only to be explored. Bombay shares this quality with Rio de Janeiro and Naples, each embraced by a curving bay, arms of land to support buildings fringed against the sky. As one stands at either end of the long Marine Drive, in turning almost a full circle one's line of vision rises and falls with the crests of distant buildings ranged in a wide immensity of human achievement. This aspect of totality in modern Bombay is most arresting. I felt it to be glorious, as though India were whispering to the Western sea: 'This we have done.'

At the flat I was given a comfortable guest room with an adjoining shower, a glimpse of scarlet flowers beyond, in sunlight shielded by soft curtains. There, after the fall of cool water into hair and skin, a shave, a warm dry towel beneath the turning fan, the change into clean sweatless bush shirt, trousers and sandals, I lay on the bed and fell asleep – just enough sleep for renewal and the hours of discovery to come.

When I awoke it was lunch time. I emerged into a wide, book-lined hallway leading to a lounge where I was introduced to Nita, Ananda's wife, a young girl of marvellous beauty. Her personality had a strength of grooming, of discipline. Her spoken English, whilst fluent, pursued some consonants with a peculiar Indian charm. She would say: 'Are you going to Calcut-ta?', strongly thrusting down the 'u', sounding the first 't' and lilting up the 'a'. Or: 'You must see the tem-ple', with a strong 'm' and a pretty, upturned 'ple'.

Lunch was of curried fish, rice with poppadums, tasty oddments, fruit and squash, all distributed by a bearer with grey hair and a little smile – the smile of one who had known the parents on both sides and approved of the living.

Ananda said that, by a coincidence, I had arrived in Bombay on a very special day, the culminating event in the Ganapati festival. It was essential that I should see the crowds in the streets, and he would take me out to see them later in the afternoon. After lunch I returned to my room for more sleep, and he awoke me again at about four o'clock. In a few minutes we left in his car for the centre of the city.

We parked the car in a side street and walked on through the dense, excited crowds. The air was full of sound, insistent drumming, motor horns, wild music and wilder yells – splashes of colour, red, yellow, green of saris and children's clothes, coloured powder flung in the air, swinging plaits and clinking bangles, hands clapping to different rhythms, sweat streaming down laughing faces. From every street were coming groups in wildly animated processions, each with its own bright new image of the elephant god Ganesh, figure of success, wealth, jollity, with full round stomach, waving trunk and human limbs. The images were large and small, each provided by a group from some part of the town and from outlying suburbs and villages. The models are made of clay or papier mâché, elaborately painted and sit aloft, some accompanied by other figures from the mythical story of the god. Round the images as they moved along, some of them supported upon lorries, others on hand carts, others carried on stretchers, young people were prancing, clapping and yelling to the rhythm of drums, with music, some coming from loudspeakers, others from instruments in the processions, all at full blast. In hundreds of faces, especially those of young men, was a seeming fierceness of pleasure, somehow aggressive, full of challenge, with shining teeth, streaming sweat and irresistible *élan*.

In bits I gathered an outline of the myth of Ganesh and his trunk, but my notion of it is only one of various alternatives. If one consults a mythological dictionary or encyclopaedia one soon discovers that there are usually several, widely differing, mythical origins of the vast number of figures in the Hindu pantheon. Most of them are the offspring of greater parents whose own origins are likewise varied. In the great religions of the Middle East, Christianity, Judaism and Islam, a dominant figure, Jehovah, Jesus, Allah, is accepted by the believer as the source of various principles of faith or conduct, but the identities of such dominant figures is not in much doubt. In Hinduism widely differing mythical origins do not cause doubts in the minds of believers but merely present choices whose relative 'truth' is not the primary concern of the devotee. The Hindu accepts a mode of 'puja', or ritual, more or less aware that mere logic cannot reconcile conflicting myths and values. His divinities are not gods and goddesses with the meanings attached to those nouns by devotees of the three monotheistic faiths of the Middle East. They seem, rather, to be symbols of human qualities with which he chooses to endow them at the moment of *puja*. Hinduism is quite the most elastic and liberal system of attitudes in the world. There is no orthodoxy, no central fount of authority, nothing corresponding to a pope. There is a mass of traditional literature, a limitless horizon of possibility, varied codes of conduct and an infinite variety of meaning.

The story of Ganesh, as I pieced it together, is not without frivolity – slapstick, I fear. He was the small boy son of Siva and his beautiful wife Parvati, each a central, dominant figure in the pantheon, and he was just like any other little boy of about four years old when events caught up with him. Siva had been away for just over four years, fighting in the interminable wars against demons and miscellaneous forces of evil. Returning on leave unexpectedly after such a long absence, understandably eager to embrace Parvati, he approached his home with powerful strides.

She, however, happened to be having a bath at the moment of Siva's arrival. As a precautionary measure against possible intruders she had told young Ganesh to stand outside her dwelling and keep away visitors. At the approach of his formidable but unrecognised father the boy bravely commands him to halt. Siva, enraged by such obstruction from a child completely unknown to him, raises his scimitar and, with a quick swipe, as though to demolish a dandelion, cuts off the boy's head, sweeps aside the curtains, advances into the bathroom and seizes his wife in a dripping embrace.

She, through a chink, had seen the dreadful act, and was as hysterical as any wet and naked goddess could conceivably have been. 'My son! My Ganesh!' she screamed. 'You, Siva! Bring him back! Make him live!' To which Siva replied at once: 'Yes! Yes! Dear me! Of course! Our son! I'll do what I can! Wait!'

He rushed out, without even removing his armour, and marched off into the nearest patch of jungle. There, in a few minutes, he spotted a young elephant grazing beneath a tree. With one mighty swing he hacked off the creature's head, heaved it up on his shoulders and struggled home as fast as he could to the sobbing, demented Parvati, sitting on a charpoy with the bloody corpse of Ganesh in her arms. Seizing the body in one arm, with the other Siva thrust the elephant's head upon the torso of his son and, with glaring eyes, uttered the single word of command: 'Live!' And Ganesh lived, and still lives, especially in Bombay.

The main point about an elephant, of course, is that it can overcome obstacles with a shove, and that is exactly what Ganesh achieves in his cosmic role. He is the god of strength of purpose, divinely conceived, divinely recompensed, cheerful, ever strong. For some reason he is also good at learning and literary achievement. Books are dedicated to him. I do not think it can be entirely fortuitous that Bombay and the western state of Maharashtra, in which India's industrial and commercial revolutions are the most advanced, are especially committed to this particular god. There can be no certain answer to the question whether the people of Maharashtra are successful because they love Ganesh, or love him because they are successful, but a coincidence is there to identify.

All the processions were moving down to the sea, where the tide was low. To get a better view we drove to the northern arm

of the bay from which we could look back and downwards upon
the whole sweep of the beach. It seemed as though the entire
stretch of it was crammed with people, several hundred thousand
perhaps. I had never before seen so dense a concentration of
humanity. The scene reminded me of those tiny sweets known as
'hundreds and thousands' which children spread over bread and
butter with a spoon, the resemblance enhanced by the predominance of certain colours, the whites of shirts and dhotis, turbans,
the pinks, reds, yellows, orange, mauve dots that were the saris
of women and the dresses of little girls, dots of distant *pointil-
lisme*, dazzling, immense. At the water's edge small boats were
being loaded with the images of Ganesh – motor and sailing craft
and rowing boats – all of which proceeded, as soon as loaded, out
to sea, some as far as the distant horizon. Somewhere out at sea
each craft would stop, and with words of incantation, the image
be cast into the water in a messy dissolution of its matter. Such
destruction seemed to me puzzling until it was explained that the
sea, and water generally, affords a blessing to sustain the god
until his reappearance the following year when the cycle of
worship and culminating dissolution begins again.

On the way back to the flat I asked myself how it had come
about that in India, but not in most other parts of the world,
religious festivals imply the participation in the streets of great
masses of people, nearly all of whom are young. Vast numbers
gather to receive the blessings of the Pope in Rome. In Hong
Kong, Singapore, Port of Spain, Rio de Janeiro and Nice
immense throngs of people, their faces glistening with sweat and
joy, watch fiery dragons or the brilliance of carnival, but it is only
in India that so many days in each year are so lavishly dedicated to
ritual whose meanings, however well or little known, have
shaped the lives of countless generations. Hinduism is not a
religion of congregations enclosed by walls. It is, rather, a
religion of multitudes in sunlight, colour and great din. The
question I was asking myself is not answered readily, but similar
questions present themselves everywhere in the streets of modern India.

My four days in Bombay were not those of a tourist. I was
taken to meet men and women in whose houses and flats there
was much talk, with meals, memories, faces, voices, gestures –
elements of portraiture. On the first evening I was taken to the

Willingdon Sports Club.* Here I was able to glimpse a mode of living that seems to have survived, virtually intact, from the past. Indeed it extends today far beyond India to other parts of the tropical world in which British influence makes itself felt in a ghostly form. The club buildings with their arrangement of big rooms on two storeys with verandahs, lawns in moonlight, belonged to memory of a similar club at Lagos, Nigeria: Edwardian lines, cream walls, big fans turning, bare-footed servants in white with flashes of scarlet and brass, deft attention, informal form, a hidden committee and notices of authority upon green baize. This world, within Bombay, is distanced beyond awareness of streets that lie beneath a glow in the sky, beyond the images of Ganesh in the afternoon – strongly a world of India's élites.

Over drinks we were joined by Ananda's chief editor, Homi, and his wife, and by a large textile manufacturer whose English speech somehow brought into a single identity the Mayfair of Oscar Wilde and a prospect of the Marine Drive from a flat twenty storeys above observable humanity. Stoutness was accentuated by pin-striped waistcoat rather too tight, fleshy cheeks above a necktie also too tight, and a moustache recalling an image of Lord Kitchener after some luncheon in Pall Mall.

Homi was big, fiftyish, with kind, witty eyes and a lounging detachment, his speech recalling Cambridge and Bloomsbury before his time, with delightful talk of Proust and Charlus now transposed to the coast of the Indian Ocean – a flexible face with laughter in its rims. And the women – his wife with fine, beautiful features, a soft, regular mouth; and Nita, too, dazzling – her voice also firm and decisive, yet to discover its inner edge.

I did not talk much over the curried chicken and lager, for the sound of the fan overhead and a little deafness in one ear deprived me of Lord Kitchener's wit at one end of the table, and he might well have been wittier than the archetype at Madame Tussaud's. But Homi, who sat next to me and saw my difficulty, turned to advise me agreeably. He had read my portrait of my father and he urged me, in the adventures that lay ahead of me in India, not to struggle with any plan or theme for another book, but simply to

*Lord Willingdon was Viceroy from 1931 to 1936, during my father's period.

allow ideas and impressions to accumulate without discipline. I forgot this until some time after I got back to London. But my diary, somehow, seems to have remembered.

After dinner we moved out to wooden chairs on an expanse of grass beneath moonlight, about fifty feet from the club buildings. Facing them I became even more aware of their seeming similarity to the other club in Nigeria long ago. Here was coffee, and mosquitoes about the ankles. I had with me a small bottle of insect repellent, which was effective. I offered it to my companions, who rejected it, and the talk made no reference to anything so subordinate as a mosquito. It drifted to the social and political scene. I was warned that Bihar, my destination, was a backward, corrupt and caste-ridden state, and that it would 'disappoint' me very much. As to the Indian scene generally, I heard on this first evening a view later to be repeated over and over again: 'We cannot go on as we are. There is a lack of *will*. Mrs Gandhi is all right as a person, but there is no *will* for her to mobilise. The British at least had will. We have no will.' This yearning for a manifestation of will is derived largely from French pre-revolutionary thought about that imaginary monster The Will of the People, received into India from British academic sources during the last decades of the Raj, the period of Jawarharlal Nehru's youth and my own earliest student years. Listening to such talk among people who remember Harold Laski but know no French, I began to consider whether or not India is on the eve of some upheaval. It was a good first evening.

At breakfast the following morning Ananda challenged me: 'And now, Richard, here is a suggestion. Why don't you wear some Indian clothes? Your father, after all, set you a precedent, did he not?' It seemed odd perhaps that the suggestion had not already occurred to me, and it was true that my father had certainly worn Indian clothes, just as he had worn Japanese clothes in Japan and whilst travelling in a Japanese liner. He would wear the most characteristic garment of the Hindus, the dhoti, when entertaining Hindus, and the long coat of a Muslim gentleman when his guests were Muslims. In the hot weather especially, he had worn loose Indian pyjamas and could often be seen in a beautiful Indian shirt with a white turban sitting in the back seat of his car as it trundled through the streets of Patna. It was clearly impossible for me now positively to decline to dress as Ananda might propose. So I replied at once: 'You are right. I will. You advise me. I will do the shopping this morning. Lend me your car, driver, and somebody to advise if you are too busy yourself.' Dressed as an Indian I felt I should look like some vegetarian mystic from a remote hill station in Devon or the latest biographer of Mrs Besant, but so be it. I would do what I had admired my father for doing, whatever his ghost might think.

For some forty minutes in the heat of the day Homi most kindly helped me to buy the necessary kit – two pairs of immensely wide pyjama-like white cotton trousers that seemed curiously stiff, two white shirts without collars, with loose wide sleeves reaching just below the elbows and stud holes down the front, nice brass studs with mother-of-pearl tops, and a pair of elegant sandals which fell off my feet in the event of unallowed-for haste. This gear had to be collected piece by piece from various shops, and since I had other bits of shopping to do, I took Homi back to his office and left him there before setting out again with Ananda's driver. This shopping, and the business of getting Indian currency and travellers' cheques, and obtaining a comprehensive rail ticket for my various journeys for a spell of days enabled me to experience the city somehow as a citizen. In a new city one must do more than stare and eat if one is to see, feel and touch its life a little.

The vast sweep of Bombay's skyline, towering blocks and seeming modernity, had led me to expect to find big department stores with lifts, soft canned music, some sort of oriental Selfridges perhaps, or at least a gilded or lacquered Marks and Spencer, and I had a distinct memory of an Army and Navy Stores during the war years. Today, however, India seems to possess few such concentrations of investment in retail trade. Bombay is the headquarters of vast banks, administrative, legislative, judicial and academic buildings, new and old, but shops, virtually all of them, are small, sprawling along crammed streets into alleys, streets with broken paving stones, blackish puddles of mud and rainwater. There are indeed quite sizeable shops, many of them long established, but nowhere in India did I see anything comparable to the scale of the department stores and supermarkets of the West. Everywhere, in corners, on the ground close to buildings, can be seen the booths and little trays or mats of solitary vendors, the levels of trade grading downwards into destitution. The display of goods itself, to a far greater extent than anywhere in the temperate zone, is out in the open air, however dust-laden or exposed to the bleaching dazzle of the sun.

I went from street to street and shop to shop, the driver struggling to get into or out of gaps for parking whilst I waited on corners, or disappearing for spells as I waited sweatily for his re-emergence from the honking mass, or waiting for me to reappear after losing my bearings. Tropical urban mobility is always a nervy, sweaty business, but in the early phases of experience the visitor from the less clinging north feels somehow challenged to enjoy the feel of heat, the burning touch of metal in a car.

The commercial areas of Bombay are much older and lie behind the Marine Drive which presents its great façade of modernity to the open sea. Most of the principal buildings fronting the sea for miles are angular strongholds of steel and concrete, painted, I suppose, with white or cream emulsion. The image of splendour survives powerfully, but it suffers from the harsh impact of the monsoon rain, from seaborne mist – perhaps also from industrial smog and the fumes of traffic. A grey, streaky patina soon develops, gutters and ledges crumble, and it is clear that the cost of maintaining the pristine gleam of such buildings is commonly prohibitive. Whilst in Bombay I was led by local people to assume that the problem is peculiar to the city. Later I found the same situation in every other urban area that I saw in India. The climatic factor is evidently dominant. India's climate is very cruel to man, to most of his artifacts and to consciousness itself. A fortune awaits the chemist who can discover a cheap method of preserving the surfaces of modern buildings in the subcontinent.

One day there was a lunch party with Homi and his family, who lived in an old, three-storey house surrounded by huge white blocks of flats. Such a house, oddly, is often described in Bombay as a 'bungalow', the word evoking some nostalgia for the past. Very few of the upper strata in the city live in houses or 'bungalows' any more, and Homi's house, gabled, crumbling and beautiful, will by now have been demolished. On a previous occasion, at a drinks party, I had been introduced to Daulet, a Parsi lady who had lived for many years with Homi's family. She was the housekeeper, in control of the servants and also of the cooking department. She and I had talked of cookery, after which she had promised to give me a lesson in the cooking of rice on the day we were due there for lunch. I was to arrive at the house an hour and a half early. I was admitted by a bearer in a red sash and conducted to a flagstoned kitchen, with calor gas, biggish utensils of iron and aluminium, and Daulet to greet me in the centre foreground. In a second she began. Principles and ingredients, rice, salt and water, are respectively strict and simple. She started at the beginning: selection of the rice in the shop, recommending Dehra Dun rice of hard quality. It must not be chalky nor crumble between finger and thumb. Then washing: she washed the rice about three times in cold, not hot, water, tipping the water away and filling up again at once. Then, exactly how much water is required for each unit of rice? How much salt? How big the flame? How tight the lid? How long? Then how to dry out the rice with a cloth over the pan? Leaving the rice to cook she led me out to the verandah where we sat talking over drinks – lemon for her and lager for me – until the others arrived.

It was good talk with Daulet that day. I remember yellow-flowering acacia trees and scarlet hibiscus motionless in the warm atmosphere of noon. Round about were the tall blocks of sunlit flats and, only fifty yards away, the form of a temple, sculptured entirely in white marble, rich with pinnacles and elaborate detail, evidently at fantastic cost. Daulet said it was a Jain temple, built only a few years ago with funds from contributions from the wealthy Jain community of Bombay. This led to talk about religions and what was happening to them. How had the growth of industry and wealth affected traditional codes of conduct and taboos? She said that, whilst people still stuck to their separate religious communities and seldom married outside them, some of the rules of each were increasingly broken by its members. Many rich people would do in public things they would never dream of doing in their own homes. She knew of Muslims who would eat pork, Parsis who would eat onions and Jains who would eat chops, all such horrors perpetrated in restaurants and hotels, but never at home where servants and children would see. The various religions were full of hypocrisy of that kind today. As for caste, it was impossible to stick to old rules in a big city where people of high and low caste had to sit or stand close together in buses or trains. Caste, she said, was still strong all over India, but it made itself felt in important matters such as marriage and jobs and progressively less in old rules about purity and pollution by contact. I did not ask whether people broke religious rules of conduct because they were rich, or had become rich because they had broken rules. Competitive efficiency in India requires an output of energy that may not be compatible with the dietary rules of some communities. The energy required to become rich is not, I suspect, noticeably generated by the kind of diet traditionally prescribed for Jains, but many are now rich. Some at least, in darkest confidence, may attribute their success to a judicious consumption of chops.

After my shopping expedition, with a parcel of Indian raiment under my arm, I was taken to a white skyscraper and hoisted to the fifteenth floor to meet an old Indian friend of my student days in London, Ravi. I had met him again quite by chance in Delhi in 1945 and, in October of that year, had been his guest for a week in the princely state of Bhavnagar, of which he had been the Chief Secretary. After the abolition of the princely states he had come to live in Bombay and had become an important figure in the world of finance and banking. Now, after retirement, he was the chairman of various undertakings and represented the government of India at certain organisations of the United Nations. He was wiry, with a strongly emphatic speaking voice, shining deep-set eyes and vigorous laughter – clean shaven, balding with strong black hair curling at back and sides, a man of masterly sparkle. He greeted me with wonderful enthusiasm.

Although it was only a little after four o'clock in the afternoon with the sun shining brilliantly, the curtains in Ravi's big office were drawn and his brown scalp glistened in the light of an electric desk lamp. Indians often prefer artificial light to sunshine in their offices, and many like to consume food that is almost invisible in the darkness of a restaurant. Indeed, the darker the restaurant the steeper the bill, more or less. Temples, too, are usually pretty dark inside and must at one time have been even more so. Darkness confers mystery and the mysterious East – carpets, curtains, screens and domes – keeps away the light that we in the grey north so yearn for in our advertisements for swimwear, canned fruit and cigarettes.

Tea in India, like other things, is of two kinds, twice born and untouchable. The tea summoned for me by Ravi was twice born,

direct from the finest Darjeeling leaf, with a strong, non-bitter
taste, scent and an exact judgment of creamy milk and sugar.
Ever since Dr Johnson's celebrated thirst we have drunk Indian
tea in Britain to excess, but most of it a poor cut above
untouchability. Good tea is encountered in Britain mostly by
accident. In India it appears always by design.

As I took tea Ravi dictated some letters of introduction for me
to various people in other parts of the country and then, at my
request, took me to a still higher floor to windows from which I
took photographs of the huge panorama below. We went down
to the street and by car to the Gymkhana Club. Again, as in the
Willingdon, I found myself in an atmosphere oddly British,
though I was the only European in sight. The people about me,
men and women sitting round tables on a long verandah, felt
British. For a few minutes we stood watching a soccer match
between two clubs, each in brightly coloured shirts and stock-
ings, green and red respectively. There, after a shower, I undid
the parcel and put on the garments of my Devonshire fastness and
the big rimmed spectacles of mystical happenings. Ravi advised
me about the studs. I felt that it was about time that he, too, put
on some Indian clothes, but could hardly make so discourteous a
suggestion directly to his face.

For many years Ravi had lived with his family in a large
penthouse at the top of an old commercial building in the Fort
district of the city, the financial centre. We were to eat there later
but in the meantime he took me for a vigorous walk to see the
main features of the district. Although the general shape of the
Fort area is not like that of the City of London, its architectural
and cultural feel is similar. In both, through the last century, men
went to church or temple among the banks, warehouses and
alleys of their work. The language of trade, English, was the
same – that of money, bills of exchange, interest, discounts,
credit: awareness of goods unseen, moving distantly about the
world to the scraping of quills, quick utterance, sweaty cuffs and
fingernails blackened by the touch of print. The City of Dickens
and the Fort of the East India Company certainly looked similar
and must have felt so. And today there is much in the Fort that
remains of that world. The Dickensian features are not in the
imposing, colonnaded Edwardian buildings, but in the streets
and alleys between, at their feet. Here in the falling light the scene

evokes images of London in some heat wave of the hungry
forties. Paving stones are broken and one steps warily, especially
in sandals, over black puddles, the trampled debris of food,
banana skins, husks of coconuts, spewings of betel juice, the
excrement of a child. Lying against blackened walls are the
figures of exhausted people sleeping, hiding their eyes beneath
greying cloth or faded saris. Among the figures a man squats
before a mat upon which objects for sale are laid in rows, combs,
studs, notebooks, bangles, cigarettes, key rings, torches, tattered
reading material about horoscopes, Bette Davis, Siva and a novel
by Graham Greene. Ravi, in shoes more solid than mine,
marched briskly ahead whilst I followed as deftly as I could with
thoughts of leaving a sandal in a puddle, of a squelching
something between the toes. He led me to the blackened
cathedral church of St Thomas where, in the eighteenth century,
the British community celebrated their baptisms, marriages and
funerals – funerals every few days during each monsoon, with
processions in black from which ladies were kept away lest their
tears should mar their parties in the evenings.*

Ravi halted at an opening beneath an old building, where broad
stone steps wound upwards into darkness. We had to climb the
steps because the lift, which was being replaced, had been
removed from its shaft. The steps, dark and dusty, led to a top
landing with a strong door which he opened with a key, and we
entered the flat. It was large and rambling, cluttered with the
jetsam of a family that had grown up and departed – old toys
gramophones, blankets, magazines, cameras, a tennis racket,
cooking pans, pillow cases, a rolled carpet stranded on a bed, a
sideboard too heavy to move, a picture rail too high and nowhere
to stand a ladder. I felt instantly that my old friend should be
elsewhere, also high up, but with space, the freedom to gaze over
the western sea. In a few minutes I found the fulcrum of his
position. His wife came forward to greet me, moving slowly,
part paralysed, able to speak a little, anxious to please me. I had
last seen her as a young mother of four children at Bhavnagar
thirty-five years before. It was clear that the logistics of any move
would be entirely beyond her strength. In a few minutes we were
joined by one of her daughters, Priti, in a lovely flowing sari of

*On the mortality of Europeans in India in the past there is no better guide than
T. C. Wilkinson's *Two Monsoons*, Duckworth, 1976.

dark blue. She was a talented musician who composed her own songs in a classical, austere tradition. We moved to a wide verandah upon the flat roof, with a high parapet, open to the stars and the red glow of the city in every direction.

Sitting over a drink between father and daughter my mind was soon split between Ravi's views on India's inflation and Priti's exposition of Indian musicology. Both subjects presented an agreeable complexity, but we were soon diverted by the arrival of a table spread with Indian food arranged in round trays of shining steel. The trays themselves were the very same as those from which I had shared meals with the family in 1945 – copper outside, stainless steel within. In human relationships a continuity of physical things can whisper a little grace.

One day Ravi arranged a special lunch for me on the seventeenth floor of the enormous building of the twice-born tea, where I was introduced to four men who had been our contemporaries at the University of London in the early 1930s. All had distinguished themselves in modern India. One had become one of the senior officers in the cabinet secretariat in New Delhi and the others chairmen of big industrial and financial organisations.

Lunch itself was appetising. Perhaps a little alcohol might have set the conversation free – we drank only lemon squash and coconut juice – but I found that none of the powerful figures at the table seemed prepared to commit himself to anything so incautious as a notion about India, her problems and prospects. They recalled instead the names of long-departed lecturers and professors at whose feet we had all sat and the titles (not the contents) of textbooks that had once tormented us. However, just before we broke up Ravi rose to his feet and made a forceful speech in which he defended the achievements of India's industrial revolution during the past thirty years. He reminded us that the country was now able to produce virtually the whole range of manufactured goods consumed in the country and was developing a thriving export trade, especially in the Middle East and South-East Asia. I would not belittle that achievement even if it does very much depend upon a policy of protection against competition and a great deal of inefficiency. Even if, as economists have argued, the whole policy can be shown to be of dubious logical merit, India's industrial revolution is a fact. Many of its deficiencies are evident, but not so powerfully as to prompt any fundamental reversal of policy. Not yet, anyway.

On another occasion I was invited to a drinks party in a flat overlooking the sea and the whole sweep of the Marine Drive. Here I met some of these men again, with an assortment of wives, sons, daughters and dazzling secretaries, each more gorgeous than the last. I found, here and elsewhere in India, that at such events women tend to gather along one side or at the end of a room, looking neglected and – however beautiful they might be – being ignored by the men. At first, in Bombay, I did not fully grasp the essentially Indian quality of this behaviour and, unthinking, assumed that most of the men must somehow be too dull or shy to join the women. If the latter actually wanted to be so segregated, why had they made themselves so devastatingly attractive? My impulse was to approach them. I did so and introduced myself to several. Some of the men actually followed my example – so the party became at least a bit more mixed than if I had restricted myself to a few chatty observations about the timetables of trains with my elderly and rather tired-looking hosts.

In America, Europe, India, anywhere, at gatherings of this kind, at which hosts are men of business in their late sixties or early seventies, the intelligence of women will sparkle: that of their men remain as dull as pewter, a mental bric-a-brac of dead deals. The distinction is especially apparent in western India, where many girls are well educated and many men are rich. The age of marriage is much lower than in the West. Before a woman reaches her forties her children are usually independent and she can be intellectually freed. No such rejuvenation awaits success-ful males. As they move steadily into bigger and grander offices with more and more subordinates and telephones, their powers of attention are increasingly confined to the vocational jargon of their work. Sensibility is blunted and, in the tropics especially, even the financial press is a bore after early sunset. However, in India such men usually eat and drink much less than their Western counterparts, and their boredom, their bewilderment, can be more dignified in the benignity of silence.

At dinner in Ananda's flat on my last evening, he asked me if I would like to see some of the night life of Bombay. I declined with thanks for, whilst I much enjoy much of what it is

fashionable nowadays to call the exploitation of women, a
prospect of stimulation without more of it to follow, on the eve
of a long railway journey, could distract attention from the
landscape. Instead, therefore, we got up early, took swimming
things and drove to a marvellous club and swam in a smooth,
sunlit pool surrounded by flowering acacia and palms. Here again
I felt that small things had not changed in half a century of time
and pessimism – the distribution of towels, yellow soap in the
showers, facilities for the safekeeping of watch and cash, and the
grace with which an English breakfast was served by turbaned
bearers on the lawn beneath a coloured umbrella. The Cooper's
marmalade suggested that the Army and Navy Stores had not
closed after all.

In Bombay I spent some hours alone, watching the urban
scene, especially in the early mornings when people were going
to work and at dusk on their return. Since I had last seen the city
the growth of its industrial and commercial life had been
immense. Energy, personal zest, is now dominant, vivid. In the
big streets is a thrusting roar of traffic, the onward sweep of
thousands of cars, lorries, buses, scooters and cycles, each with
its own brain-locked will. On the pavements people walk fast
and smartly to work and, in their morning demeanour do so with
aplomb – a grooming of hair, features and form to defy the past.

More than in other big cities of India, the sections of the
population that are destitute, living close to exhaustion, are shut
away, less by any laws or regulations than by the opacity of the
cliff of modern buildings facing the great curve of the bay, and by
the location of economic life to landwards. Beggars appear
suddenly between the lanes of traffic, maimed, feeble, cripples
with broken, twisted, hacked off limbs, struggling, reaching
upwards with entreating eyes. The visitor to India is soon warned
by his hosts and by authorities not to 'encourage' begging and,
despite the huge growth of population, I was less beset by
beggars in 1980 than I had been in 1943, the year of the great
famine, and of war.

It is important, I think, for the Western visitor, whose view of
the world is obscured by the security of his own welfare state, to
appreciate implications of city growth in tropical countries the
bulk of whose people live in rural settings. In 1936 I travelled for
some thousands of miles in the Soviet Union which I then

believed to be the land of socialist promise. I met beggars in the towns, but very few of them. Rough as urban conditions were, the urban poor were a good deal better off than people in the Soviet countryside. In the tropical world of today, and especially in the areas fringing cities where the destitutes and the 'scheduled castes' live, the poor are considerably worse off than most of the rural peasantry. There is a logic in this. In the mid-1930s the Soviet authorities were in the midst of the early five-year plans of industrialisation. These implied a great migration from the land into the towns where new industries were being established at fanatical speed. In order to prevent the towns from becoming uncontrollable slums, the system of internal passports was used. No person was allowed to travel to any town unless his pass showed that, in the town to which he was going, he already had a job to go to and somewhere to sleep. Such regulations were strictly applied, and only by means of them was it possible to maintain in the towns a general standard of living higher than that of the people in the countryside. In the Soviet Union in those years the words 'dictatorship of the proletariat' were endowed with various interpretations by party activists and other ideological practitioners, but their meaning was hardly mysterious to a destitute peasant who might be hoping to find a job in the motor car plant at Gorky or the tractor plant at Stalingrad merely by purchasing a rail ticket and going to make enquiries. In those days I was full of enthusiasm for the Soviet achievement and far too jejune to realise what it meant. I gave no thought to the fact that, in Britain, I carried no internal passport and could not be prevented from travelling about at will in my own country by any officially appointed representative of the People spelt in that way. The word People always implies tyranny over people.

I did, of course, encourage beggars in Bombay, on an *ad hoc* basis without much consistency. I did not give money to strong, tough-looking children, but gave a little to people obviously helpless. On one occasion, as Ananda's driver was slowing down in a swirl of traffic, a loosely clad young woman appeared suddenly at the open window with a naked child held on a hip in her left arm. She regarded me for a second with a tiny smile. With her disengaged hand she quickly pulled aside her faded sari to disclose a pretty breast, moving a little in the hot sunshine. I recall her mischief more clearly than the coin I gave to her.

Ananda had been most helpful to me, both in the task of obtaining an 'Indrail' comprehensive ticket for travel anywhere on the Indian railways and in the even more cantankerous business of arranging a reservation on the Rajdahni Express for Delhi. Both jobs involved much traipsing about from office to office, form filling and argument in the sweaty heat. The train was due to leave in the mid-afternoon.

On that day Nita lunched with me at the flat in the absence of Ananda, who had to entertain an author from afar. She took me to the station in the car, found the train at its platform, identified my compartment, my name in block capitals in the list on the open door, and the seat itself. All was accompanied to the lilt of her unforgettable English, adding 'Pat'na' and 'Cut'tack' to her repertoire of downward 't's and upward 'a's. When the sound of a foreign language grates upon the ears, its place names sometimes rescue the heart.

2

Rajdahni Express

As the train slid out of Bombay, I reflected that there would remain only about an hour and a half of daylight in which to look at India, and that hundreds of miles of it would be denied to me before dawn, by which time we should be in a different climate far to the north. Tiresomely, the window glass is darkened – chiefly to avoid glare but also, I was told, to discourage people on platforms from staring in at passengers. Every now and then, through chinks or through an open window at the end of the coach, I could see the continuing brilliance of sunlit land or the silver grandeur of the monsoon cloud.

The train sped northwards on embankments over partly flooded land stretching away to the sea beyond the horizon. Cultivated land consists of low-lying, green paddy fields of rice, much taller millets with feathery pods, sugar with bright green fronds and strong stems, fields of pulses of middle height, taller than rice, shorter than sugar. Dark mango trees, finely symmetrical, stand among the huts of villages, with glimpses of red tiles, earthy alleys and children at play. Few human beings could be seen in this landscape, however, and much of the land, though covered with wild vegetation, is clearly a saline waste. From the air, when approaching Bombay, I had already seen something of this country and knew that, to the west, it sank away into sand dunes and the widening estuarial wilderness of a river, to the greyness of discoloured sea.

To the east, only a few kilometres away, stood steep, jungle-covered hills, rising to peaks two or three thousand feet or more above the land. Occasionally, poised as though in a painting by some Indian Claude or Poussin, a small white temple stood upon a slope, pointing to the sky, some little place of pilgrimage, accessible only on foot very slowly by a thousand steps of granite.

As the train moved north-eastwards the land became less

flooded, water more confined to man-made channels and the beds of streams. More cultivation appeared, more people everywhere, busy to complete their work before the rapid dusk. From now onwards, throughout my travels in India, I could never look out over agricultural land without seeing people. In Britain and northern Europe one can gaze from a moving train or car over rich land worked only by invisible powers that leave but the trace of tractor wheels along an edge of field. The land of India has not thus been emptied for postcard photography. In every direction, along tracks and roadways, people are seen in all the months of cultivation and harvest from mid-June to the end of February perhaps, walking barefoot, moving between the rectangles of their crops, working in the fields. Fields are divided, not by hedges but, for the most part, by little bunds, walls of earth a few inches high, to hold water for the growing of rice and to mark areas of property or control. In the slanting light faces and figures are lit in colour, vividness. Sweat gleams in each face. Grey-black stubble glistens on the jowls of turbaned men. The colours of saris and children's garment's glow. The people walk in single file with arms upraised to steady metal tools and vessels upon heads or shoulders. Sometimes several women in a row – a line of elbows jutting, hands balancing wood, bundles, brass vessels, baskets, a bangle slips to a forearm, a hand lifts a sari to avoid a bush, a pool – all are moving to the end of the day, to the village in the middle distance.

So long as the land remained visible I tried to avoid my companions, but later felt required at least to smile if any of them addressed me. And as soon as I turned towards the man in the opposite corner he began to speak to me. He had obviously been waiting for me and I sensed at once, from his face, what I could be in for, a session with a religious or political obsessionist. He was youngish, black-bearded, with burning eyes, formidable teeth and a bald head designed as an offensive weapon. In a few seconds the obsession was out and challenging. How, he demanded loudly, could I explain the coexistence in India of abundant coal and iron and the great poverty of the workers? Yes, I replied, adding, in silence, a square full stop. He went on in a burst of partially audible garrulity, all about exploitation and surplus value. I nodded amicably, hoping he would subside and get on with his Marxism in silence. To my surprise and relief he spoke

not another word and got out hurriedly at Baroda accompanied
by a bulging briefcase of very tired looking newspapers.

I had three other companions. On the upper berth opposite
was another bearded figure, also quite young. When he entered
the compartment in Bombay he was dressed in a spotless white
Indian loose cotton shirt (of better quality than mine) and
pyjamas. This costume suited his gold-rimmed spectacles and
somewhat academic air. Guessing that I might be British he
announced that he had a brother in Birmingham who was a
doctor. I smiled and said something like: 'Oh yes? There are lots
of medical men from India in Birmingham.' He said nothing
more to me and I felt that I had said something disturbing to him.
I asked him in a friendly tone if he himself was a medical man. He
said 'No', looked the other way and, in a few minutes climbed the
steps to his upper berth and went to sleep there. When he got out
of the train at Delhi he had abandoned his Indian clothes and was
dressed in ordinary trousers, belt and a bluish bush shirt.
Younger members of the intelligentsia in India shift frequently
from Indian to Western clothes and vice versa. Western clothes
are more conventional in the hours of work and daylight. Indian
clothes relax a man after a shower at dusk, and go better with
sandals, a little scent and a long chair on a tiled verandah.

Opposite in a corner was a tall Greek with heavy black
spectacles and moustache, who, all the way to Baroda, which we
reached about midnight, sat reading (or otherwise examining)
what appeared to be children's magazines and picture books in
Indian languages. Presumably he was concerned with the
manufacture and distribution of such matter. At Bombay, after
Nita's departure, his wife and two small children had sat in the
compartment, preparing to say goodbye to their father and
playing about my feet with toys. After saying farewell to them all
he mentioned to me, in English, that he had intended to travel
with his family but that reservations for them had not been
possible. Such frustrations are frequent on the railways. The
Greek had an interesting face. I suspect that his talk would have
been more technical than obsessive.

My next-door neighbour was a handsome man in his late
forties with short smooth hair and greying temples, clean shaven.
He was clad in a smart khaki bush shirt and trousers, well cleaned
and pressed. He left the train in the early morning clad in white,

Indian-style shirt and pyjamas, looking as handsome as ever. I thought at first that he could be a staff officer in one or other of the armed services but, on my inquiry, he made it clear that he was a very senior officer in the administration of the railways. He spoke with me in a quiet, reserved, unflappable voice – a responsible sort of man, I thought. I asked him to explain a few strange features in the passing landscape – the identity of this or that crop, the timing of this or that agricultural process, and his replies seemed always dependable, especially when he admitted that he did not know an answer. Unreliable people do not like to admit such things. I asked him about the gauges of the railways and about catering arrangments. I remembered that, during the war years, a train would stop at big stations for an hour or so to enable passengers of various classes, castes and faiths to take meals on the platforms. For first-class passengers there were attractive tiffin rooms for this purpose and I had certainly enjoyed travel in that way very much. He explained how all that had vanished long ago. The democratic process had downgraded services the world over, except possibly in aircraft. I realised that a railway station could no longer be associated with aromatic curry, Bombay duck and poppadums, with a glass of lager, bearers with red sashes slanting across their white tunics and trays held aloft. First-class travel was no longer grand. The evanescence of grandeur is one of the prevailing features of Indian democracy today. Wealth is in a bank, not in the upholstery of an elephant.

In due course a meal did appear, preceded by a young man with a notebook who inquired whether each of us wanted vegetarian or 'non-vegetarian' food. I soon got used to this negative description of something I had imagined to be positive. The young man wore no uniform and looked like a student – perhaps he was. The food arrived later, an aluminium tray with a flat cover and sunken cavities for the various items being handed to each passenger. My own assortment included plain rice, a little lamb curry, dahl, yoghurt and a couple of chapattis – not bad but everything a bit tepid, a condition caused partly by the chill of the air conditioning, which I had not the effrontery to switch off, even if I knew how. My first and only belly trouble in India was caused by the cold of this compartment, which made it imposs-ible for me to sleep for more than a very short time. My companions I noticed, had all brought blankets. At stations I

would get out on the platform to enjoy the warmth of the tropical
night and drink some hot, sweet tea purchased from an agreeable
person bearing a kettle of fully made tea and a pile of little
earthenware cups. After drinking the tea one throws the cup out
of the window. The civilisation of India is only now approaching
the epoch of plastic and cellophane litter.

Travelling in the Rajdahni Express, with its cleanliness and
bright metal fittings, its smooth plain synthetic upholstery, I
assumed that future long journeys by train in Indian would be
similar. Looking back it seems strange that my neighbour
omitted to warn me of what was to come.

I awoke to find daylight. Slipping on my dressing gown I eased
myself gently past my sleeping companions, slid back the heavy
door and went along the corridor to an open window to watch
the scene. The reader who, in a northern summer of rain and
slate-grey mist, has travelled overnight by train down the valley
of the Rhône to the different world of Provence, of the
Mediterranean, will have shared something of my experience
that early morning in India. I remember waking up at Arles after
such a journey – the still wonder of tender colour everywhere,
ochre, yellow, orange, and the atmosphere itself pink, like the
bloom of peaches – a clump of dried grasses near the line, a dove
on a platform roof, two young people asleep on a blanket with
rucksacks at their heads – warmth held in the weeks of harvest,
shade beneath limestone and pine. Now from the train I could see
a corresponding transformation in the Indian scene. The clouds
had gone and the air was still; a haze of coral light covered the
immensity of the plain. Tall crops of millet and sugar cane,
peeling and dry, angled by as the train moved gently on and on;
rectangles of rice in many shades of ripeness from honey to light
green, bushes of dahl, some in yellow flower, solitary palms
whose fronds hung motionless. Already people were at work –
women, five or six of them squatting as they collected weeds
between the crops, putting them into little open baskets to be
carried on the head towards a distant village. Weeds are food for
cattle. In India very little land, except perhaps beneath a clump of
trees, can be spared for grazing and the sun, in any event, very
quickly dries up growing grass. Some rectangles of rice had
already been cut by women using small sickles, leaving only
stubble. Sometimes a man could be seen wielding a heavy hoe

like an axe, breaking stubbled land, preparing it for the next crop, wheat to ripen after the turn of the year. Sometimes a man with two bowing oxen, guiding a plough, would move slowly in a paddy field, cutting lines of soil. Glimpses, too, of small children – leading a group of fawn cows or, standing near the rail embankment, flinging water from gourds over the motionless bulk of a black buffalo.

Sometimes the train passed through a new industrial complex – big, windowless walls, gleaming tubular chimneys, rigid and curving equipment of heavy engineering or petrochemical production, with the crowded shanties of workers stretching for hundreds of yards along the lines of rail. Heavy industry in India towers over all the life about it. Just as, in the dynastic history of the country, great forts, palaces, tombs, mosques and temples stood strongly over long-vanished huts and shelters in the heat beneath their walls, so now immensities of steel and concrete stand above the same frailty today. The land of India's agriculture is ruled by man with his notions of gods and goddesses. He does not rule the factories. Sometimes the domination of things over the living seems as grim as any dynastic cruelty of the past. The train rumbled slowly through an area whose central feature is a plant where rock is crushed for the manufacture of synthetic stone shapes for the building industry. Here dredger-like machines with moving metal containers lift loads of rock fragments and drop them heavily into great structures in which they are pounded by hammers into powder. This passes into furnaces. The entire plant looked like a dream of hell in the mind of Hieronymus Bosch, a dream drained of the colours in that painter's mind. The air is hot with soot-blackened flames, dense smoke and stone dust. The incessant bang of hammers obliterates the loudest human shouts, reducing all communication to gestures of lips, teeth and reddened eyes. Black-edged flames thrust from furnace doors. Here, along the rail embankment, are the dust-smothered habitations of people, the games of dusty children with voices silent in the din. As we rolled through this inferno I recalled a similar scene from a deck of a ship on the east bank of the lower Volga during a journey in the Soviet Union in the summer of 1936. An American professor and I stood watching the riverine panorama of the town of Volsk, entirely devoted then to the manufacture of cement. Every habitation along the river bank, timbered shacks and small brick houses, and all visible humanity, was smothered in white grit and dust. The water in the river was white, the exhortatory banners of the local Communist party stretching across the roadway were faded with the dust of cement. 'How would you like to live *there*?' asked my academic companion. As one who, in youth, had gone to the Soviet Union to *feel* the exultation of its message, I found myself without words.

In a little while the train was moving slowly into Old Delhi and, for a few moments, I had glimpses of the long-remembered outlines of the great Jamma Masjid mosque and the massive walls and turrets of the Red Fort. But there were other buildings and scenes, especially in New Delhi, which belonged more vividly to my own past.

3
Days in Delhi

In Bombay Ananda had kindly booked me a room at the Ranjit Hotel in Old Delhi, just on the border of New Delhi, and asked his local representative to meet me at the station. He, Mr Banerjee, singled me out almost before I could step down to the crowded platform. A man in his middle thirties with a strong, cleanshaven face, he was energetic and helpful to me, getting a porter at once and driving me to the hotel. I invited him to call back and have tea with me in the afternoon.

The Ranjit is not luxurious but it is new, clean and imposing enough for visiting tourists and international cadres of ping-pong champions, or experts in librarianship and the probation of offenders, who touch down in groups when the time is ripe for conferences at key points round the middle of the planet between the Philippines and Mexico. Representatives of such categories were rising from their coffees with handbags and briefcases as I entered the dining room for late breakfast.

After a shower I slept for an hour and then took up the telephone, made appointments with various people for the next three days and went out with sunglasses into the hot dazzle, to be a tourist at least until some kind of lunch snack somewhere. Above all I wanted to explore the great complex of sandstone buildings designed by Lutyens and Baker early in the century where, in uniform, I had worked between July 1944 and December 1945. I summoned an auto-rickshaw.

This vehicle, especially in the relatively advanced cities of India, is probably as ephemeral as the tonga of my earlier experience. Very few tongas are now seen, but in the recent past they provided the commonest form of urban transport plying for hire. The tonga was a small, two-wheeled horse-drawn trap, high off the ground with bench seats behind the driver enclosed by woodwork, usually varnished three-ply. One entered the vehicle with the aid of a step and a small door at the back. In the spacious, tree-lined avenues of New Delhi could be heard the clip-clop of hooves and there was everywhere an agreeable scent of horse dung. One rode in a tonga in one's bush hat or side cap, accompanied by a kitbag or a girl but seldom both.

The auto-rickshaw of today, presumably gone tomorrow, is a three-wheeled motor scooter. The driver sits on a saddle with his legs astride the tank and engine. One or more passengers are perched behind on a padded seat with a rest at the back, partly sheltered by a flimsy hood, often a bit tattered. The thing splutters along, weaving through dense traffic in a fuming din of haste. These machines, products of a vast nationalised enterprise, are all equipped with identical hooters whose music resembles that of a panic-stricken wasp. Nearly all the cars, also national-ised, emit an identical high-pitched metallic sound like a burst of mechanical hysterics. These uniformities of sound in the streets at least enable drivers to identify unseen dangers to the rear of them.

The New Delhi of Lutyens – of the 1920s – consists of three big functional areas, each with its own grandeur and separate importance. My ride towards one of them took me briefly through parts of the other two. The hotel is just on the edge of the commercial area. This is dominated by Connaught Circus, a white-columned circular arcade with handsome buildings in a uniform plan rising above it, and streets of similar design radiating from it in various directions. The arcade is full of shops and business offices, hundreds of booths, the mats and wares of pedlars. In our recollections of urban scenes we remember the form, colour and atmosphere of major artefacts, but forget dimensions. I found the Connaught Circus of reality to be much bigger than my memory of it. In memory it was a ring of dignified white columns, a few big shops beneath the arcade and a comfortable view of its proportions from a first floor, with the smell of coffee at eleven.

Modern Indian civilisation has imposed its own vitality, another imagery, upon the commercial area of New Delhi, upon the architectural design of the late imperial decades. In the following weeks I was to discover the same imposition upon design in every other town that I saw. And yet, although the scene is fundamentally Indian, in the sense that no photograph of it could be mistaken for a scene in any other country, it shares certain features with the modern world as a whole. Modern society, whatever the contents of its holy books, whatever anybody may intend, implies domination by the middle grades of urban humanity. These grades do not actually rule, for only individuals do that, but they provide the scene, the din and the values from which no escape is possible. It is for them that the products of India's industries fill the shops and bazaars, theirs are the textiles, the colours, the saris and bush shirts, the scooters, cars and the drinks, mostly soft. For them the loudspeakers blare tunes from the films of the Bombay studios, for them the hoardings in Hindi, Urdu and English rise garishly above the Connaught Circus of memory. Their values and life styles do not extend to the urban poor nor to the vast rural hinterland, though in a longer perspective, far, far longer, that may change.

Branching off from Connaught Circus are several thorough-fares. My auto-rickshaw sped along one of them in a stream of traffic, overtaking cycles, crowded buses, lorry-loads of timber, a camel with disdainful look and two stationary cows which, standing athwart the traffic, flipped at flies with grey stringy tails. In the surging din I glimpsed a most Indian happening, a woman perched side-saddle upon the pillion seat of a fast-moving scooter. Some Indian girls wear jeans and some, usually in jeans, drive scooters. More common is the pillion rider in a bright sari, sitting gracefully aside with her back to the traffic, sandaled feet pointing to the kerb, handbag slung over a shoulder, a flutter of drapery flying. Thus poised she cannot grip with both hands either the waist of her Sikh or any part of the machine. Neither can she safely permit herself to slump. She sits erect, curvaceous, nonchalant, her predicament dissolved in the presentation of her torso to a wonderful advantage.

In a few minutes we left the thoroughfare and travelled for almost a mile along one of the residential avenues which constitute the second main area of the Lutyens plan. These radiate from the central complex of governmental buildings, in a manner reminiscent of the radiation of fine avenues from the Arc de Triomphe in the Paris of the Second Empire. Along such avenues are the bungalow-style houses of India's élite, with deep veran-dahs and gardens, the same dwellings in which senior British officers, civilian and military, had also lived in my father's day and during my own period in the city.

I stopped the rickshaw at the end of the Jan Path, the long

straight ceremonial drive that used to be known as Kingsway, leading from the magnificent central government buildings to the India Gate arch standing upon a distant horizon.* The buildings, huge twin structures designed by Herbert Baker in consultation with Lutyens during and after the First World War, are reached by a broad, up-sloping roadway between them. This slope,† which I used to ascend daily with a bicycle to reach my office, leads to a flat area of flower beds, fountains and pathways between the great buildings on either side. With my camera in a satchel I walked up the slope in hot dazzling sunlight, wondering how I should rediscover the scene at the top. An interval of thirty-five years is usually sufficient for the betrayal of memory, but nothing in the scene I beheld implied the smallest structural change. Even the flowers, some of them zinnias, seemed unchanged. I found that the building on the left, where I had worked at all hours of the day and night, known in the British period as G.H.Q., was now occupied by the Ministries of Defence and External Affairs. A few military vehicles, less battered than those of memory, stood nearby and I suspected that, if I were to walk through the central gateway into the cool darkness of the building and turn to the left along a certain stone corridor, I could open a certain door and perhaps see within some young Indian major or captain sitting before a buff file with spectacles on his nose and notions for the evening in his mind. Vaguely enticing, the odours of onion and curry from the tiffin room would not have changed.

I walked to the parapet and looked down upon the broad Jan Path, lined by wide grass verges and trees beyond which, on either side, rise important buildings – a vision deriving from Versailles, from Schönbrunn, from the Winter Palace, moving out and onwards over the centuries, into South America, to the East, here at last into the red and yellow stone of India, dissolving into another vision of the same antiquity, that of the Moghul world.

From the parapet I turned left to look at the other block of buildings, its twin, occupied by the Departments of Home and

---

* Formerly called the All-India Memorial Arch, designed by Lutyens in 1920.
    † During the war we used to call the slope 'the biggest ramp in India' – not without affection.

Financial Affairs. Then I walked towards the domed palace at the rear, formerly the residence of the Viceroy, now that of the President of India. Here, as I stood near the railings, there was something more to recall. Some time during the hot weather of 1945, when Wavell, the Viceroy, was away at Simla, I was strolling in this area during a lunch break when I recognised a senior British officer emerging from a gateway in the railings. In 1940, when I was a rifleman in England, he had been my company commander in one of the battalions of the 60th Rifles. I had been privileged to scrub out his office on Sunday mornings with a scrubbing brush and a pail of grey soapy water – it provided a wholesome alternative to church parade which, he knew, was then repugnant to my notions about the nebulosities of religion. Later, defence of the kind of liberalism implied in a choice between the genuflexions of prayer and scrubbing became for me the single war aim, among so many, in which I could feel intellectual confidence. In those days we exchanged war aims between the songs of Vera Lynn.

The officer, now a lieutenant colonel (I had become a chairborne major), was a member of the Viceroy's staff. Greeting me warmly, he asked me to lunch with him on the following Sunday at the palace and to swim beforehand in a pool somewhere in the grounds. And so eventually, on a rickety bicycle, I rode in stupendous heat to the palace, handed the machine to a turbaned bearer, and was led through the gardens where the colonel, in a nicely ironed bush shirt, met me beneath an arch of roses. We swam in a little pool somewhere on a terrace overlooking ornamental gardens reminiscent of Hampton Court. We had a very English lunch of ham, salad and cold beer, and talked of the past, the toughness of training on the Wiltshire Downs, of his childhood in India, his love of the Indian regiments and of the North. He could see only a greyness ahead.

My few days in Delhi were largely occupied in making arrangements to visit Mussoorie in the foothills of the Himalayas above Dehra Dun and for the journey to Patna, capital of Bihar. In all this I was greatly helped by the staff of the British Council. It is clear that the work of the Council is now of crucial value to Britain in her dealings with the rest of the world, and the more so the weaker she becomes in the economic and military fields. In India I met many intelligent and friendly Indians who lamented

that Britain is now virtually 'done for', insular and narrow, and
that the rest of the world can obtain the kinds of goods
manufactured in Britain cheaper and more reliably from other
producers. The trouble with Britain, I was told, is that the British
people had lost their own awareness of the true reasons for which
Britain is still respected. These have little to do with trade or
defence but a great deal to do with the contents of British books.
The libraries of the Council in India are full (almost literally so),
not of elderly Indians with long memories, but of earnest young
people with the future before them. The books they read indicate
the values they seek to discover and to preserve. These British
books were not written as communications addressed to these
Indian readers, but to readers in Britain in the past, recent or
remote. The libraries merely order whatever books happen to be
in demand by Indian readers. Whilst this helps the British balance
of payments, it performs a function vastly more important,
namely, dissemination of the contents of the books. It is not at all
obvious why intelligent young Indians should today be expected
to seek the contents of books intended for a very different
readership, especially when British links with India are now so
intangible and British policy so insular and inward-looking as it
is. The English language itself, I believe, is the key to this.

I did not, of course, wish to consult the librarians about British
books, but about Indian ones. This was beyond their responsibilities, but they helped me none the less. Mr Biswas gave me the
titles of several good Indian books about changes in Indian
society, especially those affecting the caste system, and the names
of people in Bihar whom I met later. In my view it is lamentable
that the jobs of the librarians and others in the offices of the
British Council overseas, and the very existence of the libraries,
should be in jeopardy.

Mr Banerjee, Ananda's representative in Delhi, came to the
hotel that day and, having somehow missed his lunch, ate a big
sandwich in my room, and we drank tea. We walked together to
his office where we talked to the clatter of traffic in Connaught
Circus. His talk was characteristic of the Leftism common
throughout the Third World, where a miasmic image of
'capitalism' is vaguely associated with another, even more
ghastly, 'imperialism'. Anti-'imperialism' is directed at the
United States with emotional paranoia. The news at the time of

our talk was about the American hostages in Iran, the Russians in Afghanistan and the beginnings of the war between Iraq and Iran. For Mr Banerjee the first of these happenings was the most emotionally charged. He insisted, his voice quiet, his teeth (very strong ones) almost clenched, that the very name of the United States implied something fundamentally evil. All American policy, every action of the United States government in its dealings with the Third World, was vicious, corrupt and sinister. He declared that the revolutionary 'students' who had seized the hostages in Teheran had demonstrated their defiance at the evil of America. I asked him what he thought the Americans ought to do about the hostages. He said that they must now apologise to the whole world, and to Iran in particular, for all American wickedness in Vietnam, the Middle East, Latin America and everywhere else. As he lashed out, his head on one side in a twisted tension, his eyes burning, I hoped that, in the ensuing weeks, I should not have to meet many other persons of this kind. As to the hostages, I told him I thought that no great power could be expected to do anything so improbable as to apologise for anything whatever. History was not that sort of a business. We must look at the world as the sort of place it appeared to be in the light of its past, not as the sort of place in which the identity of power was likely to be transformed by anybody's doctrines. It is about as difficult to understand history as to attempt to change it, and the two tasks belong to different kinds of persons anyway.

In Bombay I had another old Indian friend, in addition to Ravi, who had been at the University of London at the same time as myself. I had met him again in New Delhi in 1944–5 when we had been colleagues. This man, after independence in 1947, had joined the Indian diplomatic service and had served in many parts of the world, both in the information department and as trade commissioner for India in several important centres. We had corresponded ever since. He and his wife, both now in ill health, were living in a suburb of Bombay, where I had visited them for lunch. He had told me interesting things about Indian economic problems, including the business of inflation and 'black money', and corruption generally. He had kindly given me an introduction to a most distinguished Indian in New Delhi, and this man had invited me to go and have breakfast with him on the morning after my audience with Mr Banerjee. I had never been out on a breakfast visit in my life before and felt that a coach and a pair would have been more suitable than the auto-rickshaw I engaged for the purpose.

My host for breakfast shall be anonymous, not because he had anything confidential to whisper to me over the coffee, but even the tiniest publicity can be ill-advised in circumstances of innocuous grace. After a career in the administrative service he had become governor of an important state, a position from which he had retired two or three years previously. He now concerned himself with good works of various kinds.

The auto-rickshaw turned into a little gravelled drive and stopped in front of a cream-washed bungalow dating, I suppose, from the early 1930s, with bougainvillaea motionless in early sunlight and a glimpse of roses at the rear. A servant ushered me into a modern lounge with bookshelves and brown basket chairs, a settee before a coffee table, and a dining room recess. My host and his wife were there to greet me, both grey and very handsome. Her hair was finely done above light features, brown eyes, a touch of pink and cream. He was strong with balding head and a military-looking moustache. My impulse was to address them as 'Sir' X and 'Lady' Y, for such non-available honours would precisely have graced their style.

My host led me to the settee and we talked over some tea for twenty minutes or so, until breakfast. He knew about my father and the background of my visit to India, and so at once asked me to give my first impressions. I had been reading a book about India's Constitution and mentioned this, which led to general talk about political trends in the country. In such talk it was natural that he should question me rather than I him, and that such questions as I did put to him should take the form of seeking his responses to my own tentative ideas. Sanjay Gandhi had recently been killed and there was an enduring political hiatus. I asked him how he thought the future would unfold. He felt that policy would tend to move in a direction somewhat left of centre. I said I had formed the impression, after reading Romila Thapar's excellent history of India, that the social structure of the country was extremely strong. There did not seem ever to have been a revolution (in any Western sense) in the whole of India's recorded history, and I could see no convincing indications of any such experience to come. I said I had been thinking about the implications of the chapter in the Constitution which laid down broad policy directives for the future. I asked if this did not have the effect of causing political parties to over-commit themselves to particular policies, merely because such policies were enshrined in the Constitution anyway? This could surely be dangerous, by causing disappointment to the followers of any party which actually found itself in power. Should not each party be entirely free to adopt any policy whatever, without reference to policies laid down in a Constitution invented by people in a vanished past? The electorate should not be committed to policies by any Constitution, but only to procedures and conduct with which Constitutions are properly concerned? He agreed that this was a danger, but thought it more theoretical than real. With a smile he said pragmatically, 'There's not much wrong with the Constitution, actually.' The inner strength of his reply would stand, I felt, not because of its logic, but because of the social strength of Indian society.

I was invited for dinner by Brigadier Goswami, retired from the Indian Medical Service. This man, in his youth, had been a medical student at Patna in my father's day. My introduction to him had come from an Englishwoman living near Oxford who had spent much of her childhood also at Patna, where the young medical student had been treated almost as a member of her own (also medical) family. (Her memory of my father was that of his rotundity and tobacco as she sat, without invitation, upon his knee on a verandah.)

The brigadier lived in a suburb in south-west New Delhi, about sixteen kilometres from the Ranjit Hotel, and I took a taxi to get there, a pretty hefty expense. For several miles we sped along tree-lined avenues of the kind I could remember from long ago, now racked with the noise of traffic. The speed of Indian traffic is not so great as that in Europe or America but the noise and the fumes seem more warlike in their impact upon the senses. Eventually we were forced to slow down by the density of vehicles and humanity, so I decided to get out and walk, knowing I should have to find the brigadier's house by asking questions. I admit I felt afraid of being mugged, but was treated by all with grace and courtesy. Indeed, despite news of every kind of violence in the press, I encountered only civility and friendship everywhere in India.

After about twenty minutes I found the brigadier's house. It was much like the many other small buildings in the area – though perhaps just a little bigger. I was greeted by a tall, dignified, military-looking man in khaki trousers and bush shirt, with a white moustache and domelike head. The house inside was modern, furnished with good hardwoods, but looking a little dusty. He led me up fawn-carpeted stairs to a lounge with a dining area raised above it by two or three steps. There were wedding photographs of young people, a bowl of fruit on a sideboard, more photographs of family groups. We sat on a sofa with Indian whisky and I asked him about his family. He told me he was a widower, his children were grown up. He seemed to be living with memories, though he was a cheerful, strong man in his early seventies, very busy running a clinic for the poor people in the district.

Whilst I thought I had been asked to dinner, the brigadier turned to me smiling and said: 'Are you sure you won't stay and take pot luck with us?' To which I replied, trying to conceal any manifestation of appetite, 'Yes – thanks very much. Absolutely anything will do for me.' He shouted, a young manservant appeared in a second, as though he had been concealed beneath a coat in the hall, a brief order was given, the servant made a small obeisance and went. In a very short time he reappeared, bringing excellent curried lamb, rice, dahl and chapatties, followed by a sweet with a milk or yoghurt base, the whole accompanied by a pleasant drink of cold coconut juice.

Over our meal the brigadier told me that he had last visited Britain about ten years before, so I asked him if he had visited the lady near Oxford. 'Yes, of course I did. Celia is a wonderful person, you know. As a matter of fact . . .' he faltered and added, almost inaudibly, 'I am still in love with her. You will think me mad, but it is true. I am in love with her.' I liked this man. In his loneliness he would have revealed to me more than he might later have wished to mention, so I confined my response to a look of understanding.

He changed the subject. 'There is a neighbour of mine,' he said, 'who lives only a few doors away. Dr Patel is his name. He knew your father in Patna and would very much like to meet you. I told him you were coming and promised I would ask if you would like to meet him. He is expecting us about now.'

We went down into the crowded street and walked about a hundred yards to another, smaller, house where we were greeted by Dr Patel, a big, ungainly sort of man, unshaven, in a crumpled shirt, old belt and uncreased black trousers. The front door led directly into a cramped living room with a stone floor, whitewashed walls, a bare, shadeless electric light and old, cumbersome furniture – an air of struggle, of relatives pressing closely into each other's lives. A small girl in a pinafore stood wide-eyed, thumb in mouth, looking at us. The large back of a woman receded into a kitchen where a bicycle stood against a hanging towel. The child scurried away beneath the hubbub of greetings. Standing back to look at me, Dr Patel said earnestly that I reminded him of my father. 'Your father,' he said, in a thick, struggling kind of English, 'was the biggest force in my life when I was young. If he had not given me the strength to study I should never have passed.' He was referring to medical examinations which he had taken after my father's death in 1938. 'I will show you his testimonial. I got it out to show to you.'

As I sank into a big settee of synthetic fibre upholstery, he produced an old file and extracted from it a small, faded typewritten letter of ten or fifteen lines, bearing my father's signature at the foot. At the top, in heavy, black embossed letters, was the address – CHHAJU BAGH, PATNA, E.I.R., the official residence of the Chief Justice of Bihar and Orissa. The letter, dated in 1935, addressed to the superintendent of the local medical college, expressed my father's confidence in the young Patel, if accepted as a student, and his ability to work hard for certain examinations.

'That letter, Mr Terrell, changed my life completely. If your father had not encouraged me by writing it, I should never have buckled to and passed my examinations.' He looked at his wife, who had returned from the kitchen: 'I wouldn't, would I?' She smiled at me: 'He was never the one for work till Sir Courtney talked to him. Oh no.' From which I gathered that the stimulus afforded by my father had perhaps not been the only one in his early (and perhaps his later) career. My father had made himself into a special British guru to many young students in Patna who used to visit him on the broad verandah of Chhaju Bagh and tell him of their troubles, their loves, their convictions and their fears. In his early life he had abandoned a medical career for the sake of a girl and changed over to law. His lasting remorse about this was expressed when he urged Indian medical students never to abandon their studies. India, he thought, could never have enough doctors. He also thought that most of the law students could be more useful to their country if they were to hurl their law books into the Ganges and take up carpentry instead.

Dr Patel spoke a little about his career, and I gathered that he had had little medical practice as such but had spent most of his life as a public health official. During the past twenty years he had worked for the World Health Organisation on anti-malaria projects in Latin America, the Caribbean and the Philippines, and had only recently returned to Delhi. In such a career, it seemed to me strange that his spoken English, and that of his wife, should be so poor, and that he knew only a few words of Spanish. He was a simple, practical man of few words, who had managed to make himself useful in the world with his knowledge of mosquitoes, the use of insecticides, water control, latrines and drains in tropical conditions.

He furnished Goswami and myself with very strong drinks of gin, lime, ice and spices mixed up in an elaborate cocktail shaker, an oblong instrument of the age of the young Fred Astaire. Then Goswami said: 'Richard Terrell has come here to find out about India. What can we tell him?' Patel said he hardly knew anything about India or politics or Mrs Gandhi and could only talk about mosquitoes. He could talk about those in the Philippines, in Colombia and Jamaica, but there was really nothing else he *could* talk about. He didn't read 'books or things like that'.

The brigadier was standing. With his glass in his left hand he bent over the table, clenched his right fist very deliberately and pressed it down repeatedly on the hard surface: 'Well, I'm going to tell Richard the truth. We are corrupt. We are lacking in technical mastery. India is now rotten, and rotting faster! It cannot go on! It cannot go on!'

He had drunk very little and his passionate words were slowly and deliberately uttered. Here was a strong, good man, gravely concerned about the condition of his country. It was clear, by his look, that Patel agreed with him. But Patel's caution was that of a subordinate official, perhaps of lower caste. He did not speak.

'Well,' I said, feeling that something of a restorative nature required to be uttered, 'as you know, I want to write a book of some kind about my visit to India. But, in Britain, America and the West generally, it has for some years been common for journalists and photographers who have visited India to describe the dreadful poverty, the beggars, the inefficiency and, in general, something they feel to be rotten, even putrid, about the country as a whole. This, I believe, causes a great many people to dismiss India as a hopeless place which must simply be left to stew in its own juice. Nobody can do anything with it – not even the Indians.'

'Anyway,' intervened the brigadier, again pressing the table with his fist, 'whilst all that may be true of India, I will tell you something about England. England is finished. Absolutely finished and done with!'

This gave me a small cue. My speech went much as follows: 'There is something rather British in all this self-denigration and mutual denigration. But, however true such statements may be, there are other kinds of truth, too, and, in my book, I should rather like to discover some of them. The population of India has grown vastly since independence. If India were indeed wholly lacking in technical mastery, as you say, such growth would not have been possible anyway. So long as people actually live and do not die, the achievement of sustaining them, whatever their poverty, is manifest. In forty years India has now become one of the world's greatest manufacturing countries, importing very few manufactures at all and giving employment, at however low a level, to many millions of people. And then, there is great beauty, too. Before coming to India the journalists and photographers had led me to expect to see a country sunk in apathy and misery. Instead I have seen energy, vast achievement and great beauty. The thunder of the traffic on the roads between the Ranjit Hotel and this place is all evidence of strength. Apathy is silent, but the silence of India is not heard in its din. The wheels of the bullock carts squeal to the energy of the men who drive them in the burning sun and the driving rain of the monsoon.'

I really did not want any more gin and wondered how I was to get back to the hotel that night. On expressing such thoughts I found my hosts sensibly concerned for me, and the party broke up, Goswami kindly going out for fifteen minutes to find me a taxi.

Apart from visiting the central block of administrative and

parliamentary buildings (the Lok Sabha), the only other sightseeing I did was to visit the immense tomb of the Moghul
emperor Humayun (A.D. 1530 intermittently till 1556), son of the
founder Babur and father of the great Akbar. I took an
auto-rickshaw for the purpose. On the way we passed the ancient
stone walls and turrets of the Purana Kila (Old Fort), relics of
Humayun's own period, including, within the walls, the attractive little tower that held his library and where he lost his life by
falling down the stone steps. The walls (at least when I was last in
Delhi) surrounded an undulating grassy area forming a small
sheltered parklike enclosure. I would sometimes cycle there,
taking a flask of coffee, some biscuits and Gibbon's *Decline and
Fall of the Roman Empire*, the first three of the eight volumes of
which I read in a period covering two hot weathers. I had
forgotten the layout of· the area and felt a strange thrill of
recognition when the auto-rickshaw suddenly passed the line of
single-storey breeze-block hutments containing the quarters in
which I had lived in the past. I had assumed that such temporary
structures, erected during the war to provide housing for a couple
of hundred Indian and British military officers for 'the duration',
would have disappeared long ago. It was very surprising to see
them apparently unchanged, as though in a dream. They are still
used for army officers and I saw young Indians in khaki sitting or
strolling in the area just as my own companions, their predecessors, used to do.

The scene having changed so little, a lasting impression of a
phase of life in India may be indicated if I digress for a moment
and return to memory. For several weeks between about
mid-April and mid-June the shade temperature, day and night,
varies between 100 and 117 degrees Fahrenheit, that is, at levels
above the normal temperature of human blood. My job involved
work at G.H.Q. on a shift basis, much of it at night, and I worked
in an air-conditioned office. The outside air was bone dry, so dry
that the moisture in the eyes seemed to dry up, giving one a slight
headache. After a night shift I used to leave the office at eight
o'clock in the morning feeling dirty, empty, crumpled and
unshaven. Coming out of the big dark building with my old
hired bicycle was like opening the door of an oven. As I
freewheeled down into Kingsway, hot air from the red sandstone
walls and the roadway would blow into my face, neck and

sleeves. I enjoyed the heat as I rode along in the direction of my quarters, thinking of breakfast and the prospect of several hours of rest, of solitude.

I would go straight to the mess for breakfast, for hugely enjoyable bacon and eggs, with rather limp toast. There would be desultory talk with one or two colleagues, Indian or British, before they rose, fresh and smartly dressed, to go off on their bicycles to their various jobs. Some were memorable for their oddities. Some had seen something of the war, in the Western Desert or, like myself, in Burma, but many, usually for reasons of health, had known only the life of peacetime India in the old Indian regiments. Some were cavalry officers who knew little of tanks, or Gunners with ancient guns. A few were Anglo-Indians from the railways or the postal system. At that time social contact with Indians was rare and there was a cynical bitterness common to Indians and British alike. Whilst many British officers yearned only to get away from India to 'leave them to rot or stew in their own juice', Indian officers disbelieved every British ministerial statement about constitutional policy for India and were convinced that all was 'eyewash', that Britain intended only to 'divide and rule' for ever and ever. The British were fed up with India and said so. They were not in the least frightened of the Congress or of any nationalist politicians, but merely exasperated by Indian woolliness. Many British of all ranks were acutely sex-starved, myself included, and the strain of solitary existence was endured as a kind of imprisonment. There would be sudden outbreaks of emotionalism, anger and even tears. Our lives were monkish without the mystical postures of real monks.

There was an Indian cavalry officer, a captain, whose appearance was memorable and who became a good friend to me. A Muslim, he was tall, aristocratic, with pale oval features derived from his Persian or Afghan ancestors, a princely figure – and I am sure that he must have been a proper prince of some sort. He was about twenty-eight years old, but looked a bit older, for he was a little stout, which suited him well. I used to call on him sometimes in his quarters where we would sit drinking sherbet and talking. His quarters differed vastly from my own. In my own little space a few doors up the line of hutments, I prided myself on the scantiness of my belongings. For, in the Arakan, all my things together must not exceed forty pounds in weight, so that I, and all the troops, could move off on foot at a few minutes' notice if required. I made a philosophy of it. By ridding ourselves of all encumbrances, in the planned society of the future, we should be good plannees, at least. Lying under a fan in my quarters in Delhi I used to find it amusing to envisage a kind of socialist universe in which the workers would be like soldiers in the Arakan: equipped only with a spare shirt, denims, spanner and kitbag, they would become infinitely plannable. Men would all live in solitary cells. Women of child-bearing age would live in beautifully appointed breeding blocks managed by the Commissariat of Health. Old persons would wash and sweep, cook and make beds, and love would occur in purpose-built arbours constructed by the Commissariat of Human Relations. Children would live with their mums in the breeding blocks.

Reflecting on all this it occurred to me that there was a contradiction between two desirable ends – namely, socialist planning, on the one hand, and its very purpose on the other. For the purpose was an ever-expanding output of goods and services in the possession of the workers. But the less goods a worker possessed, the greater his mobility as a plannee and the easier it was for the commissars to make plans. Workers encumbered with houses, furniture, old bikes, broken washing machines, perambulators in the yard, electric irons and books, would just get left behind. Only kitbag types like myself could survive in the inevitable socialist world of the future. In fact I felt very fit.

The quarters of the prince were very different. When I called I could hardly open his door for junk. Huge and costly trunks surmounted his cupboard to the ceiling, there were shelves of shiny leather boots and spurs, several Sam Browne belts glittering on pegs, dress uniforms waiting to be dusted by an obsequious bearer, dressing gowns with crossed swords above them hung against the wall. A beautiful book with pictures of the regimental uniforms of the world lay open in the centre of a round table, hemmed in by bottles, cut glass and boxes of cheroots. The whole den could have been reassembled in the Fulham Road as a successful business enterprise.

He sprawled in a regulation arm chair and greeted me with a wave of his arm: 'Have a spot of sherbet, old man!' His voice belonged to the age of Curzon, itself a confection of the English Moghul past. He himself belonged to a Persian painting in the palace of a king. There, in the picture, he sat upon a silken cushion, his lips about to receive a sip of yellow wine from the hand of a courtesan whose lashes and mysteries the painter had revealed to him, and to us, in the tiniest strokes of colour. For the moment he seemed to have stepped carefully out of the painting into a Fulham Road of my imagination, leaving a dent in the cushion and a whispered promise to return.

Two things the prince said in our talks affected me after leaving India in December 1945. At that time the whole subcontinent was comprised within the Indian empire and there was no Pakistan, no separate Muslim state. But Mr Jinnah, the future President of Pakistan, was already determined that such a state should be established, and political discussion turned upon its prospects. So I challenged the prince to tell me what he thought. He said something like this: 'You will, of course, have noticed that, in India, whatever the nationalists and socialists say or think, the whole of our society, whether Hindu, Muslim, Sikh or Christian, is deeply hierarchical, stratified into layers, each with its own aristocracy, its own élite. Nothing will ever change that. It is the most important fact about India – something which your British Labour Party will never understand.

'Now then, if you compare the elites of the Hindu community with those of the Muslims, you will find that the proportions of the Muslims who belong to their own élites are much smaller than the corresponding proportions of the Hindus to the rest of Hindu society. They have far more intellectuals and trained people to go round than we have. There are historical reasons for this. Most Muslims are the descendants of low-caste Hindus or untouchables who were converted in the past. Few of them belong to our élites, who tend to be descended from a small class of military invaders and rulers from the North West. Modern British India depends on a huge official class, including the whole officer class, civilian, military and judiciary, to keep the system going. This means that, if and when the British leave India, the Muslims will simply not have enough educated people, a big enough élite to fill all the necessary posts in the predominantly Muslim parts of India. But the Hindu community has a huge surplus of trained people and these will spill over into the vacant jobs in the Muslim areas. If that were to happen it would not be long before *all* power would be in Hindu hands, just as all power in Ulster is now in Protestant hands. So we must have Pakistan, a separate country where we Muslims can manage somehow without being swamped.'

The prince's theory, right or wrong, affected my later life profoundly. When in the spring of 1946 I had to appear before the Civil Service Commission as an administrative candidate, the Commissioners, knowing I had just arrived from New Delhi, invited my opinion about the prospects of establishing Pakistan. The theory seemed to the Commissioners sufficiently novel to persuade them to accept me into the service.

On another occasion, when I was telling the prince about my Stalinist views of the world, with an air of total conviction, he said something like this: 'The famous standard of living which socialists and communists go on about is nothing but a substitute for a philosophy of life. People who talk glibly about "raising the standard of living", as though that were the main object of policy, have in fact only a sausage machine in mind. The Americans have nothing whatever in their minds but a sausage machine. Nor have the Russians. That is why they hate each other. Rival sausages. More of everything! Always more and more! So long as there is more, nothing else matters. That is the grand illusion of the West, of the Industrial Revolution and the optimistic notions of your K. Marx of Bloomsbury and Highgate Cemetery fame. The addiction of Marxism is due to the terrible ease with which the drug is swallowed. But you, Terrell, are able to think. Think then!'

The tomb of the emperor Humayun stands in a wide green garden enclosure forming an attractive park, and is approached by a gravel pathway about a hundred metres long. It is a big, domed and turreted structure of red and yellow sandstone and contains the sarcophagi of royal descendants of both sexes down to the period of the Mutiny in the middle of the last century. I accepted the services of a tall, dignified guide of about sixty years of age, a rather impressive man who spoke very good English, was well informed about India's history and was able to discuss it sensibly. He seemed emotionally affected when I said I had visited the scene years before and that my father, in a real sense, had belonged to India. He told me he had retired from some quite responsible position in the public service and was doing the guide work occasionally to add a little to his pension.

Humayun's tomb and, indeed, the dozens of other relics of the past in the country round Delhi, such as the Lodi tombs, the Kutub Minar, the palace of the Tughlak kings, the Red Fort itself – all of which I had explored long ago – indicate, it seems to me, certain enduring features in the past of India. Virtually all the monuments and relics recall dynasties of power, successions of rulers distinguished by the styles of their authority, their strength and their weaknesses, each with its own achievement and cruelty, dissolution and style of ruin. Forts, palaces, mosques, temples and tombs, that is all. Each relic commemorates and commits to oblivion a man, his line, his power, his will. Of the people who laboured in heat and rain, only faint, anonymous tracery remains – small undulations in the land with fragments of pottery, beads, a broken bangle, a crumbling sword. The 'proletariat' in Roman times implied the class which contributed to posterity only the labour of its offspring, the 'proles'. That definition was fitting for the slaves of Rome. It did not, and does not, fit any class in the history of Europe since medieval times unless within relatively short periods of decades. This is because of the great social mobility of the class structures of European society over the centuries. The social history of Europe can almost be described as the endless story of the emergence of new rulers from the middle ranks of society which, in turn, are ever emerging from the strata below. But it fits the social history of India far more effectively. For India has never, I believe, experienced social mobility comparable with that of Europe during the past thousand years. That, in my view, is the most important fact about India.

Another feature is closely connected with this. The climate of India – certainly of those parts of it whose soil is richest and where population is most dense – is so harsh as to destroy the stamina of any rulers who fail to protect themselves strongly and securely from its bodily impact. In the Red Fort, in all the palaces of kings, the mansions of princes, the houses of rich zamindars, in the best official residences, in the hill stations of the British Raj, great ingenuity of protection from heat and cold has been evident throughout history. Such protection always implies luxury, austerity, authority and the subordination of the ruled – in short, inequality. Western socialists and Indian 'democrats' revile the 'exploitation' of the Indian masses implied by the eternal social reality of the country. But the climate of India does not change and the technology of protection from its implacable power is of limited effectiveness and extremely costly. A thick bandage of non-historical padding is firmly strapped over the eyes of critics of India's inequality.

4

To Mussoorie

The train to Dehra Dun left Delhi about seven thirty in the morning and did not reach its destination till five in the afternoon. What is described as first-class travel on most Indian trains, apart from the Rajdahni Express and one or two others, is very rough by European standards. The dark green upholstery in hard synthetic fibre and the old paintwork in the compartments are grimed with irremovable dust so deeply ingrained as to make most surfaces appear older than their years. Windows are usually smeary, gadgets look grubby whatever rags and hoses may have been applied to them. Hard, tough and very used, all my trains in India, except the first, were very old soldiers indeed. Yet all reached their destinations on time even after late starts. The taps may not have worked in the dusty loos but the engine in front functioned. (In fact, the loos were much cleaner, on close inspection, than a mere glance would suggest.)

The distance to Dehra Dun, the rail terminus at the northern limit of the plain in the Siwalik Hills lying below Mussoorie, is only a little more than a couple of hundred miles, but the train journey is extremely slow, with stops at many stations. I had several companions but only two, a young army officer on leave with his wife and baby, remained for the whole journey, and there was very little talk.

The rail does not go directly to Dehra Dun but, after running north-eastwards to the old military cantonment of Meerut, turns north for about a hundred miles to the city and rail junction of Shaharanpur. It then goes south-eastwards to Reorkee before turning north again to Hardwar and Dehra Dun. In this zigzag it traverses a much wider extent of the great plain than a direct journey would involve, so that I was able to see a considerable stretch. Although the land seems very flat it lies at a higher altitude than the vast expanses of plain to the west and the east. For this broad belt between Delhi and the Himalayas is actually a low plateau forming a watershed between the two main river systems of the North, of the Indus and the Ganges. This area includes parts of the states of Haryana and Uttar Pradesh where India's 'green revolution' in agriculture has made impressive progress, of which much is visible from the train.

Now, in the first days of October, colours were overwhelmingly green, from the pale tenderness of rice ripening in the sun to the darkness of mango trees beneath which animals and people shelter from the heat. As the dry season continues colours become steadily less green, more yellow and golden, the atmosphere more and more suffused with haze and pastel colours. This last quarter of the year, including the tail end of the monsoon and many weeks of the ensuing dry weather, is perhaps the most active time for the peasantry and rural labourers all over northern India.

The major crops do not, as in north-western Europe, all stand at roughly the same height, but are either much taller than European crops or much shorter. The tallest are millets and sugar, each growing in thick, grasslike stands with poweful stalks rising to well over fifteen feet – millets with varying seeds, some feathery, some in clusters like cigars. The pulses, lentils and chick peas are of several kinds and grow as bushes, some five or six feet in height, others much smaller than that. In many parts of the plain rice is succeeded by wheat to ripen late in the dry season. All crops are grown in rectangular areas that are much smaller than the big fields of Western Europe, say in East Anglia, Hampshire or Normandy. This breaks up the expanse of land and gives agriculture a look somehow heftier than the wide, lakelike green of rice cultivation that I was later to see in Bihar.

The aspect of villages varies greatly. The plain itself contains virtually no stone and all relatively durable building materials are brought from a distance – glass and metal from the towns, stone from the mountains. For this reason villages and small towns along the railway or accessible by lorry contain more stonework, steel and concrete, brick and glass than the majority of villages out in the rural plain where transport is restricted to rough muddy tracks negotiable only by bullock cart, shovable bicycle or on foot.

The walls of most buildings are of mud or brick. The bricks are not the strong bricks familiar in Europe, but small, powdery, fragile ones, lighter in colour, which give to dwellings, walls and shops an unfinished appearance. Woodwork, very seldom painted in the heat and dust of the plain, looks frail, dry and old. Heat, driving rain and wind, thick dust, are severe tests for all the exposed surfaces of buildings in northern India – these, indeed, are cruel implications of the harshness of the climate for all humanity. The tourist who sees India only in the gentlest weeks of the year should try to envisage the grimness of her climate at other times and its effects upon the work, life and habitations of her people. The plain is dotted at intervals with brickworks, situated usually quite close to the railway lines, most of them with two narrow tapering chimneys of metal. All over the North stacks of bricks, often ill-protected from rain or thieves, may be seen standing near roads or railways.

Mud buildings and walls are often protected by thatch, usually grey and tattered-looking, or by odd rusty pieces of corrugated iron; windows consist of open, seldom framed, holes. The only protection against insects is afforded by the loose cotton garments of the people and perhaps by a little oil of citrus – rarely a mosquito net. When darkness falls most villages dissolve into invisibility or reveal themselves only by the glimmer of tiny flickering lamps of vegetable oil.

In India the difference in appearance between a small town and a remote village is not merely that of size. As I have said, towns along lines of rail or motor roads include buildings of stone, metal with concrete and glass, all of which are rarely seen in remote villages. Another big difference is that trees appear sparsely in the small towns, leaving the populace to swelter in the glaring sun, with little shade other than that of makeshift awnings and shelters over market booths along the dusty, curbless streets. The feeling is of a dense, coarse existence of struggle, anxiety and sweat. The aspect of the village is vastly different. The only vehicles are bullock carts and a few bicycles, virtually the only sounds those of voices, animals and birds. People are barefooted, their movements seemingly relaxed beneath the shade of trees, mangoes, peepul, banyan or plantains. Children play about the unpaved alleys, women squat, preparing vegetables, making chapatties, washing rice, moulding cowdung into flat round pats to spread in the sun to dry for fuel. At dusk men, women and children return in single file along grassy tracks, feet and hands earthy, bodies sweating after the labour of the day. In the village the small, dark habitations are relatively cool. There is nothing idyllic in this world and much that is grim in rural India. The visual differences, however, are real enough, whatever notions one may derive from them.

In the great plain villages stand, usually much hidden by trees, on small elevations of only a few feet above the arable land about them. Gazing out over the scene from the train, one suspects the existence of a village whenever, in the middle distance, one sees a green density of trees, a little white temple or shrine, a small turreted tower to indicate a mosque.

As for the green revolution, signs of technical ingenuity are frequently visible. Occasionally a new-looking tractor could be seen or a motor-driven pump with water gushing into irrigation channels between growing crops. These exist in the same areas in which the traditional, laborious methods of irrigation survive. Water is raised in a metal, dish-like container, or in a leather skin, by a pair of bullocks walking slowly round a capstan perched over the well, the water being tilted out into channels on the land. Water is lifted from ponds – often from the hollows alongside the railway line, or beneath the embankments supporting roads – by means of a kerosene can or a long wooden container which looks like a dugout canoe. The can, or one end of the wooden container, is attached to the end of a long pole (usually of bamboo), with a weight attached to the other, the pole being perched on a high tripod. A man holding a rope attached to the can or one end of the wooden container, pulls it down into the water to fill it. The weight at the other end of the pole is then allowed to lift the can or container which is tilted over the irrigation channel and emptied. Sometimes a tube well, hand-operated or worked by motor, is carried about in a bullock cart. It can be sunk anywhere at will, for the soil of the plain is uniformly soft and in many places water exists only a few feet below the surface for some weeks after the end of the monsoon. Whilst tractors and the most effective pumps require imported oil fuel at high cost, there are strong incentives to develop fuel-saving devices in agricultural development. I heard of, but did not see, a metal frame equipped with most of the tools for tillage normally drawn by a tractor, but which can also be drawn by bullocks. I saw land upon which piles of animal manure had been laid in rows ready for digging in or dispersal, and vast quantities of chemical fertilisers are now manufactured in India. In this northern part of the plain the ryotwari systems of land tenure by independent peasant families (either as owners or tenants) has for long prevailed. Following the tradition of service in the famous Punjab regiments of the old Indian Army, soldiers will save much of their pay for eventual investment in capital equipment for the improvement of their family holdings. I was told repeatedly that this tradition lies at the root of much of the green revolution in this part of the plain. When I got to Bihar I found a very different situation, with problems of absorbing interest concerned with land, its tenure and development. There the more primitive methods of tillage and irrigation prevail.

As the train moved northward from Hardwar a small upward gradient made itself felt and I gazed north-westward and north-eastward for the hazy outlines of the hills. My surprise came when the train changed direction and the Siwalik hills appeared quite close, only a few kilometres away, dark, jungle-covered forms rising to several hundred feet above the green plain. At one I was reminded of scenes in north-western Burma, where similar hills rise abruptly from paddy fields along whose edges we had trudged in dusty denims. In a few minutes the train was moving into a valley between the hills and, on either side could be seen jungle with occasional tracks or foot paths leading away to invisible clearings and tiny farmsteads. The jungle here, as in hundreds of miles of South-East Asia, consists largely of teak – middle-sized, rather straggly trees with large, ragged leaves, the raggedness caused by caterpillars, red ants and bees. Just as the bark of plane trees and eucalyptus looks injured and ragged, so do the leaves of teak, hanging motionless in the heat.

At Dehra Dun I followed the young military family out into a scruffy street where taxis and the bus for Mussoorie stood waiting. In the queue at the booking office I eventually bought a ticket – an extremely cheap one – and went over to the waiting bus. During this visit to India I saw hundreds of buses but never set eyes on a new one. Those I saw were gravely bruised, battered creatures of great rumble power and authority, more like ancient rams, buffaloes or elephants upon the roads of India. Most of them bear in front the dusty but prestigious letters ASHOK LEYLAND or TATA.

I climbed into the grimy, crowded vehicle and steered to a seat next to a window, immediately behind the young officer's wife with her baby. In a few minutes all the seats were taken, people sitting with baggage on their laps, jamming the gangway. There followed a very lengthy process of examining tickets, a semi-uniformed, part-shaven youth struggling to reach outstretched hands bearing tickets that were passed back and forth for perhaps twenty minutes, whilst dusk fell and lights appeared in the street. Then, in a venerable shudder, we started off.

Dehra Dun is a straggling town through which a long, broad avenue lined with trees runs upwards gently to open country and the hills. I got a good view of the scene on the return journey a few days later. There were stops at two or three villages and a halt where a small visitors' tax is collected, presumably as a contribution towards the cost of maintaining the stupendous zigzagging road up to Mussoorie which we reached less than two hours later. Unable to see anything from the windows I watched some of the passengers, but my attention was held mainly by the mother and baby. I talked a little with the family. They had a week's leave and friends with whom to stay in Mussoorie: it would be quiet and cool there, good for baby. Meanwhile, baby had to be fed, the preparation of milk powder and boiled water from a flask being undertaken by father under the guidance of mother whilst she, holding baby, was immobilised in her seat.

The spectacle of mother and child in an Indian setting, village, field, street, train or bus, forms an archetypal image in which sartorial form, curves, colours and fragilities, gestures, hair, eyes and laughter, the infant's smile, thrusting, curling toes, are enduring features. Emerging from a painting by, say, Andrea del Sarto in the Italy of the Renaissance, the Indo-European maternal form persists in an Indian bus about four centuries later. There is, however, a difference between West and East in prevalent attitudes to archetypal form. In the West, even from remote times, consciousness has been dominated by yearnings for human perfectibility, by utopian vision and aspiration. Every technical change, the smallest apparent improvement, seems to indicate a direction away from archetypal form towards dream-come-true. The words 'progress' and 'fashion' imply this. Fashion is felt to be no mere change but, especially when we are young, a forward movement, even in the grace of an earring or a slipper. There is fashion, of course, in India, but it is only a tiny infiltration. In the West the drive of human aspiration into the future has broken the pursuit of archetypal forms of every kind, leaving the roles of modern man, director, priest, professor, milkman, footballer or disc jockey, to be undertaken by figures who, at least at weekends, are more or less indistinguishable. Mother and non-mother cannot be told apart. In India human beings, perhaps most of them, seem consciously to strive to appear in archetypal roles within a powerful society of caste and form. India teems with such forms, bearded, sandalled, saried or naked, walking in the sun. Democracy in the West implies the upthrust of lower orders whose visible and audible uniformities dominate the social world. In India democracy is experienced, not as a single upthrusting heave to uniformity, but as a mulitiplicity of yearnings of relatively lower castes, each striving for the privileges of relatively higher ones in an infinite hierarchy of archetypal forms. In India it is a yearning. In the West fulfilment has exhausted the momentum of direction. Archetypes have gone: only fashion remains.

The use of cars in Mussoorie is strongly restricted by law, and the buses from Dehra Dun do not enter the town but halt in a parking area at the foot of a wall which runs along the main street at a higher level. To get to the street one climbs steps or walks up a steepish slope. I was not aware of this when I climbed out of the bus in the dark, and had no idea of the location of the hotel in which a room had been booked for me by the friends in the British Council in New Delhi — let us call it the Rosebelle. So I walked over to one of the waiting taxis and asked to be taken to the Rosebelle Hotel. The driver repeated my instructions, smiled a little oddly, took my bag, and we started. He took me rapidly zigzagging down the hill again in the direction of Dehra Dun. After a few seconds of this I felt anxious. 'Is this all right? Rosebelle Hotel!' I shouted. He made no reply but kept on downhill with no loss of speed. Suddenly the car turned and went up hill again, presumably by a road to some other part of Mussoorie. It swung round and halted, and I recognised the bus station from which we had started out. 'Rosebelle Hotel,' said the driver. 'Must walk now.' The hotel could be reached only on foot by climbing a few steps and walking about fifty yards along the road, then up another flight of steps to a comanding site on a steep slope. I had, of course, been slightly hijacked. However, having eaten practically nothing since breakfast I was not disposed to contest the driver's demand for a sizeable sum in payment for his services. Moreover the thin mountain air had not improved my ability to climb steep steps carrying a case. It seemed better to pay and feel green than to explode and drop dead. In any event the energy with which the driver had bounded up the steps dissuaded me from contest with such a goat. This is a suitable point at which to warn the visitor to India to be careful. I do not believe India has more thieves than most other countries. But Indians are curious about money. Unless you really are of a litigious nature, avoid allowing an Indian, however pleasant, to become your debtor.

At the hotel, apart from a dim light at the reception counter, I found the place in darkness and silent, though it was still quite early in the evening. A dishevelled young man at the desk, aware of my name, required me to furnish a long list of details of my identity, past movements and future plans, the questions framed as though all my movements must be finely calculated to the nearest half hour. He took my bag and led me into the building, switching on lights as we proceeded along passages, up and down short flights of stairs and round corners. In a distant passage he inserted a big, old key into the lock of Room 17 and turned it clumpily. We entered a musty room whose contents, like garments in a museum of departed styles, evoked a mode of living long vanished – two much hollowed beds with faded coverlets, two deep arm chairs and a settee each stained by cigarette burns of forty years ago, the seats low enough for the drunk or exhausted, a crooked picture of cattle in the misty bogland of a Scottish fastness and another, almost straight, of a hunting scene in Leicestershire, a standard lamp with no bulb and a tangle of electric cables vaguely across the floor. There was a lightable bedside lamp and a rickety glass covered dressing table upon which a letter might possibly be composed or a diary upkept. Adjoining the room was a slated and tiled area with shower and loo. A robust spider, conceivable in Cornwall, advanced wisely up the wall. I expressed my thanks and said I would come to the dining room after a shower; and a little to my surprise the shower worked, eventually with hot water. The spider looked on.

Hanging on a wall near the reception counter was a framed glass case containing a pleasantly printed account of the building. It had been erected in the 1870s for a prince and used by his family as a hill-station residence till 1952, after which it had become a hotel. The glass-case story is typical, not only of old buildings in Mussoorie itself but of such relics in every part of India.

The dining room was a big, tall, gloomy place with a glass and timber skylight but no windows. Hanging from beams on long chains were two immense imitation candelabras of glass crystal-line shapes, each candelabra containing but a single naked bulb of low power. Two long narrow tables were covered with white cloths, one of them crumpled at one end, with food stains of recent date. Also in evidence were a few well-acclimatised sauce bottles, with sticky tops, and two large dishes of fruit, possibly real. Along one side of the room, below waist height, ran mahogany shelves on which stood a few books, an almanac and faded copies of *The Strand Magazine* going back seventy years, some sloping, others flat, lying crookedly as though tossed aside by passing waiters. In a corner stood a very tall hat stand, unutilised. Along the opposite wall were enormous glass cases in which, on broad shelves, stood silver-plated soup tureens, covers for joints each marked with a princely heraldic design and initial, complicated cruets, egg stands for the very small eggs furnished by Indian poultry, vessels in red Venetian glass, hefty ladles, carving knives and forks, elaborate toast racks and coffee pots reminiscent of Osborne or Sandringham in a shadowy past.

I turned from the glass cases and surveyed the used table in search of a spot relatively free of stains and equably distant from the sauce bottles. It struck me that the absence of any smell of cookery meant simply there was no one in the kitchen; but then a waiter appeared and asked me laconically, 'Vegetarian or non-vegetarian?' Happily incredulous, I asked for chicken, dahl, rice and chapattis. After about twenty minutes he reappeared, bringing the dishes in successive missions extending over a further fifteen minutes or so. This was the first of many similar meals I was to consume in India in hotels or circuit houses. It was tepid (presumably because of the great distance it had to be transported from the kitchen), feeble and watery in flavour, and very hard to chew. But then the Indian chicken adapts ideally to a culinary disaster: it is extremely small, it is cooked almost immediately after slaughter, and it is apparently reared on a diet of sashcords and old matting. It even has its disciples. My fellow guest, a kindly old Englishman from Croydon, enjoyed the food immensely.

Apart from breakfasts, I took only one more meal at the hotel, the gloom of which depressed me, and sought other meals at cheap restaurants in the streets. Breakfasts, however, were more cheerful, making demands only upon shops, not cooks – bowls of genuine fruit including good apples and bananas, a local form of wheat flakes, toast, butter, almost English marmalade, and eggs. The eggs were presented in the wonderful stands from one of the glass cases.

After breakfast I set out to find what might still remain of the Charleville Hotel where I had stayed during a hot weather leave in 1944. At the reception counter of the Rosebelle I was told that the Charleville no longer existed as a hotel, the buildings being now used by the Lal Bahadur Shastri National Academy of Administration for the senior grades of the all-India public services, a sort of national administrative staff college. The buildings of the old hotel, including chalet structures arranged in a group round a circling approach drive and ornamental gardens, are used as classrooms, a library and administrative centre. Most of the students, some with families, live in recently constructed flats nearby, or scattered about Mussoorie. The centre is about a mile and a half from the town bazaar, on steeply sloping ground beneath the quiet roadway.

The layout of Mussoorie itself is not easy to describe. The main bazaar is along the roadway above the wall, facing down to the Siwalik hills and Dehra Dun, more or less to the south. The roadway lies a few hundred feet below the crest of a ridge through which a gap takes it to the other side, with a northern prospect of the Himalayan mass far away in white cumulus cloud, with snowy peaks occasionally visible like distant crystal in the sun. Between the road and the distant mountains rise a succession of shadowy ridges, each silhouetted against the haze of the one behind it. Forest-covered slopes descend steeply into a huge valley immediately below, its other side heaving in rocky aridity across the entire foreground, several miles away.

The bazaar was packed with people, pedestrians or rickshaw passengers – the rickshaws being pulled by four or five men of the hills, swarthy, with slightly mongoloid features. Two kinds of people are at once distinguishable – visitors from elsewhere in India, and the local people who serve them, tough-looking men and youths who pull rickshaws, bearers, other servants, lodging-house owners and the staff of many institutions, educational, religious and others, including various kinds of Christian organisations. Columns of boys or girls in school uniforms, young students and teachers are seen everywhere. Life in the town involves a continuum of cultural activity, concerts, shows, dramatic events, exhibitions of craftsmanship, bands, processions and festivals. All this shrivels away each year when the snow descends in winter and during the heavy thunderous monsoon rains. No visitors remain in those months.

Rising from the trees, at various levels above and below the winding roadways, stand structures similar to the Rosebelle Hotel, mostly white, dazzling, some of them the mansions of a former élite, or hotels of the period of the Raj, clubs where, in uniform, we danced so passionately, slept late and awoke in sunlight and pine-resined air. Most of those buildings are now shut, some, like the Rosebelle, pretending to be alive, with warm, glass-covered verandahs, dead flies, lizards and spiders undisturbed. The modern visitors seldom frequent such places, but live in small, crowded boarding houses or furnished rooms, doing their own catering.

Thronging the bazaar in vivid colours, the Indian crowds of visitors are vastly larger than the smaller numbers who went to hill stations in the past and included many European wives and children, joined for short spells by their husbands from the great heat of the plains. The Indian visitors, nearly all of the new, ever-swelling middle grades and castes from the cities, now live in the world of sauce bottles, snacks and plastic bags. All are too young to have witnessed a silver soup tureen or engraved joint cover at the tiffin of a prince, his family and friends. India's democracy is that of loudspeakers and Coca-Cola, picture postcards and bicycles, buses and din.

In the trade of the bazaar, chain stores and large supermarkets are wholly absent, and this is true of all India, even the biggest cities. Virtually all shops, by Western standards, are small family affairs, and the great volume of trade is carried on less in buildings than in the streets. As in the rest of the world the nature and quantity of goods for sale indicate the social strata to which they are sold. In the West a large proportion of the goods in the shops can be seen in the council flats and homes of the people who produce them. In India the corresponding proportion is far smaller. Peasants and factory workers produce the contents of the shops, but such goods are purchased predominantly by middle grades who are neither peasants nor 'workers', but the vastly expanded strata who now dominate every urban scene. It is much simpler to reduce death rates with drugs and insecticides than to enrich the larger population which ensues. And it is easier to enact a democratic constitution for a people than to democratise the products of their labour. The life of India is a demonstration of these truths. Whatever may happen in politics, this situation is unlikely to change significantly unless, of course, for the worse. Worsenings, the world over, are simpler to arrange than improvements.

As in all country of forested hills, the walker can seldom leave man-made tracks of one kind or another for more than a few minutes. Had I had a companion, as my father did decades before, I could have set out with a rucksack and a good survey map to walk down a winding track to the bottom of the valley and find my way up to the crest of the first range of hills which interposed themselves before the distant snows. I could perhaps have had a swim in a stream and sat near it in the sun, reading a novel by Nayantara Sahgal which I had in my pocket. I could find no suitable map for sale locally (which indicates the non-walking *modus vivendi* of Indian visitors) and to walk to such an area without a map and without a companion implied taking the risk of a mishap – a fall, a twisted ankle, say – to prevent my visit to Bihar, which must be achieved.

As I walked along the asphalted road, crossing pools of shadow between sunlight, I heard voices from the trees below and saw the figures of two young Indian women with rucksacks and jeans, climbing up a stony track towards me. I watched enviously and greeted them as they reached the road, sweating, laughing and rosy. They seemed happy to talk with me, much interested in my identity and purpose. British people are very seldom seen now anywhere in India. Australian girls investigate the Himalayas before settling down as dentists' receptionists in London or New York, American hippies in beads and sandals recline in rickshaws before deportation and drugs overtake them, but the British, being now ghosts, are seldom witnessed. And their descendants in Britain are indifferent to the ghostly vocations of their forebears. British absence of mind has survived both the establishment of Empire and its evanescence. The two girls seemed astonished to encounter a seemingly able-bodied Briton who was apparently not unconscious like any other Briton they might have heard of. Both were former university students, recruits to the senior public service, fluent in English and now attending a three months' course at the training academy. One, like myself, had a degree in economics, so I asked her a few questions involving a vaguely remembered jargon and was charmed to find that she was aware of my old teacher, Professor Hayek.

We parted, waving, and eventually I reached and recognised the complex of buildings of the old Charleville, a couple of hundred yards down a slope to the right. Stretching across the approach was a large white signboard with black lettering, indicating the training academy and making clear that only properly authorised persons were admissible as visitors. So I walked down a track into an area called Happy Valley, to see if I could recognise paths along which I had walked long before. After a few minutes I saw a group of large wooden buildings on the other side of the valley a few hundred yards away. Someone had told me of the existence of a community of refugees from the Chinese invaders of Tibet. The buildings ahead were a school for Tibetan children, many of whom could be seen running about in blue uniforms, with jolly-looking faces. It was now about two o'clock and I was thinking of going to one or other of two Chinese or Tibetan cafés I had noticed near the road, when I saw ahead of me a white-haired European woman. I greeted her and we introduced ourselves. Her name was Nancy Cooper. She was a teacher, formally retired but still teaching the Tibetan children English and other primary subjects. She was tall, handsome, with hair swept back closely, blue eyes and a nose that might have belonged to the Guermantes. Despite such equipment her fluent English retained something of the curiously Welsh sound of the English spoken by Indians. She had evidently spent virtually all her life in the country. Indeed, I found that she had actually been teaching at a famous school at Simla at which an old friend of

mine had been a pupil until 1924, and that she remembered him
clearly. By a strange coincidence my friend, now in his middle
sixties, was on a visit to Simla to attend a prizegiving at the school
at the same time as my own visit to Mussoorie. There is nothing
mysterious about coincidences except the feel of them, a feeling
to which man, eternally blinkered, attributes his various beliefs.

When I asked Nancy to advise me to which of the cafés I should
apply, she said firmly (speaking as a Guermantes): 'I shall take
you over to the school staff canteen and they will give you
something.' She took my arm and led me to a cheerful place full
of young Indian and Tibetan teachers of both sexes, talking,
eating, drinking sweetish liquids, tea and coffee, smoking – in the
mid-stream of their day. An aproned Tibetan bearer fetched me a
paper napkin, a glass of squash, a bowl of Chinese-looking
food and a bottle of soy sauce. After seeing me served Nancy
said she would return to her cottage for her own snack but come
back to collect me in about half an hour, which she did. When I
offered to pay for my food a small bill was produced. The school
was financed and run by the Government of India, the principal
being an Indian and the rector a Tibetan. There was a large staff,
two-thirds Indian and one-third Tibetan. The Tibetans of Happy
Valley practise various crafts, mainly the making of textiles and
basketware, and are gradually being absorbed by India. The
absorption, I suspect, will be of the kind which India has evolved
in the long ages of her history, a process of accretion, not
dissolution. The unity of India is an ever-moving pattern of
accretions, none of which ever becomes wholly fossilised or ever
disappears.

Nancy collected me and we walked back up the track together.
I was hoping that she might show me her cottage but, on the
way, we saw a young, fair European woman walking down
towards us. Nancy introduced me. She was Janet Rizvi, the wife
of Sayed Rizvi, a senior member of the Indian Administrative
Service, now in the role of deputy director of the training centre
at the Charleville. We went, not to Nancy's place but to Janet's,
an old, small house with a garden and terrace, flowers in a wide
arc, approached by a gravelled drive beneath the steep, forested
hillside. When Janet heard that I was bound for Patna in Bihar she
said she knew it well, for she went there during most years to visit
her parents-in-law, her father-in law being S. Q. Rizvi, a retired

Chief Commissioner of police of Bihar. She was aware of my father's name. On the strength of these coincidences, tea was assembled on the terrace where we sat in deck chairs, talking. She had two sons who went to school daily in Mussoorie – they would be back from school shortly. Bicycles stood about the garden and against a whitewashed wall of the house. Bookshelves within were visible – old things and new, cushions, blankets, the things of family living. They had been stationed for two years at Ladakh in remote Kashmir a few years earlier, and she had written the manuscript of a book about it.* She told me about the tremendous rain they had had during the monsoon now virtually ended, the great thunderstorms, clouds of mist through which rain crushes down the leaves of teak trees, streams roaring over stones and rocks to the flooded rivers of the plains below, to the Ganges far away.

After Nancy had left us Janet invited me to walk with her to the training centre to meet Sayed. I felt a ghostly recognition as we entered the central block where the old reception desk had been, now a lobby with pigeon holes and a blackboard with chalked announcements for the students all around us, young men and women from every part of India. We entered a pleasant office where Sayed Rizvi rose to greet us. He was tallish, slender, good-looking, in his late thirties – perhaps the best period in administrative life, when the rigidities of decisiveness have not yet injured the elasticity of intelligence. Glancing at a large wall blackboard with firm and fluently chalked words and columns upon it, I gathered that he had both teaching and administrative responsibilities at the centre. After introducing me Janet looked at her watch, decided to leave us together, and returned home.

The British member of the old Indian Civil Service was, of course, an alien ruler. Yet the strength, as well as the weakness of his position, apart from personal qualities, was enhanced by this remoteness. Many of the decisions he was required to make, whether administrative or magisterial, demanded a detachment from conflicting communal, caste and cultural interests which surrounded him during every day of his life. This detachment was assumed and valued by the people of the country, whom he encountered at every level. Members of the service commonly

---

Ladakh, Crossroads of High Asia, Oxford University Press, New Delhi.

served the whole of their careers within the boundaries of a single province. This deepened their understanding of the local people and their languages, enabling potential responses to alternative policies and decisions to be assessed with shrewdness.

Just as the strength of the old I.C.S. depended largely upon the remoteness of its members so, I believe, does the modern Indian Administrative Service depend for its strength upon a remoteness of its own. It is a remoteness of a different kind. First, its members constitute an Indian, not an alien élite. Second, the caste structure of Hindu society strongly reinforces the authority of any élite selected largely on educational grounds. Members of the traditionally priestly and most venerable caste, the Brahmins, are supposed to be endowed with wisdom, whatever their learning, and the Kshatrya, or princely caste, are expected both to practise wisdom and to demonstrate courage. There is, therefore, an understandable presumption in Indian society that an administrative and judicial élite largely consisting of members of these castes who have survived severe intellectual tests will not be lacking in the kind of detachment required by tradition in the services to which they belong. In all this India is a little like France. During the past two centuries, French politicians and statesmen, however ostensibly radical and revolutionary their utterances or intentions, turn out to be pretty respectable bourgeois in the manner of their lives; so, too, top Indians, whatever their notions of socialism and democracy, are usually pretty near the summit of their own ancient society.

The authority of the Indian senior public services, and of the officer cadres of the armed services, is sustained also by certain Indian attitudes that are as ancient and deep as caste itself. These may be encapsulated by the word 'adulatory'. I shall have more to say about this later. Indians are adulatory people. By this I mean that any human experience considered to be fortunate or praiseworthy engenders among Indians an impulse to express recognition of it by a gesture. The gestures take many forms – placing a garland of flowers or tinsel about the neck of an individual, speeches, flattery, embraces and physical gestures of tenderness. The administrator or magistrate, officer or judge, is much sustained in his role by adulation which the role itself requires. Incidentally, this quality, which pervades Indian life, endears India to people and individuals from the outside world whose cultural tradition or personal history has been relatively deprived of the experience of adulation. The personal life of my father was deeply deprived in that sense, and his love of India, not understood by himself, was rooted in the adulation bestowed upon him by Indians. In the Protestant North of Europe a sense of sin has caused whole peoples to be deprived of the experience of adulation which Indians bestow upon all the living. The guilty feel guiltier and relish their own guilt by eschewing the adulation which the human psyche craves. My father earned what he got, but he needed it, too.

The young Indian graduate who joins one or other of the senior services will, as likely as not, have received all or most of his education within a particular state. The country is so large that his experience of other states and his awareness of India as a whole will be fragmentary. Apart from classroom instruction during the basic training at the academy in Mussoorie, by meeting colleagues from all over the country he rapidly becomes acquainted with all-India matters, such as the structure of the Constitution the distribution of powers between the states and the centre, relationships between legislatures, executives and judicatures, and, of course, a great deal about the financial and economic structure of the country. After initial training the recruit is posted to a state, not necessarily his own, and in due course may return to the centre for specialised training in this or that particular field of responsibility.

From this summary it will be clear that, by broadening and deepening the perspectives of their outlook upon India, the training strengthens still further the detachment with which members of the senior services are able to view the mission of their lives. This sense of mission is derived from the past, but I believe it is very strong indeed in modern India. The English language is itself vital to its survival in a unitary form.

The Indian Administrative Service of today has changed in many ways since independence, but its structure is clearly derived from the old I.C.S. Within the government departments in New Delhi and in the secretariats of the state capitals, the main function of the service is both to brief and advise ministers and to execute the policies of governments. In the British period, even after the India Act of 1935 had established a large measure of provincial autonomy, the advisory role was a relatively minor one, the exercise of authority within an administrative hierarchy being much stronger than it has since become. Out in the countryside the role of the 'collector', or district magistrate, apart from the collection of revenue, is now mainly that of a coordinator of the activities and policies of the ever more numerous agencies of the central and state governments – he is essentially a chairman. The territorial areas for which individual officers are responsible, for that reason, and also because of the growth of population, are smaller than they were during the Raj, but the coordinating role is an exacting one, certainly more desk-bound, because of the proliferation of public agencies and the vast growth of the private economic sector. The administrator has become more faceless, less of a person. As man and master he is less known than his British or Indian predecessor. Even so, his position in the field is far more authoritarian, solitary and exalted than that of any local authority in Britain since manorial times. The unity of India is heavily dependent upon the preservation of his position within the structure of government. It is the function of the training academy at Mussoorie to promote the attributes required to sustain it.

I asked Rizvi about the quality of recruits to the senior services. Was it declining, or well sustained? How about corruption, rumours and reports of which were evidently so newsworthy? He believed that the quality of recruits from the universities was exceedingly good, showing no sign whatever of decline. There were, however, long-term factors in modern Indian society which put great strain upon members of the senior services. He did not elaborate, but I was to hear more about such pressures later in my tour. He said that great damage was being caused to the 'norms' of administrative conduct derived from the old I.C.S. and the British tradition. I did not like to press him on this, and there were other things to discuss before it was time to part and he drove me back in his car to the hotel.

Here is an extract from my diary:

Sunday, 5 October 1980, 0940 hrs.: At about 5.20 yesterday afternoon I heard the sound of drums, bagpipes and brass approaching – a demonstration? I went round to the terrace of the hotel and saw in the street below, approaching from the left, a long procession headed by a scarlet-coated band –

overhead banners with big inscriptions in Hindi, arms swinging, marching figures, hundreds of young people in rich colours lit by the afternoon sun, small children to teenagers of both sexes, divided into many little groups. In a few seconds the band was just below me, deafening – just behind followed a group of girls in pale mauve saris and tunics, boys in dark blue, other girls in brilliant red, a little group of girls in bright, tinselled saris, a float bearing a big banner in English: 'God is Pure' – this representing the movement of Mother Teresa in Calcutta – another group of girls in delicate pastel draperies, dancing in a moving circle along the street.

It was some time before I could get any explanation from the hotel servants. The procession was a celebration of the autumn, perhaps rejoicing at the end of the rains and the beginning of the dry weather. All the children are resident in Mussoorie, belonging to many schools and miscellaneous organisations and religious groups. Whilst in Europe a seasonal festival may include different groups, it is seldom that very different kinds of faith will be represented. And, in Britain at least, the show of colour, dress and mime would be subdued. Here, where the people live in tiny dwellings in cramped conditions, with very little comfort, the occasion is one of wonderful display, rich in colour, grace and artistry. The coexistence of multiple identities is the integral feature of Indian social values. Parents, especially mothers, devote meticulous attention to the dress and deportment of their children on festive occasions. And, among adults, the attention to dress, the grace of women in the cities as they go to work, is a strong, vivid achievement in the midst of poverty.

5
To the Eastern Plain

After a solitary, ruminative final day in Mussoorie, I boarded the crowded bus for Dehru Dun soon after breakfast. The road itself, zigzagging down the rocky hills, is a great feat of civil engineering. Blasted out of the rock, the outer edges support stone walls which require constant maintenance to repair damage caused by heavy rain and falling rock. The lower slopes of the hills contain green valleys, orchards and much arable land, and reminded me of scenes in Alpine country. As the bus approaches Dehra Dun substantial houses with gardens appear, all, so far as I could see, in a condition of neglect, though not unoccupied. Most of them had presumably been the residences of British officers, military and civilian, years ago, but some have always belonged to landowners, merchants and professional men. I saw several that were evidently used by religious organisations, Hindu, Buddhist or Christian, but all these seemed very seedy in appearance – with unpainted wrought-iron gateways rusting in the sun, broken window frames, unpainted woodwork, a ragged path, neglected gardens and litter-strewn verges – not unlike aspects of inner city squalor in Britain. Indeed, throughout India I saw Indian manifestations of social changes familiar to us in the West – the unpredicted shabbiness of life that ensues from ostensibly democratic or egalitarian policies and pressures.

The bus descends gradually into the town along a broad avenue of considerable length, but the whole stretch of it, apart from the trees themselves, is melancholy, with houses and gardens in various stages of decay. Low salaries and the tendency of the wealthy to live mainly in city flats, their wealth no longer spread out into the landscape in the forms of mansions and gardens, elephants and show – these, I believe, are the basic causes of this decay. It may be due also to a certain inward-looking quality of the Indian mind. People who look inwards do not concern themselves with the appearance of their homes and lives.

The train waiting at the station was not crowded and I had few companions on the long, slow journey to Delhi where, empty, crumpled and grimy with dust, I arrived at about half past ten that night. I went in search of an auto-rickshaw to take me the short distance to the Ranjit Hotel. Unlike British travellers, Indians are not disciplined queuers and the drivers of rickshaws and taxis are men of independent decision. Indeed a vigorous form of *laissez-faire* dominates the entire private sector of the Indian economy. After observing the evanescence of various attempts by citizens to form queues, I spotted a young auto-rickshaw driver, walked over to him and asked to be taken to the hotel. He grinned.

We moved away from the station and plunged at once into a narrow, crowded lane in almost complete darkness. I had no plan of the city and darkness obscured all the outlines that might have afforded clues for me in daylight. I was fully aware that we were not taking the direct route to the hotel but I was powerless to utter a sensible word to the driver who, anyway, seemed to know no English. The lanes through which he drove were cobbled, pitted and bumpy, lined by small shops and full of people. I began to steel myself to the assumption that I was now, after all these years of liberty, being hijacked at last.

Then the rickshaw, spluttering and smoking, emerged from cobbled lanes into a main street jammed tight with traffic. For a long time we were immobilised amid huge lorries laden high with bundles and surmounted by humanity. Hidden in dark recesses people lay close to buildings, sinking into fitful sleep, waking to a child's cry or to hit away a rat. Four big camels in single file towered above my head, a cow masticating a large sheet of newpaper was urinating into an absent meadow– the night air, foul with thick yellow dust, vibrated with the roar of engines. Our own stopped and was restarted a dozen times by the young driver, whose face and body streamed with sweat. Finally we turned a corner and I recognised a railway bridge not far from the hotel. In a moment we were there. The driver jumped down, beamed at me and demanded a hefty fare. I paid it without question. The journey which, a few days before, had taken ten minutes in the early morning, had now required fifty. It was easy to say – as people did to me the next day – 'You were taken for a ride'. Was I? An Indian reader who knows the streets may answer the question with authority. I can only tell the story. In the hotel they found some soup for me, a banana and some yoghurt.

I could have travelled to Patna overnight in a smart modern train like the Rajdahni Express but chose instead to leave Delhi at ten 'o'clock the following morning in another old slow one, in order to see as much as possible of the plain to the south-east. The taxi journey to the station again took only ten minutes. At the station I followed an old, red-shirted and turbaned porter to the office of an official whose massive responsibility it was to decide which passengers should be permitted to travel. Sitting behind a big black table by a cupboard festooned with cobwebs was a heavy, unshaven man with an enormous ledger in front of him. Standing behind and about him was a group of subordinates in various states of dishabille, apparently quarrelling but possibly not. On the floor squatted a barefooted man in grubby cotton garments, with a hammer. Above his head the cupboard door was open, revealing thousands of rectangular printed documents loosely piled on shelves. The man was engaged in arranging these papers into regular blocks each a few inches thick, through the centre of which he was required to hammer a long nail, thus transfixing them before removal to a place of storage elsewhere. In front of the table sat several prospective travellers of both sexes who, like myself, wanted to know whether or not seats would be allotted to them on trains. The work of the big man was to scan the pages of the ledger, lift and lower his spectacles in a manner of decision, make authoritative statements of affirmation or denial and fill in spaces in the ledger with marks with a fountain pen. All this he achieved with firmness, solemnity and calm, undisturbed by the blows of the hammer or the cobwebs above his head. After I had stood watching the scene for fifteen minutes he glanced up at me, lowered his spectacles and said: 'Mr Richard Terrell. Patna. One seat.' He handed me a small piece of paper indicating the coach, compartment and seat on the train which stood at the platform. I bowed and thanked him, much relieved, but his dedication did not permit any acknowledgement of my smile.

The train moves south-east to Agra before turning more directly east and it seemed only a few minutes after leaving Delhi that we were travelling again through wide open country. I began now to feel a pleasure that was to recur again and again leaving urban areas in India, whether by train or car, and especially in the huge Gangetic plain. For almost the only attractive features of Indian towns are ancient buildings, palaces, temples, mosques and tombs or perhaps a general panorama such as that of Bombay. There is in most towns an occasional house of dignity, perhaps with old wooden balconies, elaborately carved and well preserved. But the open, earthy land beyond, with its villages and little shrines, seems to reveal an eternal quality which is brutally assaulted by the metal, concrete, brick, dirt and dust, the din and brashness of urban growth collectively known as 'the bazaar'. The Indian commercial town is a squalid precipitate of unwilled consequences, however benign the individual aims of urban man. I suspect that British absence of mind must, in history, have contributed much to this. In the past British industrial towns sprawled much as they did in nineteenth-century India. Just as in Britain, between the last few decades of the eighteenth century and the first five of the nineteenth, our slums were almost taken for granted by rulers whose personal lives were remote from the scenes of urban growth, so in India 'the bazaar' was something in which the Company, the Service, did not interfere. The minds of India's present rulers, it would seem, are also preoccupied by greater concerns. Landscape, as in England, remains superb, at least as I discovered it on October days in my journeys of escape from urban scenes.

Land, crops and villages between Delhi and Agra present a scene similar to that between Delhi and Dehra Dun to the north-east – fields of standing sugar canes, tall, feathery, rushlike millets, smaller paddy fields of glistening rice, light green, fresh, yellowing a little in the sun. Where millet or sugar had been cut I saw stacks of such crops drying or awaiting transport from the land, the stubble being weeded by women squatting, pulling the weeds with their fingers, collecting them in little baskets to take to their villages as cattle fodder. Sometimes a tractor could be seen drawing a plough, sometimes a man hacking at hard earth with a heavy hoe, sometimes a pair of bullocks and a primitive plough, a barefoot peasant driving them forwards patiently. I doubt if urban Indians feel much yearning for the land. For people throughout the tropical world pine for their towns and escape into them. We Europeans, and especially the British, pine for the land we have lost and escape into it from our towns.

The train spent a long time – about two hours, I think – standing at a platform in Agra, slowly shunting through suburban areas, advancing again, presumably to get itself transferred to the main line to Kanpur (formerly Cawnpore) and the East. At Agra many students, books under their arms, ballpoints protruding from pockets, boarded the train, half a dozen of them entering my compartment. With them was an older, stouter, black-bearded man in a turban who seemed to provide for them the intellectual and moral services of a guru. Presumably he was a professor or lecturer, but his status within the group seemed to correspond to nothing familiar to me from my own student years. Whenever he uttered a word the young men nodded in appreciation. If, when their voices were raised in animation, he smiled and said something from his corner seat, there would be a hush. At some station not far from Agra they all trooped out, leaving empty silence in the upholstery. I had been watching a small manifestation of the adulatory relationships which pervade the world of India. When one knows nothing of a language one interprets the chamber music of its use.

From the train at Agra I was not able to see the Taj Mahal itself, though I visited it years before. Occasionally between buildings close to the railway could be seen glimpses of other great buildings of the Moghul era, and these are always exciting for, here in the north and north-west of India, they stand out powerfully from all structures of later periods. Although basically of Muslim design, they express something as deeply Indian as the spirit of princely rule itself, of whatever faith. Like the Red Fort in Delhi, all have three distinct features. The first is defensive power, manifest in towering walls of sandstone, rising perhaps to a hundred feet above barren ground, shielding the prince from attack, separating his person from the rabble beyond, seemingly impregnable. The second, witnessed only within, is luxury, a mode of living sensual, watchful, envied, hated, worshipped – ending in blood upon a marble floor inlaid with agate and cornelian. The third is a visible grace. In the ruins themselves this is seen in the forms of red sandstone turrets raised upon slender columns above walls and gateways, symmetrically poised for the watchmen of old and for the spectator today. Shielded from the burning sun beneath such turret domes, the sentries long ago would gaze into the distance, watching for the movements of an enemy king, his canopies, elephants and guns moving in a cloud of dust upon the horizon. Long vanished now, perceived only in paintings and textiles, costume, music and the dance, another, human, grace moved within the walls.

After Agra the wide land opens out again. By now it was afternoon. Soon darkness would conceal from me a great stretch of country to the east and I wished I could stay somewhere overnight, in order to see that panoramic view. I now began to see less sugar and more millets than before, more rice also, and the slanting sunlight seemed to extend the horizon further. All colours were now vivid – the forms of a family group resting beneath a thorn tree, a flashing bangle, a little gold nose ring, the gleam of a bicycle lying on its side near a motionless black buffalo.

In the compartment, after the departure of the students, I had for some time two military companions: a Major Singh whose grey moustache and stoutish, middle-aged appearance suggested that he was probably concerned with supplies, the administration of a camp or the pay of troops, and a young subadar on his way to join a unit somewhere near Calcutta. I was now accustomed to eating food bought on railway platforms and my two companions, both of whom knew a little English, were helpful, telling me what to buy and where to queue – sometimes most kindly queueing for me. I would have little balls of millet dough, rolled out flat and flung for a few seconds into boiling vegetable oil in a black metal bowl over a charcoal fire – a spoonful of potato, cauliflower or cucumber with a chilli and a few curls of onion, dahl in curry sauce, a sweet called *rabri*, milk-based, a banana or an apple. Little bowls for food are made of wide, vinelike leaves, their shapes formed by pegs of thorn. Tea comes in small earthenware cups which, together with the bowls, are thrown out of the window after use.

As the train drew slowly into Kanpur station in the early evening, we passed an enormous new industrial plant whose outlines I could see through the window on my right – great shining metal cylinders reaching up into darkness, jets of steam, darting flames. One of my companions leaned forward to tell me, with a look of pride, that it was the biggest fertiliser plant in India, a joint Government of India and I.C.I. project. The immensity of the plant was evidence of something of great importance in modern India. The public sector of the Indian economy consists essentially of massive contributions to the infrastructure of a mixed economy. During my tour I was more readily made aware of criticism of such projects than of pride in their achievements or the policies they represent. As to the criticism, I was never able properly to assess its merits, for a man's bias can usually be detected in the grounds of his complaint. Left wingers always blame management. Right wingers always blame trade unions. Others blame technical factors, shortages of spare parts, etc., etc. The disposition to criticise is attributable partly to the British liberal tradition but also to the public nature of the projects. In the private sector the main criticism is of black marketeering of various kinds, but not of technical inefficiency. For in that sector weakness is self-eliminating and success rewarded. In the public sector all defects can be attributed to human agency, to the evils of power and authority.

After Kanpur I had four companions, businessmen of sorts in their middle forties. I noticed with envy that each had brought with him something in the way of a pillow and a light blanket, and that they were very neat and tidy as travelling companions, sleeping either in pyjamas or in various phases of undress. I lay in my clothes, using as a pillow my softish shoulder bag whose curves were sophisticated by the knobs of my camera and the angularities of a book. I gazed for long periods at the windows, hoping to see an occasional light in a village, but there was hardly a glimmer – sometimes a few points of yellow light from the wicks of small vegetable oil lamps in the huts of peasants.

I awoke at five o'clock. We were due to reach Patna at seven. Slipping on a light dressing gown – I had managed to put on some pyjamas – I slid open the door and went to the end of the coach where, through an open window looking northwards, I could see the land in early daylight. In soft, pink haze the wide earthy scene lay unobserved by other eyes, every feature still in pastel colour. Overnight the train had moved a couple of hundred miles down the plain, and the word 'down' is important. For now the surface of the land was only a few feet above the still far distant sea. The appearance of flatness was enhanced by a great diminution in the quantity of the taller crops of sugar and millets, superseded now almost completely by rice which, of course, is much lower to the earth. Although villages could be seen huddled for shade beneath mango, bamboo and palm, the impression was of a vast levelling away into distant haze. As with each moment the light grew stronger, delicate variations in the ripeness of rice, from fresh light green to the palest primrose, formed an ever clearer pattern, like an infinitely extending watercolour touched with strokes of tenderness.

6

Days in Patna

The city of Patna stretches for several miles along the underside of a wide curve on the south bank of the Ganges. Far in the distance across the river can be seen low sandbanks and bushes, beyond which lie paddy fields and a few hamlets lost in haze. A visitor to the city who had not previously seen a map could be oblivious of the river. For, despite its importance, people in the town do not see it at all unless they actually go to the embankment by walking through narrow streets and lanes between buildings, houses and gardens which conceal the stream from view. This rather odd invisibility of the river at first deprives the visitor of what would otherwise be the obvious guide line to the general plan of the town, just as the Thames, the Seine or the sea at Bombay instantly afford topographical clues to the cities themselves. A big town can make little sense until one has managed to plant in one's mind a notion of its general layout.

In very ancient times there was a substantial administrative centre, Pataliputra, from which the name of Patna is derived. Virtually nothing of Pataliputra remains, though the museum contains delightful terracotta figurines and other exhibits from the site. The area, including the ancient centre of Vaishali, just north of the river, became the centre of the Mauryan empire, of which the last and greatest ruler was the convert to Buddhism, Ashoka. Despite the historical importance of the Mauryan period the present city of Patna is basically a development from the early nineteenth century and the British period. Until 1912 all this part of the country, together with a great stretch southwards and south-eastwards to the Bay of Bengal, was administered from Calcutta as part of Bengal. For linguistic, cultural and administrative reasons Bengal was then partitioned between a Bengali-speaking province to the east and a large new province called Bihar and Orissa to the west and south, where the dominant languages are Hindi and Oorya respectively.

The railway from the west approaches the south-centre of the city and, after leaving it, runs parallel with the Ganges for about a hundred miles before turning in a more south-easterly direction towards West Bengal and Calcutta. The city is of a narrow rectangular shape about a mile deep, lying more or less between the railway and the river, the rectangle including distinct functional areas. To the west is a very large region of spacious, tree-lined avenues and gardens, cream-washed houses and stately buildings. This is what is known as the 'government' area which goes back to the establishment of the province in 1912. Here is the palace of the governor of the state, the parliament buildings and the large buildings of the secretariat, many blocks of flats for civil servants and the houses, each in its own garden, of the senior officials in the various branches of government. This whole area presents an image of grandeur, imperial vision, authority and ineffable social distance from the rest of the city and the country as a whole. Within the government area two balancing features are dominant. The older buildings express the authority of official strength, of the Indian social and caste élites which have succeeded to the former cadres of the British Raj. The newer, shining white parliamentary buildings express the popular political, libertarian aspirations enshrined in the Constitution of independent India. The former is the historical infrastructure of the latter. Neither, I believe, can subordinate the other: that is to say, neither could do so, whatever its dominant figures might have in mind. The government area, in my own view of the underlying forces, expresses attributes derived from Europe and now completely drawn, spiritually, into the heart of India.

Radiating northwards and eastwards from the railway station are the main roads of the commercial town, with many smaller lanes between them. This is the bazaar. These are mostly long straight roads whose English names are still used though not actually inscribed on any walls – Main Road, Exhibition Road, Dak Bungalow Road, Fraser Road, Bank Road and several others. Such roads are full of shops, old and new buildings, some of the old ones with carved wooden balconies and overhanging roofs, the newer ones of steel, concrete, brick and glass. A great deal of scaffolding is to be seen and there is a feel of brashness, rough living, din, dust and dirt. The impression of the bazaar upon myself – I lived in the middle of it – is difficult to communicate to the reader who has never been to India, to any part of the East or, indeed, to any part of the tropical world. In a painting or photograph an impression is transmitted instantaneously. In sentences of print such immediacy is not possible unless the reader, before looking at the words, already retains in his own memory a similar experience. It is possible to introduce a scene only feature by feature, in a sort of single file. In doing so I may begin with one common to virtually all commercial streets in tropical conditions: streets, that is, which are not used by any restricted class, rich or poor, but by people of all kinds in a general population. In such streets there is usually a much greater density of humanity than is normally seen in the corresponding streets of cold countries. Masonry in tropical towns can provide more shelter per unit of area than is required by people in cold countries. In the cold city artificial heating and much thicker walls are needed for all. Heating requires space for chimneys, complex equipment, all to be contained within the dwellings. Again, the warmer the climate the greater the proportion of the people to be seen in the streets. In cold countries many more people are shut away from view, indoors, leaving streets relatively deserted. In the tropics people cram the streets, day and night, many sleeping there, simply to be out of doors.

People in the crowded streets, their skin glistening, are clad in cotton and light synthetic textiles. Among men there is a predominance of white cotton and a broad division of styles between Western and Indian dress. In Bihar especially there is a tendency for certain kinds of men, both Hindus and Muslims, to wear purely Indian dress: for Hindus the white cotton dhoti – a loose abundance of soft cotton somehow knotted round the waist with one leg, oddly, more apparent than the other, a long shirt with no collar and short, open sleeves of elbow length; for Muslims, rather close-fitting, wrinkled cotton trousers and longish jackets. Similar traditional styles, often stained and earthy and soaked in sweat, are worn by peasants, labourers, rickshaw pullers and miscellaneous manual workers. Greatly outnumbering those in such traditional dress is the great mass of youngish men in Western clothes, coloured shirts, singlets, bush jackets and trousers. The men wear sandals or shoes and socks whether the rest of their attire is Indian or Western. Umbrellas, very seldom any kind of garment, are carried for rain. Virtually all women wear saris, though Eurasian and Christian women wear Western styles. All small children wear clothes that seem Western in appearance, little girls with charming ribbons in their hair. Looking at them I was reminded of a description of little girls in Mexico by Anaïs Nin: 'The little girls with short black hair and bangs wear butterfly bows of satin in bright colours, the butterfly bow that, as a child . . . I was so eager to have tied so it would stand like a butterfly about to take off.'*

Broadly, it seemed to me that the dress of people in the streets of Bihar generally was less colourful, drabber than that 'of the crowds in Delhi and Bombay. I do not believe the difference is explained entirely by relative poverty, though Bihar is indeed poorer than the regions to the west, but by a prevailing difference in outlook, a lower vivacity.

Apart from an occasional smart shop, a photographer's, a dress shop, a shop with jewellery or rows of attractive bottles and delicatessen, most buildings in the bazaar have a rough, unfinished look about them – walls of unpointed brickwork, loose bricks protruding and about to fall into an untidy alley or yard, dirty or broken glass, rusty metal, dust lying heavily in corners, upon the ledges of windows. Along the sides of most streets are rows of dark, rough stalls supported upon poles, branches of trees, sawn timber, roofed over by corrugated iron, black tarpaulin, brown, faded palm fronds or loose tiles. Many of such stalls are used for cooking and the sale of cooked snacks, with charcoal fires burning beneath black, sooty pans of boiling oil – the odours of onion and turmeric everywhere. Cooking, indeed, casts over many of the street booths the blackness of soot and oily steam. Here, too, soft drinks, cigarettes, raw fruit, yoghurt in big bowls, are sold; a kettle boils for making tea in glasses or small earthenware pots, as on railway platforms. Squatting in the shade in dust near or beneath such stalls people eat, are shaved or sleep; women comb and dress each others' hair and naked children play, or calmly defecate.

The surfaces of urban roads differ greatly from those in the Western world. Pavements for pedestrians are rudimentary, in the sense that, whilst some stretches of low pavement with

---

* Anaïs Nin, *Journals*, vol. V, p. 151.

kerbstones can be seen, all are in need of repair if judged by Western standards. Flag and kerbstones are often missing or broken and the walker must take great care to avoid falling into rectangular drain holes two or three feet deep, the covering metal grids being frequently absent. I narrowly escaped accidents, halting only just in time. During and after rain large puddles of water and floating filth appear everywhere. One's shoes and legs are soaked and blackened by the ooze formed by deluged dust. Long stretches of roadways in the bazaar have no pavements at all.

The central parts of roads, both in town and country, are usually asphalted sufficiently to provide a driveway for two or three lanes of traffic. Along both sides of the roads are wide areas of grit, dust or sand beneath which a solid layer of broken stones or brickwork provides strength and soakaway drainage. During the periods of several weeks when I lived in Patna there was a strike of the sweepers in the city and in the other municipalities of Bihar. The streets became progressively dirtier and the atmosphere more and more foul. Much of the filth consists of refuse from wayside cooking, fruit debris, used tea, discarded leaf bowls and broken earthenware, scraps of paper and cellophane. I do not suppose the scene would have been quite so atrocious had it not been for the strike, which coincided with many days and nights of religious festivals that brought a great influx of people from the countryside.

In the north-centre part of the city is a wide open grassy space, an elongated rectangle in shape, with curved corners, several hundred metres in length and about two hundred in depth, known as the Maidan – a feature common to many towns in India. The Maidan in Patna is ringed by trees, a good pathway beneath them, parklike bushes and flower beds and stone benches. Such areas, planned by the British long ago, were used as camping and parade grounds for troops and also for recreational space, processions, competitions and displays of many kinds. Throughout my stay the Maidan was in almost contant use for public events. It is virtually the only suitable public open place in the city, apart from the river embankment. I used it a good deal for walking, reading or watching the people, sometimes talking with them.

Between the Maidan and the big government area to the west is an area known as Bankipore. This includes not only the main banks, many old residential houses and quiet streets, but what remains of the estate of Chhaju Bagh. The big house of the same name within the grounds was, and still is, the official residence of the Chief Justice – my father's house. Further west are several important buildings, the High Court, the circuit house, the Patna Womens' College, the Pataliputra Hotel and many public offices. Quite near the Maidan to the north-west stands a strange building called the Golghar.*

Beyond a main roadway running along the north edge of the Maidan and far to the east through miles of extended bazaar, stand many fine buildings whose backs and gardens extend to the river embankment, a distance of perhaps a few hundred feet separating the road and the river. Seen from a distance most of these buildings are classical structures with wide colonnades, rows of pillars, spacious grounds and formal dignity. One of the finest of them, Patna College, was formerly the mansion of a Dutch indigo planter. These buildings form the student area of Patna and are most of them colleges of one kind or another, with various research organisations and libraries. In their grandeur

---

* The following description of the building is from the *Bengal District Gazetteers – Patna District*, by L. S. S. O'Malley, ics, dated 1907: 'This is a brick building, 96 feet high with walls 12 feet thick at the bottom, built in the shape of a beehive or half an egg placed on end, with two spiral staircases on the outside winding to the top: it is said that Jang Bahadur of Nepal rode on horseback up one and down the other. This dome-shaped structure was erected 16 years after the great famine of 1770 as a store-house for grain, it being intended that the grain should be poured in at the top and taken out at the bottom through the small doors there: owing to a curious mistake on the part of the builders, these doors were made to open inwards. The following inscription is on the outside: "No I. – In part of a general plan ordered by the Governor General and Council, 20th January, 1784, for the perpetual prevention of Famine in these Provinces, this Granary was erected by Captain John Garstin, Engineer. Completed the 20th of July, 1786. First filled and publicly closed by – ."
'The storehouse has never been filled, and so the blank in the inscription remains, whilst the opening at the top is closed by a great stone slab.'
The gazetteer states, however, that the Golghar was used during another famine in 1874, but was later abandoned because the stored grain was affected by insects, damp and other unforeseen difficulties. In 1907 it was being used by government as a storehouse for furniture.
According to the gazetteer dated 1970 by N. Kumar: 'It is now used as a Government grain go-down.' At the time when I climbed to the top to see the magnificent view over the city and the Ganges, and to take colour transparencies, the cover at the top was made of wood, not stone, and I was informed that the Golghar is indeed still used as a grain store. Presumably the technical difficulties, after nearly two centuries, were overcome somehow. I saw no grain anywhere, however.

they express the vision of imperial and educational policy in the Victorian and Edwardian decades. That policy was derided by many people, including my father, not because of its Western philosophy, but because it was too literary, too academic for the social and economic needs of India. It was, however, of immense importance and, I believe, glorious. It was glorious just as, however fragile, the vision of the Second Empire of Louis Napoleon in mid-nineteenth century France was glorious, setting a pattern of inspiration for many generations to come. When we visit Paris it is that vision which survives in the grey beauty that we see about us. The intelligentsia of modern India was moulded to another vision, expressed in the styles along the river bank at Patna and in other Indian cities.

So much for the layout of Patna and the look of the people. Traffic in the streets is very different from that in Bombay or Delhi. The difference is due to the enormous number of cycle rickshaws and bicycles which entirely dominate the traffic of all towns in Bihar. There are also many motor vehicles of all kinds, but their rate of progress is greatly restricted in the towns by the ever-pedalling mass which sets the pace. In Patna one is more likely to be pushed over gently by a rickshaw than smashed to death by any car. The bodywork of the cycle rickshaw is made of light metal alloy and its shape is usually somewhat upright and tall, with a flimsy hood, usually a bit tattered. Sitting in one of these things one looks upwards at lorries and buses, camels or elephants, but downwards into the surrounding cars, downwards, too, at the neck and back of the rickshaw man who sits on a saddle in front, ringing his bell almost incessantly. The cycle rickshaw is the commonest form of public transport for short distances, and the machines are owned by substantial companies. The 'pullers', as they are called, seem to have an active trade union, but it appears to cause less nuisance to the public than the union of the municipal sweepers. There are many bus services for long-distance travel and the buses are as battered-looking as those in which I had travelled between Dehra Dun and Mussoorie.

For some time before leaving London I had been corresponding with the Chief Justice at the High Court at Patna, K. B. Narayan Singh, about my impending visit. He was aware that I wanted to make Patna a headquarters from which expeditions could be made to places mentioned in my father's letters years ago. I wanted the sort of accommodation in which a room and food would be available without my having to eat in restaurants, where I could leave belongings in safe keeping for several days and to which I could return without previous warning. I wanted something like the kind of catering rest house that I had known in Nigeria thirty years before – such arrangements being cheaper than a hotel but rough by comparison. The Chief Justice had promised to arrange for me to be met at the station and taken either to the state guest house or to the circuit house.

When I got off the train at Patna at seven o'clock in the morning my belongings were instantly seized by a porter who asked with enthusiasm 'Taxi, sahib?' I signalled to him to halt whilst I waited for some emissary from the judiciary to appear. We stood for a moment or two in a great hubbub of echoing loudspeakers and other miscellaneous din, the porter with my suitcase balanced upon his turban, but with no welcome from any quarter. This seemed odd for, as the only visible white man on the platform, I felt somewhat recognisable. Ill equipped by temperament to endure suspended decision, I said to the porter 'Taxi', and we advanced to the street in single file, myself at the rear of the column. When a taximan, adjusting his dhoti and then his hair parting, stepped forward, I said to him 'State guest house', adopting the air of one as able to navigate a taxi to that destination as himself. I tipped the porter – perhaps too much, to judge by his reaction – and we set off somewhere to the north-west, to the eastern part of the government area. We stopped in a grassy space before a biggish building which I vaguely recall as rather like one of the old clubs in St James's, classical in form with a pillared entrance and steps. A slightly bewildered-looking man in a turban led me up a flight of broad stairs – my suitcase left in the hallway below – to a large room in which there were several beds, a sort of dormitory, not originally intended for any such use – perhaps at one time a club lounge or reception room. Here, near the beds, were men in various stages of early-morning toilet. I was invited to sit on an imitation leather settee while a manager or secretary was summoned at what was not, of course, a very convenient hour – still before 7.30.

After some minutes a dishevelled man, very unshaven, appeared who was able to speak a few words of English. He went to telephone the Chief Justice. After about twenty minutes he returned. The Chief Justice had been under his shower. I would not be able to stay at the State guest house (I had already decided that I did not wish to live for some weeks in a dormitory anyway) because it was full up, but I might stay at the circuit house instead, and an officer of the court would arrive shortly to collect me.

The assistant court officer, Mr Uma Shankar Prasad, was in some distress, having somehow missed me in the crowd at the station where perhaps I should have waited a bit longer. Having failed to identify me he had arranged for me to be hailed over the loudspeakers on the platform, so part of the shindy I had endured whilst standing with the porter had probably included something I was supposed to listen to. Now in a successful move to relieve my presumed distress, Mr Prasad smiled, put his head on one side and handed to me my first letter from home. With glee I thrust it into my pocket and he took me at once in his car a short distance to the circuit house, where I spent two nights before moving to a hotel.

The circuit house, though large, is typical, in the amenities it affords, of many other such buildings run by government. It is an old, rather imposing structure in cream-washed cemented brick, a colonnaded semicircle of tall rooms, each with its own concreted shower area attached at the rear. Furnishings include a bed, an old tattered carpet, a mosquito net, overhead fan, luggage rack, dressing table, writing table, armchair of rough folding woodwork and oldish cushions, a couple of upright chairs, a cupboard and a towel rack. Common to nearly all the public buildings that I saw in India were dangling or tangled electric flex cables. Overhead near the ceiling were two spluttering and very dirty strip lights with gently waving cobwebs. Attached to a pile of flex was a wobbly bedside lamp on a wobbly table. Beneath the colonnade a few yards away was a small office in a scruffy recess with one or two untidy-looking custodians, a much-fingered ledger with columned pages for details of arrivals and departures, a wallboard with keys hanging and a telephone which sometimes functioned.

Mr Prasad said that the Chief Justice, who would be in court that day, would send a car to collect me for a meeting of the Bar Association and tea at the High Court in the afternoon and that, after tea, I should be taken to meet one of the judges, Mr Justice Sarwar Ali, at his residence on the Chhaju Bagh estate.

In travel small happenings, little doings, make up the feel of each place known. In India the traveller flings off his sweaty clothes into a heap upon a floor of stone or concrete, rarely tiles, pushes the heap against a wall with a foot and hopes soon to explain to somebody, a bent sweeper, some bedraggled bearer, perhaps a trousered figure in spectacles, that the things are for the dhobi, or washerman. He steps to a platform beneath a grey metal shower and reaches to turn a leaky tap. The big dry towel feels good and tucks well round the waist. The fan is too fast, making a confounded wind. If one turns the brass thing to the left any more it will stop and one will sweat again. Breakfast arrives. Plenty to eat. Tiny wobbly eggs but no egg cups. No spoon for the cereals. Big knife provided for the banana, however. No bell. Must put on dressing gown and walk about to find somebody who can understand enough English to know about spoons, etc., salt too. The non-traveller, locked into his environment, masters it. The traveller cannot master the environment. He can only try, doubtfully, to master himself. Spoon arrives somehow, transported by important man in trousers.

I slept for two hours as the hot day grew, then wrote a long letter, wrote up the diary. Then, after asking questions at the office, I walked some distance into the bazaar and found a bookshop where I bought a crude map of the city and another Indian novel, then back to a lunch of sorts – rice, chapatti and non-chewable chicken. I decided to move next day to a hotel. The telephone at the office in the circuit house seemed always to be out of order. There were many people I wished to meet, but a dud telephone, like a strike, is a bore. I was told, moreover, that meals were only to be had at the circuit house at a minimum of four hours' notice. Most visitors at the circuit house merely slept there and took their meals with friends or in restaurants.

In mid-afternoon a car drew up at my door and a slender, smiling man, tactful and middle-aged, stepped forward to greet me. He was Mr Banerjee, the Chief Justice's private secretary. It was instantly comforting to be greeted by such a man, a successor to my father's private secretary of long ago, and to be aware that this man knew already of my correspondence with his chief, of my own plans and hopes – and, not least, the contents of my book about my father.

Whenever I encountered Mr Banerjee thereafter, his knowing

smile engendered this feeling of comfort. A good private
secretary, in his or her own gestures of greeting, provides a
warming threshold to the presence of a warm chief. Ideally, the
warmth of a secretary should be a degree or two greater than that
of the presence into which a visitor is ushered. A cold chief
however, requires a cold secretary, but just a tiny bit less so.
Every chief should know about this kind of thing and have the
authority to select his own secretary. Lack of such discretion can
be detected in most bureaucracies.

The driver took us to the High Court through an area of lanes,
puddles, rough grassy verges, smallish offices, flats, booths and
shops, crowded everywhere with men of all ages on bicycles, in
rickshaws or on foot – all obviously civil servants and various
personnel connected with the courts. The building itself is of
great size, quite as big, I suppose, as the law courts in the Strand in
London or in any capital city in Europe. At once, ascending some
steps, we plunged into a big, dark, crowded corridor lined with
shelves bulging with old files and bundles of papers bound in
string. At every turn could be seen crowded offices, all of them in
semi-darkness, badly lit. Each seemed to contain more furniture, more clerks and more paper, more ledgers than could
possibly be tolerable. Each presented the same oddities – dusty,
streaky whitewash, dangling flexes, random switches, fans
and lamps, crooked calendars hanging on rusty nails, waste-
paper baskets crammed and spilling, hundreds of men seemingly
busy with complexities in hubbub and fatigue.

Running the whole length of the building was a high-
ceilinged, dignified corridor with the names of judges
and other important figures printed on jutting signs above each
door. At the very end was the chamber of the Chief Justice. Mr
Banerjee stopped, took the handle and turned it softly. His smile
vanished for a second as he motioned me to follow.

The Chief Justice was alone. Mr Banerjee bowed and smiled,
bringing his palms together for a second. Here was strength and
weight; the desk, wide and deep, stood out into the middle of the
room. From the centre of the ceiling hung a clean, slow-moving
fan. The Chief Justice was a handsome man, regular features,
black wavy hair, spectacles, neat military-looking moustache, a
flash of gold in a tooth, another flash upon a finger, a warm smile,
athletic build. All his movements were quick – a little birdlike,

very alert – and he had a nervous laugh. He wore a long black jacket with white judicial tabs beneath the neck.

Mr Banerjee withdrew and we were alone for about fifteen minutes. After a short exchange of civilities he told me that this room was almost unchanged since my father had sat in the same chair at the same table as long ago as 1938. He went on to say that my father had been one of the most remarkable, most respected Chief Justices of the past, not only in Bihar but in all India too. The big red-patterned carpet, still so bright and apparently so little worn, had been put down in my father's day. Such a carpet would not be provided by government nowadays. Life was greatly changed, but the spirit of the courts had changed little – that India would preserve. 'In Bihar you will hear many stories of your father. You will be surprised how well he is remembered and known, even by many who are too young to have met him personally.' The Chief's speaking voice, though fluent in English, was Indian in its sound, and fast – his lips moving in a seeming stutter, very slight.

The door behind the screen opened and I heard the low voices of several black-coated men who moved into the room, each smiling and greeting the Chief with hands together. He had asked some of the judges of the court to meet me. Most of them seemed youngish men, tall and short, thick-haired, grey, balding, variously spectacled, each less or more judicial in his mien. Indian greetings are always elegant, so much so that the foreigner feels challenged somehow to respond with a fitting grace. He feels at once that his slightest nuance will be observed, weighed. Presenting in my person links with a stronger figure in the past and with the distant Raj, I could only attempt to appear aware of nothing but satisfaction with moments passing, eyes, faces responding.

We trooped out into the corridor, round a corner into another where I could hear the sound of many voices. Then we passed through open doors into a broad, high-ceilinged room crowded with men, sitting and standing. Above the brown-timbered walls, ranged all round, hung the portraits, paintings and photographs, of legal figures of the past – the meeting room of the Bar Association. As we entered, led by the Chief Justice, talk subsided suddenly into soft sibilance. The room was so full that there was barely room for us to edge into the seats in the front row kept vacant for us. The Chief Justice stepped up to a low platform and stood for a moment facing the meeting. On the back wall behind him and to his left, a few feet above my head, hung a draped rectangle of cloth, concealing a new portrait to be unveiled. He raised his hand. There was silence and he began at once to speak in English. His main purpose was to unveil the portrait of a distinguished advocate who had died three years earlier, and. most of his speech was in praise of the man's memory. There was another long speech by the senior advocate after which the Chief Justice pulled a cord, the piece of cloth fell and the portrait was duly unveiled. The picture seemed impressive to me, a handsome painting of a very clearly defined character – indeed a much better picture than most of the other paintings round the walls. I noticed that neither speaker made the smallest reference to the artist. On a similar occasion in the Western world the painter's achievement would surely have been recognised – though in the distant past, before the centuries of the Renaissance in Europe, perhaps the painter of a portrait would have been ignored as he was that afternoon in Patna.

After the speeches, at a signal from the Chief Justice, the whole assembly rose, moved out into the corridor and thence to gardens at the back of the court building where, along a gravelled pathway between beds of flowers, stood long trestle tables extending for about sixty feet, lined on both sides by chairs and covered by white cloths and a fine display of things for tea. I suppose a couple of hundred of us sat down, the Chief Justice directing me to a seat opposite himself. Close to the court building, some thirty feet to the rear of the long tables, was another, smaller table for about twenty finely dressed women, including the wives of judges or advocates and a few women who were themselves lawyers. Throughout my weeks in Bihar I found that, at most gatherings, women did not mingle with men but stood or sat at the rear of a room, silent or talking only among themselves. Very occasionally at a dinner party men and women would sit round a table together as in the West but, even in private houses, I usually found myself exclusively with men. Sometimes a daughter – very seldom a wife – would help the servants to distribute food, but she would usually withdraw discreetly from any but the lightest talk.

In a little while I was taken by Mr Justice Sarwar Ali in his car to his residence in the Chhaju Bagh estate. The overwhelming majority of other members of the intelligentsia in Bihar belong to the Hindu community, and very few of the judges at the High Court had Muslim names. I felt that it would never be possible to question Sarwar Ali about his life among the dominant community and that if I were to attempt to penetrate such private territory, his response would take the form of the briefest glance, impenetrably gentle. I liked him very much and met him briefly on two or three subsequent occasions.

He introduced me to his two daughters. The younger, Rahab, aged twenty-one, was a third-year student at the university, taking a degree in political science, that precarious misnomer for something quite different, and it was intriguing to find that some, at least, of her mentors in print had been my own in a long-sealed past. The elder sister, Sheema, married to a business-man and mother of two children, was a barrister working as a legal assistant in the chambers of a senior advocate. The availability of servants – not so numerous, however, as those employed by the same social strata in India years ago – enables the cultured woman to do responsible vocational work of many kinds in modern India. The position of such women is much better than that of most educated women in the Western world. The privilege of having domestic gadgets is always a poor substitute for that of having servants.

With the judge's family I was given another tea, less photogenic but otherwise similar to the one at the High Court, after which Rahab offered to accompany me to the bazaar to help me to buy some oddments. She imparted to me a little of her own self-confidence so that, on subsequent occasions I was able to walk about in the bazaar with an air of bogus familiarity.

Some weeks before I left London I had received a letter from an Anglo-Indian, Angus Brown, who was the son of my father's private secretary. About my own age, he had known most of what there was to know about my father's private affairs as well as his judicial life.* Some time in the early 1930s, when I was still

* My father's private secretary, Kenneth Cyril Brown, a young civil servant in Bengal, had transferred to Patna in 1912 when Bihar and Orissa became a separate province. In 1914 he became private secretary to the Chief Justice and served all the Chief Justices of the province till he retired in 1945. In 1931, on my father's recommendation, he became Commissioner of Oaths at the High Court and also received the honour of the Companionship of the Imperial Service Order.

a student, my father asked me to meet Angus who was coming
on a visit to Britain to take his examinations for the Indian Civil
Service. I had little recollection of him, except that he was tall,
fair and good-looking, I heard no more about him after his return
to India until I received his letter in 1980. He had now retired after
a distinguished career in the service in Bihar and represented the
Anglo-Indian community in the Bihar Legislative Assembly – a
nominated appointment. He was on a visit to London, had read
my book and wanted to meet me. We met in South London at the
home of his sister Anne who had married and settled in Britain
years before. Just before I left for India he gave me letters of
introduction to three people in Patna, each of whom was of great
assistance to me.

Two of these were Romesh and Sita Pande. Romesh was a
member of the Indian Administrative Service with a responsible
job in one of the economic departments of the state government.
About forty, he was an open-complexioned, cleanshaven man of
genial rotundity whose eyes, behind spectacles, alternated
between seconds of gravity and knowing laughter. The grave
seconds expressed a certain pessimism, the laughter an escape
from it. Sita, much younger, was very shapely. The word pretty
is not right for a pretty woman who is more so. She was petite but
long-featured, with eyes large, wistful and laughing in quick
flashes. Later that evening, with her image in recent memory, I
envisaged her as a possible model for Gainsborough two
centuries ago. As such, should Lady Howe let him down in a fit
of petulance, Sita could have sat for him instead. And the
Countess, in that event, could today have graced Kenwood
House with a look less baleful than that with which the artist
found it necessary to equip her.

They took me in their car to the Rajasthan restaurant which, I
suppose, must be the best in Patna. Here a wide variety of
vegetable curry dishes can be had in fashionable semi-darkness,
with red velvet, a gleam of brass, broad cummerbunds, cushions
and plush. Of alcohol there was none, but in Bihar I soon became
accustomed to tasty meals entirely without alcohol. Many
Indians will drink whisky or gin at home before going to a
restaurant, but seldom in public. Wine is very seldom seen –
indeed, at the economic level of my own adventures I saw
none at all. Alcohol contributes very little to the animation of

dining out in India. Wit is therefore more cautious than on such occasions in Europe, talk is less and ideas more tentatively moved.

Talk about my movements led to Indian affairs about which I sought Romesh's opinions. At once, looking serious, he said quietly that there was an abysmal lack of 'will' in India. I had heard that before. However, Romesh gave it a meaning of his own. He meant that there was a lack of concentration of policy upon limited objectives. Instead, politicians at all levels and in all parties tended to aim at all and any desirable ends but failed to attain most of them for lack of the necessary concentration of will. When I asked how this had arisen, he said the explanation lay in the nature of the electorate. Simple, illiterate people, mostly peasants, were not divided among themselves by any broadly conceived political ideas, as people were in a country like Britain. Such notions as 'left', 'right', 'centre', 'socialism', 'capitalism' could mean absolutely nothing whatever to them. The effect was that the politician, seeking popular votes in his constituency, could only hope for such support by promising all sorts of goodies his audiences could be expected to want. There are political parties, of course – any number of them – but their various identities are not understood by the electorate. Romesh said that, in contrast with the Indian village voter, the British elector tried to make up his mind between the merits of different *but limited* objectives of the political parties. This required an understanding of the issues and powers of reasoning that were quite beyond the Indian voter who did not *read* about politics and *then* go out to vote. He listened to and looked at a man and voted for him if his charisma and promises seemed convincing at the moment of utterance. Indian politicians were all trying to appear more democratic than their rivals. All politicians, everywhere, were natural windbags. The trouble with the Indian bags was that they were all full of contrary winds and nobody knew of any other kinds of bags or winds. Romesh, as I said, was pessimistic, so I did not ask him to elaborate the future. As a congenital optimist I felt rather less despondent than enlightened by what he had said. My optimism might have been shaken had he caused me to feel that any particular politicians seemed likely to monopolise the sources of wind.

Reflecting later on what he had said, it seemed to me that the

condition of political democracy in India now has something in
common with the situation in Britain for many decades during
the nineteenth century, except, of course, that Britain did not
then have universal suffrage but only a steadily expanding one.
In the age of Disraeli people voted for men, not parties, whatever
the parties themselves suspected. The words 'floating voter'
meant not the elector whose support for this or that party varied
from election to election but the member of Parliament himself
who would, and often did, cross the floor of the House, knowing
full well that he had been elected to make exactly that kind of
judgment if *he* (and nobody else) thought fit. Such flexibility is
perhaps the essential feature of our parliamentary government
and is its finest virtue. Loyalty to parties implies eventually the
doom of Parliament and its replacement by the tyranny of party
activists who never represent more than a tiny minority of any
electorate anywhere.

The Chief Justice had earlier suggested I should make
a list of all the places I wished to visit. My list was handed
to an assistant registrar of the High Court who worked out what
seemed at first sight like a detailed programme for me, indicating
the methods of travel, by bus or train, and timetables. After
studying it, however, I realised that I needed a good deal more.
Since I spoke no Hindi whatever, I should have been entirely
helpless in the small towns of Bihar. In each place I must be met
by some English-speaking person, accommodation and food
would have to be made available and people would have to be
alerted to my presence, so that I could meet and talk with them.
Without such assistance I should have been as ill-equipped as a
non-English-speaking Manchurian or Bantu trying to make a
tour of Devon and Cornwall for literary and non-intelligible
purposes of his own. None of this seemed to be appreciated by
the otherwise helpful assistant registrar.

Angus Brown's second letter was addressed to Mr Arun
Pathak. He was a senior civil servant, the Commissioner of the
Home Department of Bihar, whose rank was similar to that of a
permanent under-secretary in Whitehall. Owing to continuous
religious festivals at that time of year and to heavy congestion of
work in all the departments of the secretariat, he was not able to
see me till 17 October, but it was due mainly to his kindness
and energy that I got away at all.

In the meantime I met other people. I went first to see a helpful and charming young man, Mr D. Goswami, who was in charge of the British Library in Bank Road in the absence of his chief, Mr Chatterjee, who was in Calcutta on leave. Goswami, his wife and small son lived in a maisonette within the library building, a fairly new, white two-storey structure approached by a little curving gravelled drive. I liked him at once and we saw a good deal of each other. He looked like an intelligent postgraduate student, which is presumably just what he was. He was the owner of a brand new, most impressive-looking bicycle which he kindly permitted me to ride several times round the drive. It could be purchased in the shops in India for less than the equivalent of £25, less than a third of the price of a similar bicycle in Britain.

Like nearly all the English-speaking Indians I met in Bihar, Goswami had never been to Britain, yet his working life was concerned with British books, with which the library is very well stocked. The friendliness of such Indians is comforting to a solitary British visitor, but it is also disturbing, for their warm image of Britain, derived almost exclusively from print and from a historical environment, could be shattered were they to attempt to live in the real Britain of today. My principal apprehension is not that they would be disturbed by the coarseness of real British people, the squalor of inner city streets or the problems of servantless living in a cold, hard land. It is rather because, for too easily forgotten reasons, Indians are much more aware of Britain than British people are aware of them. Our language is widely used in India. Goswami himself, though living in Bihar, was actually a Bengali who, though able to speak Hindi, the language of Bihar, could not read or write it fluently and spoke to educated Biharis in English. For generations Indians have read our literature and our textbooks in their educational system. Their laws and system of government are largely derived from the British Raj. British people are hardly aware of any of this. They very seldom read books by Indian writers and their civilisation has derived only a few tiny traits from India. The British Library in Patna contains on any day fifty or sixty Indian students, most of them young, eagerly seeking knowledge about us. Many Indians share our deepest values. Our people know nothing of Hindu mythology, little of Islam, little of Buddhism, virtually nothing of centuries of Indian history, including the many years of the British Raj. So crassly ignorant are wide sections of our society that virtually all persons who appear to come from the subcontinent can be dismissed by our lower castes as 'Pakis'. The English-speaking Indian who visits Britain for the first time has no real awareness of the vast preponderance of the lower castes of Britain within our society as a whole. Statistics are lifeless unless the reality is seen and felt in the streets of our cities. The celebrated coldness of the British, as experienced by Indians in Britain, is twofold. The British are cold anyway, irrespective of India or anything else. But coldness pervaded by ignorance, however understandable, on the part of people whose predecessors ruled most of India for about two centuries, is an exceedingly painful reality for Indians to discover. It was a relief to me that the few Indians I met who had at some time visited Britain were not embittered.

When I told Goswami that I wanted to move into a hotel he at once sprang into action with wonderful eagerness. He produced a list of hotels with their charges and services, helped me to select one reputedly clean, telephoned the hotel to confirm that a room would be available at the stated charge, ordered a rickshaw, accompanied me to the circuit house, helped me to escape from it, went to the hotel with me, examined the room, questioned the staff on my behalf and came to lunch with me at the kind of inferior establishment that I could afford. Finally, as I left him outside the library, he made sure that I would not get lost on my way back to the hotel, locating it carefully on my plan of the city.

The Hotel Republic stands in one of the brashest, noisiest highways, Exhibition Road, a sort of Indian Tottenham Court Road but wider and scruffier. The building is of newish concrete and during my stay was still partly under construction. Workmen arrived at break of day and were usually audible all day long. I could seldom see them, however, for their activities were conducted on balconies behind large concrete structures of a kind often seen in hot countries. Such structures, covering window areas, prevent blazing sunlight from entering rooms. From the rooms themselves, even when rough French windows are thrust open, one can see the street only through diamond-shaped holes in the structure, each hole a few inches in width and length.

I was in the hotel for three spells, the longest being the first, the other two after returning from tours. It was clean and the staff were good to me. My first room was rather crude, with green emulsioned walls, bright red synthetic fabric furniture and somewhat garish lighting. The food in the dining room (which had no windows at all), though abundant, was invariably dull and unappetising. There was a bar, but it remained permanently closed; I never drank anything but water and a little bottle of Indian whisky that I bought in the bazaar and kept in my room. However, I grew fond of the place and felt at home there, mainly, I think, because the faces of the staff at all levels always seemed to light up when I approached, and most of them accompanied their little services by words and gestures indicating some kind of approval. To be handed a message at the reception desk was a pleasure, and there were a lot of messages, for India is still the land of chits. The staff seemed pleased whenever I wanted a message delivered, a letter stamped and posted, a newspaper fetched, a suitcase stored or handled, a rickshaw ordered or laundry collected. Laundry, of course, is one of the prides of India. The sun, killing creatures great and small, does at least dry the shirt spread upon roof or maidan. Cleaned, ironed garments appeared each day in a fine, unwrinkled paper bag at the foot of my bed, curiously cool in such a 'world of heat. I was never furnished with anybody else's pyjamas, nor did any garment reappear minus its buttons.

The official residence of the Chief Justice, Chhaju Bagh, had, I suppose been the focal point of my visit to India. For more than half a century, since March 1928, those two strange words have possessed for me a special potency. More than any other words, they evoke the image of my father, his personal ascendency and the meaning of India in his life. He had sent me a few snapshots of the house but my notions of it had been derived otherwise only from his letters. These contained vivid accounts of what went on in the house but nothing of its physical appearance. Now that I have at last seen it, the house, the city of Patna and the vast land itself, I realise more than before that my father viewed his environment overwhelmingly as a human, social one. His letters are full of the images of people, of Indians and Indian children especially. He looked at a man, a woman, and identified a mind, a body, to challenge or to love. He did not notice the tree, the chair, the hat or the flowers. He won prizes at horticultural shows, but it was the speech, the prize and the handshake which he described, not the plant. Actually he dearly loved what he called his 'toys' – cameras, tripods, optical instruments, camping gear. His letters mention but do not describe them. Nearly all his photographs – he was a master photographer who made and used his own darkroom at Chhaju Bagh – are portraits. My own are landscapes and people say to me anxiously, 'Where are the people?' My father would never be asked that question. The pictures he showed to people were portraits, often of themselves. His letters contain some contempt for people, yet he loved them, for it was they who seized upon his mind and whose hands he grasped. He never lost his people but preserved them in his letters, in his heart. His heart, moreover, was exceedingly strong.

On my first Sunday in Patna I received a visit early in the morning from an Anglo-Indian woman, Hazel Morrison who, with her husband, Frank, had received one of Angus Brown's letters of introduction and became close friends for me in Patna. Hazel, a few years younger than myself, was the daughter of my father's principal clerk or 'judgment writer', Mr Francis.* She had promised to take me on a sightseeing tour of Patna, for which the Chief Justice had kindly lent his car and driver. We returned to Chhaju Bagh for coffee and light food about midday, after which the Chief took me over the house and gardens.

In a major earthquake affecting hundreds of square miles of North Bihar in January 1934, the old house had been seriously damaged. My father and aunt, who then occupied it, had moved out to a small guest house in the grounds and remained there for almost two years whilst the old house was demolished and a new, somewhat bigger one of broadly similar design, was erected on the same site. The Public Works Department, as a concession to my father, accepted many of his ideas about the design and included a number of unusual features at his suggestion.

The old Chhaju Bagh, like its successors, was a very large bungalow.† The word, in common English usage, is associated

---

* Osmond Wilton Francis (1880–1961). For many years he had been Honorary Secretary of the Anglo-Indian Association in Bihar and had dedicated much of his life to the exacting work of seeking educational opportunities for Anglo-Indian children and helping them to obtain employment. His wife, Hazel's mother, had been the first woman to become a medical doctor in Bihar, and she was a distinguished public character in the province.

†From the Gujarati 'bangalo' and from the Bengali 'bangla'.

with somewhat restricted living, but in India it does not have that association. During the period of the Raj and ever since, perhaps the majority of the residences used by the responsible social cadres, whether Indian or British, have been bungalows. In my father's snapshots the old Chhaju Bagh was broad, with round white or cream pillars supporting a spreading low roof and a deep, shady verandah, an impression of clean washed surfaces, a wide frontage with a few broad steps descending to a lawn suitable for garden parties and other social events. The house is approached by a winding, asphalted drive beneath old trees, cars drawing up beneath a heavy portico at the side of the building. More than any other house in Patna the modern Chhaju Bagh is characterised by a feel of low, spreading strength and depth. Most of the other important houses in the city are not bungalows and are visible from the street. Chhaju Bagh, concealed by trees within what remains of a secluded estate, expresses a distinctive style of its own.

The portico opens into a vestibule lined with legal volumes and reports, with a central table and chairs for small meetings chaired by the Chief Justice, or for visitors waiting to see him in his private office. On a mantelshelf are old photographs – groups of judges, magistrates, groups of lawyers in bespectacled dignity. In such photographs, especially in India, there is a wonderful air of vocational glumness.

To the right is a door leading into the Chief Justice's study, a room also surrounded by shelves of legal books. The furniture that I saw in the study was clearly far more abundant than my father would have endured – a desk too big for the room, filing cabinets, mahogany chairs, lampshades and a big fan suspended from the ceiling. Bundles of case papers and files seemed to be everywhere. This room and all the others in the house, being shut off by French windows from the wide verandah, is rather dark, a common feature of rooms throughout India. The study has a crammed look. One remembers the feel more than the detail of a room one has seen but a few times. On a later occasion I sat in the study opposite the Chief Justice who, for a few minutes, continued to work at a file with a textbook open before him. I felt that, had I been required to sit in his chair behind the desk, I should have cleared it of all objects not connected with the case upon which I was engaged. Perhaps, as Europeans, we intuitively impose a willed detachment upon the surfaces of desks. Indians are less compulsive and will sit at their work surrounded by extraneous matter, things in confusion. No such statement can be altogether true, but the European in India feels it to be true.

Beyond the vestibule are curtains through which one passes into a large, tall-ceilinged living room with French windows leading out to the deepest part of the verandah, overlooking a great lawn with trees beyond. To the left of the vestibule is a dining room in which twenty or more people can sit down to dinner, and there are half a dozen other rooms or screened-off areas which serve as sleeping places.

Hazel and I were greeted by the Chief Justice in the vestibule. The rest of the family, apart from an older man in his seventies, described as a brother, were not in. The Chief took me over the building, showing me especially features associated with the memory of my father – a large space more or less in the middle of the house that had been his bedroom, the area he had fitted out as a darkroom, another screened-off area that had been used by my aunt and a remarkable shower with an immensely wide rose. He had designed this himself and had it made by a local smith. The shower was still used by the Chief. He told me that it had originally been in the open air at a secluded corner of the house, my father cheerfully taking the risk of being observed standing nude beneath it by servants or callers at what, in the language of trade unions, could be called unsocial hours. The Chief had had a small extension of the walls made to provide a secluded area about the shower. Nearby, in the garden, in a part of a rockery that had once formed the inside of a big greenhouse, was a concrete tank, perhaps twenty feet long and six feet wide, no longer containing water. My father had used the tank for holding live fish from the Ganges pending dinner parties. One day a fisherman, aware of my father's interest in pets of various kinds, presented him with a couple of baby gharials, the crocodiles of the river. My father had them put in the tank to see if they would survive. Supplied with immense quantities of fish they grew rapidly into such formidable beasts that they had to be transported in a bullock cart back to the river. The Chief led me up a winding iron stairway to the flat roof where he showed me remarkable tanks which my father had had made to collect rain water for the shower below during the monsoon. As soon as the first thunderstorm broke my father would go up and stand naked in the deluge. The gadgetry seemed quite complex to me, but it appeared to be working perfectly nearly half a century since it was first installed.

Within the estate, perhaps a hundred yards from the house, is a narrow lane of small, two-storey white buildings, linked in a terrace, that were used as the servants' quarters – and are still so used, though the total number of servants, with their children, is probably not more than a dozen, compared with about thirty in my father's time. Whilst we were looking at these quarters the Chief introduced me to one of his sweepers, a tall, strong, cheerful, unshaven man in his early sixties. He was the son of one of my father's sweepers, having been a child in my father's time. For several years until his death my father held regular parties in the house for the children of the servants, and was very fond of them. On these Sunday afternoon occasions he would dress in Indian clothes. He would engage a conjuror, a man with performing birds or a snake charmer to amuse the children, and play games with them, such as hunt the thimble, oranges and lemons, blind man's buff. Large and stout, he loved to be the blind man, catching the children in his arms and guessing their names as they squealed with laughter. Eventually the children would be sent off with presents of sweets. Among them was a little girl who had been an infant when he arrived at the house in 1928 and must have been about eleven when he died. Her name was Mohinia. He clearly loved the child and took many photographs of her. * I asked the sweeper if he could remember Mohinia and what had become of her. He remembered the whole family and, with eagerness, took me to the little house in the alley where they had lived and where she had played every day. The family had come from Lucknow. Mohinia had died there a few years ago, leaving two children of her own and her old mother to survive her.

Then I was introduced to another man on the estate. He was a powerfully built old man of eighty-two, upright and thickset, his hair and military-looking moustache dyed glossy black. He spoke excellent English. He had been driver and mechanic to my father and to successive later Chief Justices and also to Governors

---

* My book *The Chief Justice: A Portrait from the Raj* is dedicated to the memory of Mohinia.

of the state. As a youth he had fought with Indian troops in France during the First World War. He remembered my parents, aunt and sister and virtually all the people described in my father's letters. On one occasion I was delighted when he met me at the hotel and drove me to Chhaju Bagh for a dinner party there. He gave me a personal message to convey to a retired English couple in Britain who had lived for years in Patna. He had attended their wedding. He was known by the nostalgic name of Jungli Ram.

In another little lane on the estate, perhaps fifty yards from the house, is the small guest house which my father and aunt had used during the rebuilding of Chhaju Bagh. It seemed now overgrown with banana palms, bougainvillaea in full colour and long grasses, the white walls streaky, crumbling a little. It is still used, however, as the residence of an Indian doctor. I stood at the gate in the hot sun for some minutes, imagining the scene as it could have been long ago – the sound of young European voices talking of tennis, a dance at the club. I could see the house properly painted, vegetation under control, beds of flowers, my father with a pipe in his mouth, emerging from the gate to step into his old green Crossley car, a young driver called Jungli Ram in front in a smart peaked cap, the bearer Ghulam carrying my father's briefcase – the car being driven to the High Court for the day's work.

This Sunday morning tour of Chhaju Bagh was not actually my first visit, for I had been there to dinner on the previous evening. The experience afforded an introduction to a style of living which, I believe, is characteristic of that of senior people in the state and in many other parts of India.

During the period of the British Raj, roughly from the age of Clive in the mid-eighteenth century to independence in 1947, important social factors had prescribed for all senior British and Indian personnel a certain life style. Such people had to appear, in the eyes of all castes and levels of Indian society, as a dominant, unchallengeable élite. This was imperative, inescapable, and implied a style of manifest authority, dignity and social elevation in a vast land of even greater inequalities in the distribution of wealth and power than had ever prevailed in Europe. In India this is understood today. In Britain the juices required for its intellectual digestion have largely evaporated.

I do not know what proportion of the senior cadres of the

Indian senior administrative and judicial officers live in houses formerly used by their British and Indian predecessors, but it must be large in many parts of the country, including especially Bihar. What has happened is that modern personnel with similar responsibilities do not enjoy the salaries and other amenities that would enable them to grace such dwellings with a life style comparable with that of their imperial forebears. The senior officers in a country area are still called 'commissioner', 'collector', 'district magistrate', 'judicial magistrate' and 'sessions judge', and a notice board in English block capitals indicating some such office still stands at the end of the drive of the residence. But, very frequently, the gate post is crumbling, the notice needs repainting and the drive is full of weeds. The officer himself is dignified, able, hard at work and obviously dedicated. But the ultimate political authority to which he is responsible has for two generations been committed to Western doctrines of 'democracy' and 'socialism', egalitarianism and austerity inspired by Mahatma Gandhi, British Fabianism, the French Revolution and the Soviet Union of about fifty years ago. I believe that such intellectual and emotional origins, as much as any financial or economic stringency, have been responsible for a modern drabness in the life styles of India's most important social strata. It is interesting that much of the same drabness is evident in Britain.

The Chief Justice sent his car to collect me at seven in the evening. For the occasion I put on my Indian loose shirt, pyjamas and sandals, all of which, though much more comfortable than any of my European things, made me feel as though I must look a lot older and frailer than I felt – a rather dotty feeling. I expected, rightly, that among the other guests only the older men would be in Indian clothes, the younger ones wearing bush shirts, trousers and belts, but omitting socks unless really set upon discomfort. My clothes caused me to be drawn to the older men for talk and a suitable gravity to be adopted in my presence by the younger ones.

The Chief met me in the vestibule. He was dressed as a European, in a brown suit, brown shoes and socks. I later found that he dressed in that way on most social occasions, wearing casual Indian clothes only privately. He led me through the curtains into the big living room and introduced me to a considerable number of men all of whom bore the name of Singh, some of them close relatives. First, however, I met his younger daughter, Anu, a very pretty girl with a sweet, open face and a pigtail. As a student at the Patna Women's College, run by the Jesuits, she was studying geography and various social subjects. She had an elder sister whom I met on subsequent occasions but not this evening.

Jitendra, the younger son, was a student of law, good-looking, well built with a fringe of beard. He seemed eager to talk with me and to tell me his views. Samerendra, the elder son, was a big strong-looking fellow but spoke very little. I cannot recall whether he was a student or already working.

Then there was S. B. N. Singh, a younger brother of the Chief – about forty perhaps. He had a strong moustache and red religious markings on his forehead – looking rather formidable. He was a senior advocate of the High Court. He joined eagerly in discussion later.

R. B. N. Singh was introduced to me as an elder brother of the Chief Justice but I doubt if he was a brother in the European sense, for he bore no resemblance to the Chief and was at least twenty years older – a gentle, guru-like bespectacled figure in a flowing dhoti. He described himself as a landowner but I think he was frail and living a quiet, withdrawn life permanently in the house. Shaking my hand very softly he said he had read my book about my father twice through from beginning to end. I enjoyed his company very much on several subsequent occasions. My father's personality seemed to have fascinated him.

Then there was Mr Justice S. P. Singh, a retired judge of the High Court. This man, dressed in Indian style, seemed to me at once to express an outlook so European and so British that I did not feel him to be an Indian at all – a long face with keen, alert eyes and an emphatic manner of speech, questioning, sceptical and firm. He had been appointed as a *munsif* (junior judge) by my father in 1933. I later learnt that since his retirement from the bench a few years ago he had presided over several important commissions of inquiry into difficult economic and financial matters, including, I believe, the wages of railwaymen. He was clearly a much-respected figure. He, too, had read my book carefully. He was very piercing in his questions about the book I hoped to write next. This I found a little disturbing, for the problem then seemed a pretty excruciating one. He expected me to produce some kind of sequel to the other book but did not see how it could be done – and neither did I.

Finally there was Dr Manik Singh, Principal of the Patna Medical College, a small, balding man of about fifty-five. He said little and looked a bit severe, but he might have been shy. Whenever I spoke he looked at me pointedly, as though preparing me for a refutation. It was not, however, forthcoming.

Apart from Anu, who appeared unpredictably and delightfully from time to time bearing soft drinks, whisky, Indian sweets and snacks, there were no women and I never saw the Chief's wife at all, though I somehow believe she was about. For some time there was a discussion of my father's attitudes, of which several of those present seemed very much aware. They all agreed that his views had been most exceptional among Englishmen in his time. Although he had seldom mentioned the subject in his letters to me, three of the senior men present told me, independently, that he had pursued a policy in his judicial appointments of preferring men not for their academic records (to which he attached little importance) but for very personal qualities, particularly those of courage, kindness and dignity, each of which he associated with the higher hereditary castes of Hindu society, and especially with the princely or Kshatrya caste. Most of the men in the room, I was told, were of Rajput ruling caste descent, to which my father had attached much importance – but exactly how true such a description might be I did not inquire. Although radical in his personal attitudes to such matters as untouchability, the welfare of his servants and all humble people, the subjection of women under the old purdah system, my father never questioned the élitism of Hindu society nor that of Britain either. He believed strongly that the British members of the senior services in India should exemplify traditional qualities of the British professional and aristocratic castes. For only men with such qualities could ever hope to be accepted in India, not only by their Indian colleagues but by the lower castes for whose welfare they could be held responsible. It was interesting to hear my father's views commended so strongly by a later generation of Indian professional men. During his own period at Chhaju Bagh the passions of the nationalist movement would have made any such discussion in the living room, whether with Indians or Europeans, quite impossible. Given the socialist views of younger Indians and the mixed social status of most Europeans, any reference to such views would have been utterly noisome. In 1980 my father's Edwardianism seemed entirely up-to-date.

When I was asked to describe my impressions of India so far, I took the opportunity to provoke a discussion which, I hoped, might be helpful to my understanding. I said that in Bombay and Delhi people had said that I would be shocked by the poverty, backwardness and conservatism of Bihar. I had not actually been shocked, but the visible contrasts were indeed great, and I wondered how they might be explained. What caused Bihar to be backward compared with Maharashtra, say?

I had already asked this question in Delhi and the answer I had received was of a different kind from the replies to which I listened that evening at Chhaju Bagh. In Delhi I had been told that the poverty of the countryside in Bihar had been due to the persistence there for generations of the zamindari system of land tenure. That system, which the British had mistakenly supported and entrenched in Bengal, Bihar and elsewhere in the last decade of the eighteenth century, implied the existence of large land-owners who were also tax farmers, privileged to retain a proportion of the revenues they raised for government from the peasantry. Contrary to original British hopes, the zamindari landlords had invested little of their wealth in the productivity of their holdings but had become passive receivers of wealth produced by the peasants. The zamindari system of tax collection had been abolished after independence long ago in Bihar and legal and administrative measures were now being pursued to reduce the size of permitted holdings of land. Such policies, however, were very difficult to apply for legal and administrative reasons. The story was much more complex than this simple account suggests, but that, broadly, was what I had been told in Delhi.

Now I was well aware that some, at least, of my fellow guests that evening were landlords, though impoverished ones. They had been compensated for loss of income attributable to their former functions as zamindars by the issue to them of bonds maturing in forty years and carrying a low rate of interest. Inflation, however, had largely destroyed the value of the bonds. They were still landlords but their position as such was precari-ous. Yet they revealed to me little of their grievance, partly, no doubt, because they would not wish-to be talked or written about by somebody like myself. They did not know my views about social matters and intelligent Indians tend, I think, to assume that most foreigners, as well as their own Indian friends, are more left wing in their attitudes than is actually the case. Socialism is vaguely assumed.

The really important causes of the special poverty of Bihar, I was now told, were of a relatively permanent and physical nature. Of the total population of about sixty-five millions, the overwhelming majority live in the vast flat plain north of the Ganges. Virtually all are heavily dependent upon climatic factors whose impact upon their lives is more unpredictable than similar factors in other parts of India. The plain is more low-lying than to the north-west. This flatness, in itself, profoundly affects the regularity of the flow of all the tributaries of the Ganges from the north and the distribution of monsoon water. Flood and drought, each of great frequency, inflict appalling damage, and both are unpredictable. Rivers change direction suddenly, sweeping away vast areas of growing crops, destroying whole villages, killing people and animals almost every year. The volume of the monsoon rains and of the smaller rains of the winter months is irregular. Then, even in years of optimum rainfall and steadiness in the flow of the rivers, the demand for agricultural labour is strictly seasonal. In the dry, increasingly hot months, between about mid-January and mid-June, the demand for rural labour shrinks drastically, and there is heavy unemployment. But, in the monsoon months from mid-June to mid-October, and during the harvest from that time to mid-January, there is actually a shortage of labour for agriculture and an appearance of some prosperity. In the dry months of unemployment villagers are heavily dependent on their savings of cash, on their stocks of food and on a family system which ensures a wide distribution of these resources in the absence of anything corresponding to unemployment benefit or public assistance. And provision of such relief in the vast expanses of north Bihar would probably not be administratively practicable anyway, whatever the financial difficulties, which are themselves very formidable.

As for manufacturing industry, factories and industrial activities have developed considerably in the last three decades, but the total amount of employment provided by them is quite small

compared with the total adult population. Moreover, most of the
mineral resources of industry happen to be situated in sparsely
populated territory far south of the river where frequent drought
and the depth of the water table have always limited population
growth.

At one stage in the discussion of all this Dr Manik Singh
intervened to say that the standard of health of the people of
Bihar, especially in the north, was inferior to that of people in
many other parts of India. This was primarily due to the severity
of the climate, its great humidity in the monsoon months and the
prevalence of insect carriers of disease.

Listening to these arguments I began to appreciate the value to
myself of further days in Patna before setting out on my projected
tour of the North. For here, in the city, I was being furnished
with ideas to consider as I went along. Had I gone on tour
without this advantage I should have had no frame of reference
against which to ask questions or to interpret replies. It seemed
clear, anyway, that the poverty of Bihar could not be explained
by the history of mere land tenure and the old zamindari system,
whatever might be thought of it in an ideological context.

I do not remember what we had for dinner, though it included
an assortment of curries, most of them vegetarian. Shortly before
we rose and trooped into the dining room a manservant appeared
with a small lamp. It consisted of a naked, smoky flame from a
wick in a small brass vessel containing kerosene, of which there
was a strong smell. He passed the lamp before each guest who
placed both hands over the flame for a second or so. The retired
judge, S. P. Singh, sitting to my left on the settee, explained
softly that the ceremony corresponded roughly to 'grace' in
Europe, fire being sacred, like water. I passed my hands over the
flame and the servant removed the lamp from the room. Talk
about poverty in Bihar did not cease during the ceremony. The
incident led me to ask questions about religions and myths, and
this led to another discussion over dinner. I remarked on the
apparent distinction between the element of *prayer* implied in a
Christian grace: words, that is, addressed to a divinity conceived
somehow as a person capable of listening, and a wordless
movement or ritual gesture that did not seem to imply any notion
of a personal entity or mind that could be addressed. The Chief
Justice and his brother, S. B. N. Singh, both seemed strongly to

accept this distinction. Hinduism is certainly not devoid of personal conceptions of divinity, though the use of the European word 'god', with or without a capital letter, is associated with meanings which are not the same as those intended by Europeans. The word 'god', whatever the language employed, means different things to Christians and Hindus and different things to different Hindus. I doubt if the meanings of the word can be sensibly defined by anybody at all. The unattainability of definition largely explains the intrinsic interest of comparative religion.

At the wide long table they insisted that I should sit in the place of honour at the end of it, as though I were the host, perhaps a reincarnation of my father. Sitting down I felt odd. Either the chair (with arms) was rather low or the table tall, but I felt a bit Mickey-Mouseish at the end of it, obliged to look up rather than down at the faces on either side of me. I had, as it were, been put in my place – though the talk about religion went on gaily.

Beyond Chhaju Bagh, in the streets of the city, could be heard a continuous noise – a distant groaning and squealing sound. This came from many loudspeakers – the loudest I ever heard – and it was associated with the annual festival of the goddess Durga. The noise started at five o'clock and continued all day, until about two o'clock every morning. It went on for over a fortnight during my stay in the city, and nearly drove me out of my mind. Remarkably vivid models of the goddess could be seen in special booths in the streets which were crammed with people all day. The goddess, a young woman in a glittering sari, with staring eyes and several arms, is represented in the act of slaying a big black buffalo with a long spear held in one of her right hands – she is a sort of female St George-cum-dragon figure. She presides over Power, her arms symbolising various manifestations of it.

At table I mentioned that I had seen the vast crowds in Bombay on the last day of the festival of Ganesh, the elephant god of success and prosperity, and said I was impressed by the seemingly vast difference between the feelings associated with Ganesh and Durga respectively. Devotion to Durga seemed to express a propitiation of cosmic power, humility and acceptance of fatality. The jubilation associated with Ganesh seemed like a worldly commercial acclamation: 'A happy and prosperous year for us all!' Could it be merely coincidental that Bombay and the state of

Maharashtra generally, where Ganesh is so popular, was experiencing an industrial and commercial revolution, whilst Bihar, where Durga is so cherished, is poor and backward?

My question divided the men round the table. Some, the younger ones, seemed rather to relish the point, though nobody went so far as to suggest that the state government might stimulate the confidence of investors by subsidising Ganesh and taxing Durga. It was clear that the older and more mystical men did not really grasp it. They evidently felt that it had been disposed of when they explained to me that the festival of Ganesh is also celebrated in Bihar, but earlier than that of Durga. It was generally agreed, however, that Ganesh is less popular in the state than in Bombay and Western India. I later had discussions with other people in Patna about the implications of Durga and other figures propitiated at shrines in Bihar. I could not, however, ever satisfy myself as to whether the Durga *'puja'* (the word cannot be exactly translated either as 'prayer' or 'worship') implies an appeal by the devotee for inner strength to enable dreaded manifestations of the goddess – flood, famine, epidemic – to be endured, or self-abasement before Power, with its infinite enormity – or both at once and, if so, in what proportions. The first is assertive, the second abject. No doubt it is no less difficult to apprehend just what Christian prayer really means to the practising believer. A special difficulty in India is that so many, perhaps the majority, of the acts of ritual are entirely wordless. In such acts as the bringing of palms together in a moment of solemnity before the image, acceptance from the priest of a touch of colour upon the forehead or a few drops of water on the head or hands, the devotee utters no words. Nor, on such occasions, does he or she seem to identify the self with any 'congregation' of like-minded persons. The experience seems to be both silent and solitary. Just as each observer of such events can furnish only his own interpretation of them, so each devotee, in India, seems to experience something private, beyond the grasp of other minds. It seems to me that Indian religious experience is so deep and so widely manifest to the traveller largely because Hinduism is devoid of any promulgating authority for orthodoxy. Priests preside over ritual but not, I believe, over the tenets of faith. Other religions, especially Christianity, are organised into congregations, each of which demonstrates its own propositions to which the faithful adhere, or change their allegiances with or without conflict. A Hindu temple can be compared and contrasted with a church or a mosque, and there are many different kinds of each. But there is no Temple with a capital T as there are Churches with capital Cs. In Hinduism the manifold differing forms of belief, ritual and *puja* evolve, grow and fade away without, apparently, any guiding will or clash of wills. We did not get as far as this over dinner at Chhaju Bagh. Such notions evolve in the movement of travel itself.

After coffee in the living room the party broke up and I was driven back to the hotel by the Chief's younger son, Jitendra. I lay under the mosquito net trying to sleep with the squealing din of the loudspeakers in the street outside. At one stage I looked out and saw the street completely empty – not a human being in sight. Yet the loudspeakers above the shrines continued to blare incessantly. How very odd people are everywhere. A noise starts. Nobody dare switch it off for fear of being disrespectful to a goddess who could probably do with time off anyway. People will fear to open a widow in a stuffy vehicle, wear uncomfortable garments, tight belts or shoes, socks too hot, endure a haircut to the accompaniment of endless pop music, all because they are too timid to utter or to act.

Here is an extract from my diary for 11 October:

At about 12.30 I went out and walked about the city till 15.10 hrs. – the hottest part of the day – by which time I was streaming with sweat and very dusty. I went to the stand-up snack bar recommended by Rahab and had a greasy thing called a chicken roll. It consisted of a sort of pancake made partly of egg and partly of chapatti, containing spicy bits of chicken and onion, wrapped in paper with the end protruding to facilitate consumption. I stood in the street and ate it, dipping the diminishing end in tomato sauce, and drank a bottle of coke labelled Thums Up. Tasty, brutal stuff. I then walked in a broad rectangle, partly to learn my way about, using the crude street plan and a small compass. Whilst there are many big buildings, the most impressive being the museum, the dominant impression is one of urban squalor, whether it is considered by Western or Indian standards. Everywhere are broken paving stones, puddles of filthy waste,

food garbage, urine and excrement. Apparently lifeless dogs lie
in the dust, cows do not look as though milk can be extracted
from them, great dollops of cowdung must be stepped over,
flies rise up in clouds. There is the occasional bright sari or
decorative pair of women in a rickshaw, everywhere a
slow-moving, dust-laden, hard life – effort and fatigue in
tattered, sweaty textiles. I saw a straggling group of communists, most of them teenagers with a few young children moving
along with banners and a drum, demonstrating for the local
government sweepers on strike because their pay is less than
that of sweepers employed by the state government.

Some of the quieter back streets contain palms, banyans,
peepul and a good deal of bougainvillaea and a sleepy greenery.
Beyond crumbling walls large houses stand now with broken
or missing windows, buildings that were gracious long ago,
with areas of dereliction that once were gardens and lawns.
One building bears the name in big embossed letters 'Lady
Stephenson Hall'. (She was the wife of the Governor in the
late 1920s.) The structure is now looking forlorn. I saw
several large school buildings, centres for arts and crafts,
colleges, groups of neat and attractive children in school
uniforms. The huge growth in the urban population seems to
be a swelling of the lower middle strata of Indian society. It
corresponds to a similar change in Britain. Even the squalor of
British inner city areas has something very much in common
with the scene in Patna.

Apart from rickshaw men soliciting fares, and a few
beggars, hardly anyone takes any notice of me. Sometimes two
or three schoolboys with a little English smile pleasantly,
standing round me as I take a photograph or try to locate
myself on the map. They seem delighted when I manage to
think up something to say to them. Once this afternoon two
groups of young men in rickshaws, one behind the other,
grimaced and made squawking noises as they passed me –
ridiculing me somehow – and I felt a little alarm, for a scene
could develop in seconds if I were to appear hostile or
frightened. One can fend off a real dog with a stick, but
human dogs require other treatment more difficult to prescribe. I smiled very weakly and was allowed to walk on with
apparent indifference. I feel that some unpleasant incident

could occur. I might have an accident, trip on a broken paving stone, put one leg down an open drain or be pushed over by the wheel of a rickshaw. I must accept these dangers, yet persist in walking – how else can I accomplish anything in this land? Presumably most of the millions of human beings in Asia, stretching about me in every direction for thousands of miles, live as I see them now. The seeming squalor is the lot of most of humanity, and it will remain thus, a little better, a little worse, indefinitely, whatever the motives, the ambitions, the hopes or the plans of any politicians or youths in rickshaws anywhere. I had assumed that the High Street of Kentish Town in London was the great world. So it is, but Patna lays bare something vaster than all the Kentish Towns.

5.50 p.m. Slept for half an hour. The heat makes me sleepy. Read a few pages of Romila Thapar's excellent history of India – about ancient Maghada and the late Guptas–Mauryan period. Now darkness is falling quickly – the sky orange – pale, dust-laden air, windless. I look again and it is quite dark. There is a power cut. No lights, no fan, no lift. I have a torch. Romesh and Sita are coming at 7 p.m. to fetch me – delightful, though I should prefer to see them at their home than in another restaurant.

In the street outside the hotel Romesh asked at once if I would like to dine with them at his club or go to their home in Circular Road some distance away in the government residential area. He mentioned that they did not have a lot of food in the house and that only a simple meal would be possible. I settled at once for home, however simple the food, so we drove off to do some shopping in the bazaar and then on to the secluded government area beyond the traffic, the loudspeakers and electronic shindy of the Durga *puja*. I greatly welcomed the silence, dignity and grace of the wide, tree-lined avenues, the well-spaced colonial houses, with their cream pillars, soft electric lights shining upon palm fronds and flowering shrubs, each house with its twin gates, little drive and seclusion. Most of the houses seemed to date from the late Edwardian period. Although older than similar houses in colonial Africa, these dwellings in soft warm light reminded me of West Africa long ago.

For an hour, punctuated by power cuts and spells of candle-light, Romesh and I talked until Sita's face appeared between curtains and we were summoned. After a few sips of Indian whisky and water, Romesh looked at me earnestly through his spectacles and said something like this: 'In India, as I am sure you will realise, we continue to think a great deal about Britain for many reasons which go back into history. And I read a lot of history – especially about India and Britain during the last century. Now there is something I have for years wanted to ask an intelligent Englishman, so please, please tell me whatever you can. Tell me why the British got rid of their empire so quickly. What was the point? I cannot understand it, and many of us Indians are as puzzled as I am. It seems to contradict the laws of history. Why didn't you hang on to the empire as long as you possibly could, fighting to the last ditch, as it were?'

Romesh's question was a purely intellectual one, not rooted in any nostalgia for the past. It is a massive question, however naïve it might seem, and I had only a moment in which to select a reply from the many available. I said that, between the end of the Second World War and the middle 1960s, by which time most of the overseas territories had become independent, there had been in Britain a steady convergence of the policies of the left and the right, but for very different reasons. The left-wing parties, including most people of liberal views, had always been opposed to what they called 'imperialism', 'colonialism', 'exploitation', and so on, on moral grounds. They wanted to get rid of the empire because they thought it was wrong, wicked. The right-wing people did not think it was wrong, but they wanted to get rid of it too, for quite different reasons, however much they had previously supported it. They believed that imperial com-mitments, especially those involving defence, had become too costly for Britain to afford. They believed that the supposed economic advantages to the British economy of the sheltered oversea markets which the Commonwealth provided were now of dubious value. For they enabled the British economy, with a lot of outdated capital equipment, to jog along at a lower level of investment and efficiency than were required in more competi-tive conditions. The forces of international competition must eventually break down all attempts to preserve the sheltered world of imperialism, whatever its constitutional structure and philosophy. Conservatives felt that if the soft but costly pillow of the empire were to be removed, and if we were to join the European Economic Community instead, the ensuing fierce competition with the more efficient industrialists of Europe would provide a greatly needed challenge. So virtually everybody wanted to get rid of the empire.

Romesh listened with interest. He had assumed, however, that unemployment and poverty in Britain (which he had never visited) must have been due, in large measure, to the loss of the empire and not (as I had said) to economic consequences of the empire itself. Now that the empire had disappeared, he asked, why was there not a tremendous economic boom in Britain, since the Conservatives had now got what they wanted? I replied that both the left and the right had been wildly optimistic. The left had imagined that, when 'exploitation' was ended and the 'downtrodden masses' of the old empire were liberated, they would be better off than under the 'yoke' of imperialism. The right had expected that, once the costly cushion of empire was removed, British energy would surge forward into another industrial revolution. But, I added, in India at least there *was* an industrial revolution of sorts and it had certainly, at least in part, been due to independence.

Romesh agreed that an industrial revolution was going on in India. Not being an economist and not, I think, attaching overriding importance to mere industrial revolutions, he was, as I have said, pessimistic. He thought that the industrial revolution, especially in the private sector, absorbed the best brains in the country outside the senior public services. A major problem was that it left another kind of man to make his career in politics. The industrial and commercial development of the country all made great demands upon people who could speak English. Ambitious men who could not master English and failed or could not face the examinations of the senior public services had little left but politics as a career. This tended to strengthen a narrow, localised politics at the expense of wider national concerns. I said I thought the situation must have something in common with that in medieval Europe when the language of the departed Romans, Latin, was still essential for the major concerns of government and policy. When Latin ceased to be used, Europe had by then broken up into separate linguistic states. Could that happen in

India? Dinner was ready before we could do much about that question. It was a very enjoyable meal indeed – by no means as makeshift as I had been expecting. Over dinner we talked about fasting. Sita was entirely vegetarian but did not fast. Romesh was also vegetarian but made a point of fasting for two whole days every week. During his fasts he ate only the lightest meals. He found it difficult to explain to me exactly why he fasted. I suspect that the abstemiousness of many intelligent Indians expresses a kind of moral assiduity engendered by determination to survive in such a severe climate. There is a conflict between the desire for stimulating food and drink which is intensified by fatigue, and the difficulty of strenuous living in conditions of heat and humidity.

Every morning a free copy of a local Bihar paper, printed in English, was pushed softly under my bedroom door – *The Indian Nation*. *The Searchlight*, another local paper in English, also appeared from time to time. I always read both with much interest. One day *The Searchlight* sent round a very nice woman reporter who interviewed me and an agreeable sort of feature duly appeared under her name. The papers are full of accounts of appalling happenings, mainly in Bihar – incidents involving violence, disorder, strikes, corruption, political violence, dacoities and what not. Here is a typical report from *The Indian Nation* of 15 October 1980:

Monghyr, 14 October. A gang of half a dozen youths, armed with pistols and other lethal weapons, raided the Mustapha House on Main Bazaar Road near Kotwalt and decamped with a box containing gold ornaments worth Rs. 15,000 last week.

The gang fired a couple of shots to terrorise the inmates, straightway entered the side room of the house and broke open the almirah in which the box and the ornaments had been kept.

The house owner had purchased the ornaments only the previous day for the marriage of his daughters.

A ninety-year-old man was the only male member present in the house at the time of the raid. The miscreants silenced him at the point of revolver while female members, including children, ran helter skelter for safety.

On receipt of information the police reached the spot. But by that time the bandits had taken to their heels.

Such usages as 'miscreant', 'at the point of revolver', 'helter skelter', 'taken to their heels' have a governessy quaintness going back to the late nineteenth century. Instead of referring to 'the spot' where some murder or explosion took place, Indian journalists will often refer with solemnity to 'the place of occurrence', a phrase used frequently in the courts. Such delights occur mainly in local journalism. The English used in the big national dailies is smooth, modern, ample and dignified, and the papers themselves are big. They are much better, intellectually,

Goswami of the British Library kindly arranged for me to visit the S. N. Sinha Institute of Social Research, an important academic organisation housed in an attractive modern building overlooking the Ganges, shielded from the traffic along the northern edge of the Maidan by trees, bushes and well-kept lawns. The Director, Professor Sachidananda, was on a visit to New Delhi. In the meantime I saw Professor S. M. Moshin, a retired sociologist temporarily in charge, together with Dr M. P. Pandey, the Registrar, a reader in economics.

As my rickshaw entered the drive at about tea time, a slender, elderly man with grey hair, spectacles, a goatee beard and white dhoti walked across the lawn, smiling, his hand outstretched to greet me. This was Professor Moshin. He led me to the shade of a big tree where he introduced me to Pandey, strongly built, broad, about fifty. We sat in wicker chairs round a table to which, in a few minutes, tea and sweet biscuits were brought. Moshin, in his seventies, talked about my father, whom he remembered from his youth as a 'colourful' figure in Patna where he could often be seen in his fine Indian clothes as he was driven about the city in his car. He told me I looked like my father, but less rotund.

I found that both men, like other people in Bombay and Delhi, attributed much of the relative poverty of Bihar and the Eastern plain to the zamindari system of the past. However, they said that the difficulties of abolishing it, and landlordism generally, were very great. The fragmentation of land holdings by the breaking up of large estates had been much frustrated by the splitting up of estates among the members of families. Fragmentation provided no inducement to owners to invest in improved methods of cultivation unless holdings were compact and of optimum size. Capital for development had to come largely from public sources, but the administrative difficulties of making compact holdings out of scattered and fragmented ones were formidable, and there were legal obstacles which greatly delayed plans. I had some further talks on this with senior civil servants after my return from my tour of the North.

To get back to the hotel I walked across the Maidan as the light was fading. For a little while I sat on a stone bench to watch the people whilst pretending to read *The Indian Nation*. At that hour the air is cooler and people stroll. A team of footballers were in training, several horsemen, police officers, were practising gallops for a forthcoming competition, groups of students passed me, laughing and talking with books under their arms. A few labourers slept on the grass beneath the trees in lengthening shadows. There was a sweetish smell of excrement and the debris of food and fruit skins. One must be careful in walking. By the end of my stay in Patna the sweepers' strike had made the Maidan so repellent that I ceased to walk there, but in the early days I did so often.

A beggar leading a small, mentally defective boy by the hand approached me. The man, unshaven, in his fifties, dirty, dressed in an old shirt and trousers, carried a small bundle wrapped in a piece of cloth. He smiled, looked me straight in the eyes and asked me, in very good, clear English, if I would give him a few paisa. His English was so surprisingly good that I felt curious and beckoned him to sit down beside me on the bench, which he did. He told me he was a Christian, educated at the Baptist Mission school, presumably the same as that to which my father had sent Mohinia and several other children during his time at Chhaju Bagh. He said that his father had been a judicial magistrate. He himself had been a chauffeur and mechanic. His most recent employer, for whom he had worked until a few weeks ago, had gone to Lucknow, telling him to find himself another job in the meantime. 'So now,' he said sadly, 'as you see, I am nothing but a beggar. May I show you my testimonials?' He undid his bundle of belongings and produced an old, black, sweat-soaked wallet, from which he took two or three faded typewritten testimonials, each praising him for his honesty and devotion as a driver. I saw no reason for disbelief. I said that I would be glad to give him two rupees but that I was careful not to carry more than a very small amount of cash when walking in the streets. He was evidently surprised at my generosity (two rupees is about enough to pay for a rickshaw ride for fifteen minutes or so), saying gently: 'That is most kind, most generous. You are right not to carry much money in your pocket. These Bihar people are rogues and liars – *all* of them. They will tell you they are rogues because they are poor. As a Christian I say that is not true. The reverse is the truth. They are poor because they are rogues. I know because I am a Christian. These people do not understand such matters. As Jesus said: "Forgive them, for they know not what they do." '

The light was falling fast now and I wanted to walk back to the hotel across the Maidan before darkness would expose me to dangers of which I had been warned. Moreover I did not share my companion's confidence in eternal verities and did not feel able to advance a more convincing confidence of my own in the eternal value of doubt. So I wished him well and departed.

Walking back I tried to imagine what it must be like to live in India as a humble member of some minority community, with no extended family, no assurance of the basic requirements of food and shelter, to be told by one's employer at a few days' notice to find another job for a spell of months till he returned (maybe). We in the West, the foundations of our life supported from public funds, surrounded by voluntary organisations, each with its own Christmas cards and resources, have now lost our awareness of the bottomless pit beneath the feet of humanity in the world beyond our small frontiers. I contrasted the position of the man from whom I had just parted with that of an unemployed man and his family whom I had watched on television in London talking to a B.B.C. reporter about their plight 'on the dole'. The man had expressed the view that everybody had a 'right to work', by which he meant that every man should be given a job to his taste by officials appointed by government, that nobody ought to be obliged to 'seek' work. In India unemployed people in cities collapse in the streets at night and are collected in carts and taken to burning ghats by day. The public is advised not to 'encourage' begging. One's hosts are careful to tell one not to give money to beggars, however pitiful their condition. The subject is changed quickly by kindly, generous people.

That evening, to my surprise and pleasure, I received a visit at the hotel from S. Q. Rizvi, the ex-Chief Commissioner of police and father of Sayed, who, with his wife Janet, had entertained me at Mussoorie. S. Q. was a tall, light-complexioned man in his sixties, fit and strong-looking. He had returned from his daily round of golf (I never saw any golf links, but the evidence was before me) and wanted to take me in his car to meet some friends for drinks. He took me at once to his house in Pataliputra Colony, an estate of colonial-style bungalows near the Ganges to the north of the government area. There, on the verandah, I was introduced to his wife. Strong, handsome, darker, she spoke hardly any English but I suspected that she would understand more than she would reveal. I was presented also to another couple, Brigadier Varma and his wife Monika,* a striking woman with intelligent eyes, whose English was fluent. It was a mixed gathering, Rizvi being a Muslim, the Varmas Hindus. Everybody in India is labelled by his name. No more than a name is usually sufficient to put anybody in his or her place. And that place is never, as it is supposed to be in the West, a small gap in society designed for the personality of a single individual, but an area for the segregation of this or that community whose attributes are assumed in advance. To say that the Indian plural society implies a plurality of communities, not individuals, is not the whole truth, but it approximates to it.

Varma recalled the West African troops with whom I had been in the Arakan and we were able to share some experiences of those years. There was talk about the Durga *puja* and I asked Varma questions about its meaning. From him I got the impression that the goddess manifested power over enemies in war as well as certain other kinds of power. This led to a discussion of the question whether her power explicitly defeated Evil or, in another sense, comprised the cosmic forces to which all great happenings and all catastrophes were attributed. Monika, with what authority I do not know, said that she was the Mother figure into whose arms the little people would sink in exhaustion and death, and so also the final comfort of the dying soldier in the field, the last embrace. Both she and her husband took the view that an important reason for the strength of the

---

*Poet, essayist and critic. Apart from original writings, her work includes translations from Sanskrit literature into Hindi and English, and she is a recipient of international awards. Her grandfather, Sir Premada Charan Banerji, was the doyen of the judges at the High Court at Allahabad for many years till his retirement in 1923, and her father also was a judge at the same court.

puja in north-eastern India was a fatalism induced by the more frequent incidence of natural disasters.

The next morning Professor Sachidananda telephoned me after his return from New Delhi and invited me to call for tea at his home adjoining the S. N. Sinha Institute. Walking back across the Maidan to keep the appointment I reached the north side about half an hour early, so sat for a while in the shade on another stone bench to read more of Nayantara Sahgal's *A Situation in New Delhi*. This time, after a few minutes, it was neither a beggar nor a Christian whom I was able to watch. A man of about sixty entered the Maidan from the street and took up a position on the next stone bench to my left, about twenty feet away. He had greying, very short hair, was upright, with good, strong, regular features. He was dressed in a soiled, long white shirt, loose dhoti and old sandals, a poor but dignified figure, probably devout. I felt that he might be a priest, though he bore no markings on his forehead and no beads about his neck. I say he 'took up a position' on the seat. Although seats, even in India, are presumably designed for the human bottom, many Indians do not apply their bottoms to seats but their feet, squatting with knees drawn up and arms extended forward for balance. This they do not by perching on the front parts of their feet, but with their heels flat on the seat, a position almost impossible for most Europeans over about twelve. I watched him, pretending not to stare, as he squatted there for some minutes. He gazed across the Maidan into the southern sky with a look of great sadness. Then he began to sing softly. With virtually no experience of Indian singing, I felt strongly moved by this man's voice, singing in a language of which I knew nothing – haunting, slow sequences breaking off on the edge of tears. Sometimes his head shook a little and his eyes closed, an expression of nevermore, as though his heart were full of grief, as well it might have been. Perhaps the shortness of his hair was an indication of mourning. After about ten minutes he stepped down to the gravelled path, tied his dhoti firmly about his waist and moved away slowly to the street. In a moment I rose and went to meet the professor.

The Director lived with his family (whom I did not see) on the upper floor of a large old colonial house in the grounds of the Institute, next door to it. To reach his apartment I climbed a flight of stairs and pressed a bell near a wooden board upon which his name was painted. He admitted me personally, dressed in cool white Indian clothes, and led me into a wide room overlooking gardens at the back – simply furnished, fawn and cream, books and ceramics. He was a good-looking, well-built, round-featured man in his middle forties, very quiet-spoken – giving the impression of a sound academic mind. The Institute, I gathered, administers endowment funds for academic projects and the publication of theses, books and other papers by scholars on a wide range of social, historical and economic topics concerning India and Bihar in particular.

Tea and biscuits appeared, after which Sachidananda suggested that we should walk through the gardens to the embankment where, at that hour, it would be pleasant to talk and watch the Ganges. We sat in a small stone shelter overlooking the river, in mid-October about thirty feet below. Although I had been in Patna some days I had not before seen the great stream at close quarters. To see it suddenly, as I did then, was a unique experience. From the windows of trains, both recently and long before, I had seen other Indian rivers, but they had not prepared me for the immensity of the scene before me. Reflecting upon this, I think that, in the millennia of history, the holiness of the Ganges must be attributed to this very immensity, discovered suddenly by each human creature in a burning land who stood upon its bank for the first time to gaze over an expanse of glistening water vaster than any memory could build. It is perhaps no accident that it was within this stretch of the river, between ancient Pataliputra and Maghada, where the stream widens so breathtakingly over the level plain, that the river assumed its special identity. In mid-October its fearful power, yellow, swirling, terrible, had become a memory of the recent monsoon. Now, a little later, far away to a distant glimpse of sand, a low green thread of land upon the northern horizon, slow-moving, limpid surfaces reflected the greys, the pastel colours of late afternoon – a liquid silence drifting slowly to the East, far away into Bengal, to the distant sea. Just near, about half a mile from the embankment, two wooden boats of ancient design, each with a slack, broad lateen sail, one red, the other green, seemed just to be moving against the stream.

Sachidananda had obtained a higher degree in anthropology at the School of Oriental and African Studies in London some years before taking up his present appointment, and he seemed familiar with trends in Britain. I told him of the origins and somewhat nostalgic motives of my visit to Bihar and Orissa, of how I wanted to write something about it. There were questions about India which afforded a huge field of study which I could never hope to penetrate to any depth. I was neither a journalist, a novelist nor a scholar. Yet, whatever kind of book might somehow evolve, I felt the need to read much more. He gave me an excellent reading list. Before I left Patna he sent me also an envelope containing several useful papers.

I asked him questions about the Durga *puja*, especially whether she was seen more as Power over Evil or cosmic power as such. I was a little surprised when he replied firmly that she did indeed symbolise cosmic power. As to ethics, it seemed to him broadly true to say that she represented Power over the Enemy, whatever enemy might be envisaged at the moment of supplication. As to the mythology of the goddess, of her other identity as Kali, her relationship with Siva and other figures, he said he would like me to meet Professor B. P. Sinha, a retired authority on ancient Indian history and culture. Later, after I had left him, he arranged a meeting for me with Professor Sinha.

During the days in Patna, both before and after returning from tours, I often visited Hazel and Frank Morrison, who were more than kind. They were living temporarily in an old, very small bungalow adjoining that curious edifice, the Golghar, almost opposite the A. N. Sinha Institute, whilst their permanent home close by was let to a Jesuit organisation. They had no telephone, so I called sometimes without warning, putting a note under their door if they were out. Frank, in his early seventies, white-haired with entirely European features, was a very practical sort of man. There was a trace of Indian intonation in his speech, which was always accurate and uttered with deliberacy, as though he were submitting advice to an administrative committee. I felt some-times that his thoughts were a little over-pragmatic, as though the non-pragmatic world of India all about him required a posture of implacable commonsense for survival. He had spent much of his life as a manager of economic and rural development projects in India and also in West Africa, on behalf of Christian Aid. He had the manner of the practical, out-of-doors man on the spot; most of his talk was of schemes and projects, their aims and

problems in Bihar. I could have devoted the whole of my visit to
Bihar to investigating the projects he described to me.

Hazel was much younger, slender, with darker, regular,
delicate features, permanently beautiful. She was a devoted
member of the Anglican Church, played the harmonium at
congregational services and gave lessons in English and other
subjects to children of all communities in Patna. Although she
had never been to Britain, her mode of life recalled that of an
English countrywoman concerned with good works and occasions. Her English speech was fluent and grammatical, with the
Indian intonation that belongs to virtually all speakers of English
in India.

[Extract from my diary] *15 October 1980. 1425 hrs.* Before lunch I
walked for an hour – to the Maidan, across it northwards.
Took photographs of a new architectural structure, the Gandhi
Memorial Meeting Hall – and of Christ Church, where Hazel
plays the harmonium, with several mischievous boys having
fun with me in the foreground – then to the bank of the Ganges.
Photographed people bathing. Walked back to lunch – simple
meal, minestrone, bread, curd, apple, coffee. Then slept for ten
minutes. The heat is great still. The climate is indeed harsh, as
Frank says. The élite of India must forever be those men and
women who, in their younger years, have been able to live
sparingly, carefully, austerely. Asceticism must be a condition
of achievement in this climate – control, psycho–physical. All
the articulate, intelligent Indians I have met, and from whom I
continue to learn of India, express in their features the
achievement of these prerequisites of authority and dignity.
The climate of the West is conducive to *permissive* achievement
– that of India is conducive to a quiescent austerity.

16 October . . For some reason, connected with the *puja*, the
noise of music over the loudspeakers is continuous day and
night. In the street below there is a structure which looks like a
temporary entrance to a booth, a fortune-teller's, a shrine; I do
not know what is to be seen inside – probably an image of the
goddess with large whites to her eyes, staring. At night the
place is illuminated with glittering coloured spangles, starlike
radiations of tiny electric lights, and from two loudspeakers
overhead the music reverberates – extremely loud. Male and

female voices, heavy percussion and a strange whistling, with moaning sounds which do not seem to emerge from an animal but from some mechanical source – a kind of rolling clangour, rising to piercing climaxes, choking, guttural descents. The bodily form of the singer appears in my imagination – rotund, big-turbaned, a long white dhoti, features strained in tension, blood vessels swelling, eyes rolling, moustache shivering. I suppose that the cultural life of India is so utterly cut off from the rest of the world as to be beyond the understanding of any other human beings. My father 'loved' India, but there is nothing in his letters, or in any record of his life, to indicate that he might or could have loved the sounds which now wound my ears. There is actually a moment of silence, presumably whilst they change a tape.

Next day. I have returned from a walk in the blazing sun – partly to buy films and partly for exercise. I bought three films for about £14, expensive by our standards, but inescapable. On my way I looked into the booth. Behind a curtain is standing a glowing, naked figure of the goddess. Her skin is white or even pink-tinted, with all her arms spread about her like the ribs of a fan. In this street alone there are three such booths, each with its own curtained figure of the goddess.

In the late afternoon of the 16th, I went to keep my appointment for tea with Professor B. P. Sinha, the authority on ancient Indian history and culture. He lived in a tiny house near the College of Engineering of the university, a few yards from the river embankment, and my rickshaw man had much difficulty in locating it. A frail, white-clad elderly man, with gentle smiles and a soft handshake, Sinha led me into his living room. Here I sat in a very low chair whilst strong, sweet tea was brought and placed before us. It was a little whitewashed room cluttered with old books and furniture too big – an old settee against a wall streaked with dark condensation from the monsoon rain. Everywhere in Bihar, in the homes of poor, retired folk, I saw walls so streaked – intelligent men who in the past had formed the active intelligentsia of the country now cannot afford the expense involved in the struggle against the climate.

In our conversation Professor Sinha said something I found

illuminating. In mentioning mythology I referred to a general similarity between the ancient Greek and the living Hindu pantheons. He accepted that there was a similarity, but added something like this: 'Whilst the myths, the stories themselves, do have much in common, there is an extremely important difference between the motives of the Greek and the Hindu artists and craftsmen who expressed them in their work. As a European, you will know that the Greek sculptor or painter was, above all, concerned with beauty. Perfection of the human figure was his basic objective, far more important to him than the myth itself, the story or incident involved. For centuries later classical authorities have argued about which god or goddess had been the central feature of a work. The Hindu artist or craftsman never left any such doubts to posterity. For *his* primary purpose was not to create beauty, though he often did so wonderfully. He was intent upon expressing the detail of the myth or story itself. The goddess must always be seen as riding upon the right animal. Her spear must always be held in the proper hand, she must always be slaying the right enemy at the right time in exactly the right circumstances. The right hand of the seated Buddha, for example, must always touch the ground with extended finger tips, for that belongs to the story. Every posture, every glance, every movement, every figure, down to the smallest, must exactly correspond to the myth. If you can grasp this essential distinction you can at once be at home in any museum, at any shrine or temple in India – except, of course, that none of it can mean anything at all to you until you know the myth backwards. Then it all comes marvellously to life, for you will know what Hindu children have known for a thousand years.'

Professor Sinha insisted that I should arrange to be in Patna on 13 and 14 November in order to see the most colourful event of the year, the festival known as Chhat. It was a very local affair, apparently not observed elsewhere in India. At that time many thousands of women, all dressed in their best and brightest saris, would assemble from villages miles about, to worship both the setting and the rising sun. He did not know of any other part of the world where the sun was worshipped by so many people on both occasions, I was advised to get to the river bank long before sunset to see the crowds assemble.

I had been invited that evening to a party at the home of one of the senior High Court judges, Shamsul Hasan, whom I had met at the High Court in the room of the Chief Justice on my first day in Patna. He was the grandson of one of the most distinguished Indians of my father's period, Sir Sultan Ahmed. Ahmed had been Government Pleader at the time of my father's arrival at Patna in 1928. Later he had gone to New Delhi to become a member of the Viceroy's Council and after Independence he had played an important part in the development of the Constitution. In 1926, as a rich man in Patna, he had built a remarkable palace, a strange building with traditional features, turrets in red sandstone reminiscent of Moghul palaces in Agra and Delhi and modern shapes suggesting Edwardian Knightsbridge. The building is now used as a government office and is one of the sights of Patna.

Hasan's house in Bayley Road, in the government area, was of colonial design. It was full of things casually assembled from a social world now almost vanished; I felt I was entering some old house in Kensington or Cheltenham. I was reminded, too, of the relics of Rosebelle at Mussoorie. In the hallway was a stand of fine old walking sticks, the head of a stag gazing down upon a vanished savannah, an ornamental sword, ivory, a large fading photograph of Sir Sultan Ahmed in dress·uniform, holding his plumed helmet in a white-gloved hand.

I had assumed that it was to be a dinner party, but instead we were offered portions of gateau, Indian sweets, strong sweet tea and glasses of soft drink – all taken from coffee tables or handed about by a turbaned bearer, without interruption of talk. The party did not last long and my own talk was confined to conversations with Hasan himself and with his brother, who owned a tea plantation in Assam. I had been in the Assam hill tracts during the war, and now heard something of the serious question of the refugees from Bangladesh and the conflict with New Delhi about it. I talked also with the tea planter's wife, Motahina, who gave me a list of Indian novels to read.

I questioned Hasan about land matters in Bihar – the effects of the abolition of the zamindari system and the so-called 'ceiling acts', legislation limiting the size of individually owned holdings of land, thus making land available for distribution to peasants and reducing the proportion of workers on the land who are landless labourers. He thought that, so far, the purposes of the

legislation had been largely frustrated by the splitting up of large
landholdings among the members of extended families. Whilst
many holdings had been reduced in size, in accordance with the
law, they had in fact often been split up among a lot of landlords
who were close relatives. Instead of creating a class of independent peasant landowners, the system had created a host of small
absentee landlords linked together by family ties. Many holdings
were scattered and uneconomic to farm by improved methods.
This, of course, is an impression I gathered from Hasan in short
conversation with others present, and not, as it were, a considered reply to a quasi-parliamentary question.

At this party, as at many others, I heard the view that India's
problems would never be solved without massive authority and
direction. In expressing such views people did not mean what
they seemed to imply. What they would welcome, in place of
corruption and torpor, is a determined policy, subject to change
by open, liberal controversy conducted within the framework of
India's existing Constitution. Even men who confessed to
pessimism about the durability of the Constitution accepted its
liberal foundations. Some would like to see the emergence of a
sort of Indian de Gaulle, but they want no Indian Gottwalds,
Gomulkas or Kadars, and no 'democratic centralism'. Hasan,
too, agreed that the inclusion within the Constitution itself of the
chapter of socialistic and egalitarian aims of policy to which *all*
parties for the future had been committed, whatever their actual
views might be, had the effect of fostering competitive dema-
gogy to the exclusion of sense and wisdom and the enactment of
laws that could not be enforced in practice.

At the party an intelligent man expressed the view that, in
India, *all* the big socialist public enterprises of the country were
chronically inefficient, beset by labour problems and muddle of
innumerable kinds. Only the private sector industries worked
efficiently. Many people in India express these views quite openly
and they are manifest in the newspapers, local and national. The
trouble, he said, is that when something goes wrong with a big
public enterprise, whether in Britain or India, it is seldom
allowed to go bust and disappear, but has to be propped up by
inflationary policies of rescue. It endures merely to face renewed
criticism later. The inefficient private enterprise is eliminated in
the economic struggle and eventually replaced by another which

works. Public enterprise just slops along, its inefficiency only finally concealed when liberty itself is dead. Liberty is killed to preserve the incompetence of the public sector.

One morning a messenger arrived from the Chief Justice with an invitation for me to dine at Chhaju Bagh that evening, together with an elaborately printed card reserving a place for me at a concert of classical Indian music later. At 8.30 I was collected by car and driven away by no less than Jungli Ram himself.

I do not remember much of what was discussed at dinner, but I had met several of the other guests on my first evening at the house. I now met the Chief's elder daughter, Neelam, very good-looking indeed. She and Anu both fussed over me delight-fully, flitting into the dining room from time to time, bending over me with little dishes, offering advice as to their contents and modes of consumption. At one stage I was able to talk alone with the Chief about my developing interest in land matters, which I had by then been able to discuss with certain civil servants in the appropriate departments and with two academic people. I told him I found it difficult to arrive at consistent and convincing views about such matters. When I talked with officials of an agricultural bank or members of the land revenue department, I was usually given what appeared to me as uncritical accounts of what was *supposed* to happen – procedures for operating the ceiling acts, etc., distribution of loans to farmers or steps to combine small holdings into viable units. Although very interesting, it was rather like trying to talk with Soviet officials about a collective farm. When I talked with retired academics about similar things I was often told that *all* government policies were 'eyewash' and that *all* officials and politicians lived on a mixture of bribes and propaganda. I should believe none of them. I felt that some officials were too committed to see the truth and that other people were too remote from it to be aware of the facts.

The Chief Justice, in his reply, stressed (a) the great strength of the radical intention of policy and (b) weak administration and very slow application of such policies. Land distribution schemes *intended* to become operative in three years tended to take more like thirty years, encumbered at every stage by slow legal and administrative procedures.

It was not till well after ten o'clock that we set off in three or four cars for the classical music concert. The event was held in an enormous marquee that had been set up in an open space somewhere near the railway station. The concert had not yet begun but the marquee was completely packed. A few hundred people were sitting in rows of chairs in the front, with many hundreds more standing behind them both inside and outside the marquee. Naked electric lamps hung to illuminate the stage and the front rows of V.I.P.s, among whom I found myself posted. Indeed I was only one seat away from the Chief Justice, separated from him by a vacant seat reserved for the Governor of Bihar, the President's representative. The Governor, A. R. Kidwai, a very handsome man in a spotless white uniform, entered the marquee to great applause at an early stage in the concert.

In virtually all other parts of the world a concert can be expected to last, at a sitting, for perhaps three hours at most, but usually less. On this occasion there was a long delay in starting, because a coach bringing some of the top performers from Delhi had been held up *en route*. Others had arrived from Madras, Calcutta and Bombay, and the whole event was clearly of importance. I was then eagerly informed by some young person that the show would continue until some time between seven and eight o'clock in the morning. As I had a 9 a.m. appointment with the head of the Home Department, miles away in the government area, I resolved that, whatever the music might consist of, I must escape by two o'clock. It seemed inconceivable that such busy people as my hosts could possibly allow themselves to be immobilised in such a place for the entire night.

The proceedings began with at least half a dozen speeches, all in Hindi. The Chief Justice, in his European brown suit, spoke for about twenty minutes, in the course of which I heard him utter the names of my father, his predecessor of long ago, and myself, and I could feel eyes and faces turning in my direction – an uneasy experience when one has no notion of what is being said. He stopped suddenly, and smilingly beckoned me to ascend the platform. As I approached he handed me the microphone and stepped down to his seat in the front row. I stood there in a din of applause, wondering what I ought to say – I do not think I had ever before had to make a speech with such little preparation. I told them briefly how I had at last been able to visit Bihar with memories of my father's letters of long ago, and of my pleasure at having been asked to speak to them, and of how I looked forward with immense interest to the concert to come. As I bowed and stepped down, handing the microphone to somebody rather better prepared, there was a further burst of applause. It is not possible to reject, unfelt, the spontaneous, uncomprehending adulation of Indian humanity.

Speeches continued till about 11 p.m. Then some electricians adjusted lights and microphones for half an hour, whilst other industrious persons shifted portions of stage property at the directions of a large man with Stalin's moustache and pan-stained teeth. At 11.30 a group of drummers started to play and went on without stopping till 12.20 a.m. My attention was closely held by the performance for about twenty minutes as I tried to form some conception of the artistic achievement as a whole. There were, I think, four drummers and a man who operated some kind of harmonium with a mobile lid to vary the volume of the sound. Each drum emitted a different sound, ranging from a light tapping or thrumming of variable key to a deep booming. It was seldom that all the instruments were played together – perhaps never. The performance seemed to consist essentially of a conversation piece in which each drum prompted a sort of challenge to one of the others. The skill of each drummer was in his power to make his instrument speak its mind, always in a dialogue with another of the instrumental souls about him. I later tried to discover what the word 'classical' implied. The instruments themselves are ancient – I was later to see the same instruments represented in the sandstone figurines on the exterior walls of the temples at Bhubaneswar and Konarak, which go back to the thirteenth century of the Christian era, so presumably such instruments are older than that. Nobody seemed able to explain to me to what extent the art consisted essentially of a traditional style of improvisation to which any performer, in any age, might make some contribution of his own, or whether every sound and gesture had to be repeated without any element of novelty, for ever and ever. Were the forms transmitted, like the English Common Law, by the evolving, ever-changing decisions of performers and judges, or were they more like statutes handed down, to be mastered but never moulded by generations of mankind?

After twenty minutes of close attention, I found that I had been watching and listening to a minutely repeated exercise. I very much doubt if the rest of the performance – another ninety minutes of it – included anything substantially new. I seemed to be able to anticipate every phrase, every sequence of gestures, over and over again. Surely no musical tradition in any other part of the world can be so extraordinarily repetitive as this? The audience clapped with passionate enthusiasm.

About half way through the drummers' performance the marquee was invaded by a huge swarm of fluttering insects like small white flying grasshoppers. They crashed into the lamps and dropped, wriggling, upon the heads of the drummers on the stage and upon the white-clad V.I.P.s in the front seats. The great mass of the audience, sitting some distance from the lamps, was not affected. My improbable appearance – in white Indian collarless shirt with wide sleeves, open sandals and white pyjamas – and my unfortunate siting immediately below one of the lamps seemed to afford an irresistible attraction for these creatures. One of the drummers, a rather stout middle-aged man, similarly clad, was sitting directly beneath a big lamp on the stage. For some moments he became so frantic that the concert had to be stopped to enable the electricians to disconnect the lamp and liberate the maestro from incipient nervous collapse. The poor man had travelled all day in a bus from Calcutta to face these bizarre attentions. Meanwhile, we attempted to preserve our critical detachment.

After the drummers there was a long interval with more speeches, and a young man most kindly fetched me a glass of squash from somewhere. Then, something new – a pair of dancers from Madras: a beautiful light-skinned young man in a golden headdress – tiny contrasting brush strokes of bodily hair, curving fingers, up-painted eyes – and a lovely girl swinging with beads, bare slender waist exposed, little toes and ankles. To the accompaniment of drums and a long, tall stringed instrument, the pair expressed in every movement a finely drilled sensuality of mutual response, never touching each other. When their bodies moved from side to side the angles of incline were always exactly together as though responding to a single, keen control. When the dance was ended and they bowed together, smiling, we could see the streaming sweat, triumphant happiness. The audience clapped and roared with delight.

Then we listened to a male singer who sat on a cushion. The tenderness and yearning in his voice moved me almost to tears, though I had no understanding whatever of the theme. On a later occasion the Chief Justice took me to another concert when I listened to the same singer again, but unaccompanied by insects out of gravitational control. I was even more moved. The Chief, sitting next to me, explained the theme of the song.

I left the marquee, during an interval, at 1.40 a.m. A young student gave me a lift back to the hotel in his old Land–Rover, depositing various friends at their homes on the way. The loudspeakers in the empty street suddenly cased to blare as I crept under the mosquito net, to sleep for three hours till the holy electronics reawakened me at 5 a.m.

Early after breakfast I was collected by Arun Pathak, the Commissioner of the Home Department, its administrative chief. He was one of those to whom Angus Brown had given me a letter of introduction, but until now pressure of work and the Durga *puja* holidays had pevented him from attending to me. He was a grey, slightly stooping man with sensitive, intellectual features. I had the feeling of being with a scholar who would much prefer to dedicate his life to the study of Sanskrit texts than to law and order in turbulent Bihar. Later I found that he was able to achieve something of both. He took me directly to his residence in the government area, a rather fine-looking house with pillared portico and verandah and a big garden containing gardeners as well as vegetation. We sat in basket chairs in the shade of the verandah.

I said that it was Pathak's 'residence'. In India and other countries in which British public service principles had prevailed, the dwellings used by members of the services, civilian or military, belonged to government, not to individuals. An officer, when promoted or transferred, went to live in another house allocated to his new grade or post, and known as his 'residence'. One 'lives' in one's home as a civil servant in Britain, the dwelling being a purely private matter. One 'resides' in an official 'residence' in India, Nigeria, Fiji, etc., the tradition having been preserved from colonial or imperial times. Until his retirement, when the officer lost his entitlement to official housing and had to fend for himself, he could reside only in such housing as was provided for him by government. Chhaju Bagh has for many

decades now been the residence of successive Chief Justices of
Bihar. I was now in a commissioner's residence. There has been
no change in these matters since the British period. Pathak and his
wife and daughter had not been living for very long in their
present residence, for he had arrived in Patna on promotion from
field administration somewhere in West Bengal, I think.

I was slightly disconcerted by Pathak's manner of opening talk
with me. He said something like this – speaking very softly: 'You
have come to India to try to understand, perhaps to write about
it.' He paused for a long time, his brows knit, his eyes looking
dreamily out beyond the gardeners into the foliage of large trees.
'This,' he went on, 'is a spiritual country. It is spiritual in
everything – everything, you must understand. Do you know
that no Indian, in any village, anywhere, will urinate beneath a
peepul tree?'

I felt that I was in the presence of an inward-looking man
whose attitudes would be repugnant to my own Western
agnostic pragmatism. While I had no wish to be identified with
any mysticism whatever, I had also no inclination to argue with
this or any other mystically inclined individual. I innocently
asked him if there was a peepul tree in the garden. He called the
nearest gardener and, when the man bowed, asked him, in Hindi,
whether or not we had a peepul tree in the garden. The gardener
went off to investigate and the subject shifted. Later, Pathak
showed me a small sprig of peepul that had taken root in a crevice
of the house.

We talked about books and he was pleased that I had read
Romila Thapar's history of India down to the beginning of the
Moghul period. He took me into the house and showed me a
collection of books lying close together on a broad table, backs
uppermost – he was awaiting sufficient leisure to arrange for their
shelving. Most of them were by British authorities and scholars
on the anthropology and customs of peoples in Eastern India,
where Pathak himself had spent much of his administrative
career. He recommended to me several stout volumes. In the
living room, in cupboards behind glass, were delightful doll-like
figures of gods and goddesses and mythical animals, which Mrs
Pathak and their daughter had made of papier mâché and careful
needlework. We returned to the verandah and he asked me about
my intended tour. I explained how an assistant registrar of the

High Court had worked out a programme for me but that I did not feel able to undertake such a tour without a great deal of additional assistance.

'This won't do,' he said quietly but very firmly. 'I shall take you to my office now and we shall do something for you at once.' This was no longer the mystic, the academic, the Sanskrit scholar; I found myself talking with a practical man of authority and will. He called out to Mrs Pathak and asked her to get his secretary on the telephone. In a few moments we were back in the car. He drove staight to the secretariat and we went up a broad flight of steps to his office. At last I felt, I am in dependable hands. This day was to have been a holiday for Pathak; his return to his office was solely for my benefit, simply because he was concerned that arrangements for my tour had been so ineffective and long delayed. He appreciated, as nobody else had done, that time and money were running out for me.

The old secretariat (there is another called the 'new' one) is a tall, long, white building with a clocktower rising from its centre over the main entrance. Pathak had led me briskly through the revolving doors, past the khaki-turbaned security guards, across a wide marble hallway and up to his office. Then he took me to see N. K. P. Sinha, Special Secretary in the Home Department.

Sinha, a stong-looking man about forty, with straight hair thinning over a fine forehead, rose at once from a large desk to greet us: He gave the feeling of authority and decision. In India decisive men are seen singly, rarely. Pathak introduced me, mentioning my father briefly. He turned to me: 'Tell Mr Sinha just what you would like to do.' When I had finished Sinha looked at Pathak and said: 'He'll need a car, a good driver and someone from the Tourist Office to go along with him. We can get the districts to look after him at each place. He can pay for oil and petrol and circuit house charges, but we can do the rest.' He tossed over to me a pad of paper and asked me to jot down a list of the places I wished to see and an indication of the date by which I should like to be back in Patna. I said I should like to be back for the Chhat festival on 13 November. Both men exclaimed together: 'Yes, Chhat – that's a must!'

Almost as soon as I had returned to my room at the hotel, the telephone rang. It was the Governor. He said he had been interested to meet me briefly at the concert on the previous evening and would like to have another talk with me. Would I please call at Government House at six o'clock – informal, 'but better put on a tie'. I was relieved to find that I had a tie and also some socks. In India socks are worse than ties, and both are avoided unless one really does intend to meet a state Governor or Chief Minister.

I arrived at Government House half an hour too soon. The building is a fine cream palace, built about 1912, standing in its own grounds in the government area. It was for me a little saddening that nobody is allowed to a take a photograph in the area, a precaution which sounds as though it might be wise, though anybody may buy a postcard depicting most things that could be revealed by a photograph. Regulations of this sort put India among the Marxist regimes of the world where the bogey of photography haunts every authority. Manufacturers of post-cards are implicitly cleared as security risks.

At a lobby I explained to a male secretary that I had arrived early. I was allowed to wait in the taxi in the parking area until he gave me a signal to advance. I was thus able to watch the arrivals and departures of other visitors and imagine what it must be like, as a Governor, to be required to receive them – a politician with betel-stained teeth and still chewing, a couple of young civil servants with boxes, a man with a large bunch of flowers.

When beckoned I entered a side door and was taken in a very slow lift to the second floor, then ushered into a great drawing room – soft light, silk curtains, pale colourings. The Governor, very handsome in cool white with flashing brass, came forward smiling warmly and led me to a settee to sit with him and talk. In a few minutes tea on a trolley was wheeled in – little sandwiches, Indian sweets and nuts. I remained with him for forty minutes and left eventually merely because it seemed right to do so, not at any signal from himself. Genial, aristocratic, gentle, he made conversation comfortable.

Round the room were beautifully made models in brilliant colours. Across a wide fireplace a procession of elephants in regalia; on a pedestal the life-sized figure of a goddess carved in brown hardwood: cabinets containing wonderfully dressed gods and goddesses, works of craftsmanship – perhaps the prize works of schools or colleges of art, some, no doubt, presented by individuals. After walking round the room to show me these things he led me back to the settee for more talk. He asked about my plans. When I told him that a programme for a tour of the northern plain was being worked out for me by Mr Sinha and Mr Pathak of the Home Department, he said softly: 'You are in good hands.'

Somehow we talked about land. Perhaps the ease of talk made me too outspoken. I asked him if it must not be very difficult in a rural, ex-zamindari society like that of Bihar, where such a large proportion of the intelligentsia consisted essentially of members of the class of landlords, to operate such legislation as the ceiling acts. Did not such a situation present a challenge to men of violence, such as that which had occurred further to the east, where landlords had been murdered and land forcibly seized and distributed among landless peasants? Kidwai told me that such dangers did certainly exist. 'But,' he added, 'we are able to deal with such people.' He meant that the forces of order were strong in Bihar. He believed that the landlord classes were increasingly aware of the dangers, and that a system of voluntary distribution of land to the cultivators was the best possible way forward. Wider distribution, with all its problems, was the only way to provide more security for the landless. 'And we must move democratically, firmly and, as your famous father would have insisted, under the rule of law.'

I still had a few more days in Patna, for arrangements were often held up by public holidays and the mounting crescendo of the Durga festival. During these days of delay people who had entertained me before continued to do so – the Pandes, the Rizvis, the Morrisons, Goswami and his wife, Mr Banerjee and the family at Chhaju Bagh, all gave me their time, talked and let me talk with them.

An extract from my diary:

All the main bazaar streets are full of piercing, raucous sound – all day and most of the night. Loudspeakers near every image of the goddess blare incessantly. Sometimes the sound is that of tunes from Bombay film studios, sometimes it is the shrieks, groans and thumps involved in the goddess's struggles with demons, the roar of the dying buffalo. Sometimes, perhaps, they are the ravings of priests – I shall never discover just what the racket is about. On my walk today I was attracted by a heavily thumping drum in a small marquee at the side of a street. I looked inside. At the back stood a large image of the goddess standing on her lion, spear aloft, eyes blazing and victim roaring. A priest stood in front of the goddess with a stick of burning incense, facing the image, moving the stick round in large circular sweeps of his arm. Behind him stood two youths with drums each about two feet in depth and about fifteen inches in diameter. The tops of the drums were decorated with large white feathers gathered into clutches like extensions of the drums. They beat out an endlessly repeated rhythm which filled the air for several minutes, stopping suddenly without warning. Inside the marquee were rows of chairs upon which sat about twenty-five small children, a few women and men of all ages, the men with religious marks on their foreheads. Some of them looked at me with expressions of silent disapproval – or perhaps their look had nothing to do with me but with some boy misbehaving himself. My problem is how to cultivate a suitable expression of sympathetic incomprehension. In India the Western visitor expresses two modes of incomprehension, sympathetic and non-sympathetic. One does not like to watch an emaciated cow chewing a copy of *The Indian Nation* in an alley of filth, broken bicycles and rickshaws. One feels sympathetic incomprehension when a very pretty family descends from a rickshaw and moves towards an image of Durga with hands pressed together, saris new, full of colour, children's hair smoothed into doll-like perfection.

1225 hrs. Power cut off. Silence. Only a motor bicycle spluttering. Now silence.

1705 hrs. Indian English: '. . . an infructuous round of talks . . .' Something about some trade unions and their successful efforts to reduce the standard of living of the population for the ostensible purpose of raising it.

1845 hrs. Goswami, of the British Library, came and lunched with me at the hotel. Nobody else in the dining room. He questioned me about the kind of book I hoped to write. I told him that (a) I do not want to write as a journalist, making smart predictions, gossiping about Mrs Gandhi, ephemeral politics, etc. (b) I do not want to appear to know the solutions to complicated Indian problems. (c) I do not want to follow

V. S. Naipaul's bitter precedent, whatever the truth in his two books about India.★ (d) I want to say something true about this country which Indians themselves might find of interest in a Western view. Goswami stressed that notwithstanding the unsolved problems – population, oil, caste, poverty, etc. – there was in India a wonderful *spirit*. He mentioned the dash and energy of people streaming from the trains each day in Calcutta, on their way to work, in the heat and sweat. I told him how I had noticed that in Bombay and Delhi – the neatness and beauty of the women workers, the surprisingly fast walk of people in the streets, the smartness and vigour of people.

He said he wanted me to meet two people – Gopal Haldar, writer, novelist and ex-professor, and his wife Aruna, also an ex-professor (of psychology), both of them now invalids. He will take me to tea with them tomorrow.

2100 hrs. Walked through the streets for half an hour. A little rain had fallen. The air is fresh. The crowds, walking and in rickshaws – small family groups, children holding their parents' hands. Both men and women carry small children in their arms. A great many of the people, especially women and children, very clean – attention to dress, coiffure, make up. Much smiling – I seldom hear a child or infant cry; many are asleep in the arms of their parents.

Watched the *puja*. Before each image, behind a small barrier, a burning wick of flame, a little bigger than that of a candle. Most of the ritual that I noticed – there must be many other gestures and acts of which I am not aware – consists of (a) passing both hands over the small flame; (b) pressing both palms together as in Christian prayer (does this derive from Christianity or did the Christians get it from other religions in the East? I need an encyclopedia of religions and myths); (c) the official or priest in charge dabs a little dye of some kind on the forehead of the devotee.

20 October. Much of the morning dealing with officials arriving to discuss plans for my tour of the North – a young man, Kishore Kumar, from the Tourist Office – he is to accompany me; a representative from the District Magistrate's office which will supply the car; Mr Tewari of the Home

★*An Area of Darkness* (1964); *India: A Wounded Civilization* (1977).

Department, an executive officer I should say. Trip starts early on 23 October. To drive all day to Purnea. Worries about traveller's cheques, cash, stationery, films, new shirt.

The last day of the Durga *puja* was 20 October, when vast crowds would emerge to watch images of the goddess cast into the Ganges, whose benedictory dissolving power would sustain the spirit of the goddess for another year.

In fact I missed the ceremony. Goswami called just after three o'clock to take me to the Haldars. The elderly couple had prepared cakes and tea and it would have been unthinkable for me to insist upon leaving early to see the climax of the Durga festival. Moreover, while we were talking the sky became overcast and it rained heavily for about an hour. By the time Goswami and I left it was dark.

I felt, as with old Professor Sinha, that I was in the company of people of distinction in the academic world who, now in retirement, were greatly impoverished, and that much of such poverty must be attributed to the country's Gandhian ethos – a code of poverty imposed by the regime. Both my hosts were evidently also in poor health. Gopal Haldar, like Professor Sinha, was thin and frail. He talked quickly and eagerly, which evidently exhausted him, in a kind of English I found difficult to follow. Aruna, poor woman, was overweight, slow-speaking and had heart trouble. Gopal did most of the talking and told me something of interest in reply to my questions about the importance of caste and the social values of Hinduism among the intelligentsia of India today. Both recommended certain boooks, some of which had also been mentioned by Sachidananda. He said I should bear in mind that, broadly, the dominant élites of Bihar and other parts of the country, especially in the north and centre, consisted of two parallel categories of men, distinguished by their educational background. The senior ranks of the public services were dominated by people trained in the British and Western tradition and able to understand the administrative language, English. The other category was trained in the Hindu classical tradition, knew something, at least, of Sanskrit and tended to speak fluently only one modern Indian language, English being much neglected. Haldar was describing a distinction having something in common with that in Russia, between

intellectuals who look back to a Slavonic and Orthodox tradition and others who look outwards into the wider world.
As for India, whilst Haldar was speaking I found myself
thinking of the Indians I knew. It seemed to me that, while
the two categories exist as logical concepts, each Indian man and
woman of my acquaintance in fact belongs to both. I had talked
with no completely Sanskritised priests nor even chief justices.
Neither had I met any completely Westernised Indians. Even the
most Westernised of my friends had stopped his car to observe a
puja before entering an office for the day's work on a Thursday
morning.

When Goswami and I left the Haldars the rain had ceased and
throngs of people were still moving out towards the Maidan, a
migration that continued far into the night. We had summoned
a rickshaw – Goswami had an appointment with a friend at a
cinema – but the rickshaw puller soon found it impossible to
move his machine in the crowd. There was nothing for it but to
walk for about a mile in a westerly direction along the highway
running south of the Maidan. Both of us lived in that direction,
my hotel being closer than Goswami's home in Bank Road.
Goswami led the way. I kept close behind, holding one of his
arms, anxious lest I might lose contact with him and find myself
alone, unable to make myself understood. For some time I could
not dispel the fear of some sudden hostility – I knew that the
District Magistrate and his staff had, all that day, been intensely
alert – but in a little while my fear subsided, leaving only the
anxiety about loss of contact with Goswami. Movement was
impossible without treading in pools of black, turbid liquid,
rubbish and excrement, human and animal; the month-old
sweepers' strike was presumably gratifying, at least to its leaders.
I was, apparently, the only white man for miles about, but
nobody paid me the slightest attention. Virtually the entire
crowd consisted of family groups, mostly barefooted young
adults with children, many babies in arms – no push chairs or
prams – the ground too broken for them even if such things
existed. The atmosphere was that of pure festival. The feminine
faces appeared to express a relaxed, placid acceptance of the basic
features of human relationships – virtually all mothers after child
marriages, marriages arranged by elders now left at home, settled
after consultations with astrologers, interpreters of horoscopes

and priests about dates of birth, stars, castes and portents, all in a plan of living unfolded in eternity. Western man and woman live always in awareness of the predicament of choice, decision, assertion, stress and will. The little people about me seemed to express, in the placid set of their features, awareness of cosmic power of which their own living was but a form.

Those images in the thronged streets of Patna came back to me later, during the second concert of classical Indian music to which I was invited by the Chief Justice. Then in more comfortable conditions, I listened again to the singer whose plaintive song had moved me late at night in the big marquee. When the applause had subsided, he turned to me and whispered: 'You enjoyed that, I think?' 'Yes, very, very much,' I replied. 'Can you tell me what so sweet a song was about?' The reply was something like this: 'The song tells how the greatest gift that any man can make in his life is the gift of his daughter in marriage.' The meaning fell upon me as he spoke, and I could not say a word. Noticing this he bent towards me and whispered softly: 'In India marriage is a sacrament, not a contract.' As he spoke, I could see again the people in the street – in whose features predicament had never been inscribed.

The few days before my departure for Purnea in the north-east were taken up with details, small meetings, plans, with pleasant evenings – one with the Pandes, another with the Rizvis and one at Chhaju Bagh. One day I spent an hour and ten minutes in the State Bank, where I exchanged English traveller's cheques for Indian ones. I had supposed that I might open an account in Patna that would enable me to cash cheques in the smaller towns *en route*, but the Indian banking system had not yet developed the cheque card device and there was no time to arrange letters of credit. Travellers in India therefore commonly use the Indian traveller's cheque.

21 October: . . . A similar operation at any bank in the Western world could have taken thirty-five minutes at most, and the whole operation would have been carried out by a single clerk, probably a girl. In the State Bank here I had first to wait twenty minutes sitting at a table, flanked by three other customers similarly waiting for clerks to appear in front of us on the other side of the table. When my clerk appeared he was civil and seemingly efficient – getting me to fill in an application form giving all the usual details about myself. I was then asked to go to another department bearing a small piece of paper and a brass disc with a number on it. Here, after I had waited another fifteen minutes in a queue, a clerk counted out for me a pile of Indian notes. These, together with the original form, I was asked to take to a third department where I filled up another form, repeating all the same data that had been inscribed on the original. Eventually I was asked to hand over the Indian notes and, in exchange, received the Indian traveller's cheques. Each operation seems to be efficiently conducted by a single worker within a very slow-moving, labour-intensive procedure. Whilst standing or sitting during the various phases I was able to glance about at the scene: white or greyish dirty walls with old emulsion paint or whitewash, fans hanging upon dusty columns from the ceiling, cobwebs connecting window curtains with neighbouring walls, a faded photograph of a staff group, perhaps twenty years old, hung crookedly on a curving wall, the glass too dirty for close inspection. Lines of electric wiring connected with lamps, telephones or fans, hung loosely down the walls and strayed between desks, each cable thick with dust; a khaki-clad soldier, elderly, leaning upon an ancient shotgun, stood at the entrance. On the floor of the main entrance hall a peon sat, before him a pile of several hundred forms, bills, invoices and records – his task to press them down upon spikes of wire, then to stack the bundles into a dusty cupboard. The Indian scruffiness – what does it imply? What kind of mental condition is indicated by the scene? I do not know. I can only describe it without being able to imagine what goes on in the minds of people whose working environment I could see. However, it seems to me that the clerical and executive procedures of most other parts of the world emulate and compete with each other, all positively seeking an horizon of unlimited improvement. Those of India are derived exclusively from the past of the country itself, and look only into their own future. India is intensely inward-looking in all her administrative procedures. The country is a vast cupboard.

Another extract from my diary, written after my visit to Mr Pathak:

At one point I asked him if he believed in horoscopes. 'Implicitly,' he replied with warmth, 'I believe in them completely.' He told me that quite recently, before going on a visit to New Delhi on business, he had consulted a pundit. In the plane he had sat next to a man of about thirty years of age. Pathak asked the man his age. 'Thirty,' said the man. 'And your religion?' 'Roman Catholic,' said the man. The pundit had predicted that, on that very day, on a journey, he would meet a man of thirty years of age who was a Roman Catholic.

Such things happen. They happen to the Mr Pathaks of the world. As Aldous Huxley wrote somewhere: things happen to the people like them.

From my diary for 22 October, written late at night:

I had been invited by Romesh and Sita to see them at 6.30 at their place in Circular Road. I decided to walk as far as I could, using my street map. I walked through bazaars till I reached the railway station, by which time it was very dark, no moon as yet – dim lights and vast crowds and noise. The darkness was so great that I could no longer find my way to Circular Road. I was advised by a man with a little English to get a rickshaw, and that I should not walk in the dark. I summoned a rickshaw man who nodded and wagged his acceptance, and we set off. After about twenty minutes the rickshaw man, old and, I think, simple-minded, dismounted and walked over to a pan-seller to ask the way. We were lost. The pan-seller waved vaguely, gesticulating to indicate turnings, crossings ahead, and we set off again. In a few minutes we found ourselves in the midst of a great throng of people, surging about a procession – a band playing, great plume-like lights of illuminated (probably plastic) feathers, dazzling white, carried aloft by about twenty bearers, followed by a prancing human figure in a hideous mask of Hanuman, the monkey god. Behind followed a big float on a lorry, brilliantly lit, containing two young men (Oorya tribesmen from Orissa), naked to their waists, carrying bows and arrows. In the crowd I spotted a middle-aged man who looked as though he could speak English. I was right. We were going in the wrong direction for Circular Road. My old rickshaw man was not only illiterate but entirely ignorant of the government area. I gave him Rs 5 (much more than the poor old creature would have expected), and my new helper, after some trouble, kindly found me a younger rickshaw man who knew a little English and apparently knew where to take me. The middle-aged man lectured him severely, shaking his finger as though to say: 'This white man is my special friend. You must take special care of him.' I thanked my benefactor warmly. So *kind* many Indians are in their ways of giving assistance. After another twenty minutes I reached the Pandes and gave the new rickshaw man another Rs5, at which he smiled happily and bowed to me with much grace.

That evening was most happy. Romesh was cheerful but said he would touch no alcohol, having fasted all day. I questioned him about his fasts. He said they were not debilitating, for he allowed himself light food, such as cornflakes and milk, or fruit, avoiding only cooked things. During his fasts, in his leisure, he read history, including especially English memoirs of the Mutiny period, upon which he had made himself an authority. We talked, and then he drove me back to the hotel.

7

To the North

Leaving my suitcase in the hotel I took with me only a light case with a minimum of clothing and a shoulder bag containing my camera, diary, sunglasses and wallet with a few traveller's cheques and a little cash. I took also a plastic bag containing a large flask of drinking water, some biscuits and fruit and a big tube of insect repellent, a ballpoint pen of course, and stationery. Thus equipped I awaited the car from the District Magistrate's office. It arrived at 9.15 a.m. with the driver and Kishore Kumar, my guide, interpreter and friend to be.

The driver, who did not speak a word of English, was a small, very wiry Muslim, Mohamed Asagar. Kishore was tall, with a softish, hesitant voice, cleanshaven. I felt initially that he lacked firmness but later grew to like him considerably. Behind that softness of speech and the weakness lay a commendable imperturbability. Mohamed was utterly different. Very handsome, about twenty-four, he had thick wavy hair, a military moustache, fine even teeth, sparkling eyes and ready laughter – a popular, tough little man of great directness and vigour of manner.

The car was an oldish Ambassador, dark blue, the commonest product of the Indian nationalised motor industry. I can drive any car, more or less, but have nothing to say about modern cars. People assure me, a little patronisingly, that the Indian Ambassador is some sort of hybrid between an ancient Morris and a coeval Vauxhall, and the description certainly fitted our model. I noticed that it had three fairly good tyres, a very threadbare offside rear one and a similarly worn spare in the boot. Later it developed some kind of electrical fault which Mohamed, raising the bonnet, knew exactly how to remedy with a pair of pliers and a bit of wire held between his teeth. It was a tough car for a very rough ride.

It took us all day, till long after dark, to reach Purnea in north-east Bihar. Purnea was merely one of a dozen place names mentioned in my father's letters. He had opened a new district court there in 1929 and had had an amusing adventure at a nameless village a few miles to the north of the little town of Araria. I had hoped to discover the village but failed to take with me sufficient data to enable it to be traced on the map.

To get out of Patna we drove through dense bazaars, past the station, up over a railway bridge and turned eastwards through the straggly outskirts of the city. The road is wide, lined with blackened booths, rough warehouses, factories, uncompleted buildings of brickwork and concrete amid a jumble of corrugated iron, hoardings, broken bicycles and abandoned cars.

Soon we were speeding along a more open highway with glimpses of the Ganges to the north, sandbanks and green water, miles of vegetable cultivation – a semi-urbanised area until, at last, clear in the morning sunlight, we entered the silence of distance, sweet to the eyes, wonderfully fresh. Before midday we crossed to the north bank of the Ganges by the Mokameh bridge – the road and rail bridges are both at this narrowing of the river (though 'narrowing' means still several hundred metres wide). I stopped the car on the bridge to watch a long, long line of black water buffaloes moving slowly from the north across the flood plain to the water's edge.

As the capital city of a state of some sixty-five millions, Patna is strangely cut off from the northern plain in which most of the people live. The river at Patna is too wide for any practicable bridge to span it, and the main rail communication, anyway, runs south of the river, east to west. An immensely long road and rail bridge a few miles to the east of the city has been under construction for some years. There is a ferry service a few miles to the west, which we used on our return from the north about a fortnight later.

A few kilometres to the north of the Mokameh bridge is the new industrial centre of Barauni, the most important feature of which is an oil refinery for processing crude oil arriving by pipeline from distant Assam. We arrived there during a political crisis in Assam, where thousands of 'students' and Assam nationalists were engaged in a campaign directed against refugees from Bangladesh, demanding that the government in New Delhi should pursue a tougher line against these people, whose influx into Assam was causing severe problems. To put pressure on the central government the flow of crude oil from Assam had been greatly reduced. All the roadways leading to Barauni were blocked by streams of heavy lorries waiting to obtain fuel there. The congestion held us up for a couple of hours during which we managed to buy a few litres of fuel ourselves at a filling station, and eat curry snacks and fruit at a stall by the roadway. About a hundred yards away towered huge new industrial buildings, shining metal chimneys, high walls of brick with steam and smoke escaping. The number of heavy lorries indicated a substantial volume of trade. The vehicles themselves, dusty and battered, were all manufactured in India and looked as though they were intended to withstand rough roads indeed. Most were decorated with tassels, hanging beads, slogans of semi-comic religious purport and occasionally images from the Hindu pantheon from Ganesh the elephant god to Durga or Kali.

To reach Purnea the road passes through several towns – Beguserai, Khagana, Gogri and Kursela, the largest of which, I think, is Beguserai. The music of their names is more alluring than their other attributes. The central feature of each town is its function as a bazaar on a motor road for a wide rural hinterland of labour-intensive agriculture, dotted with villages accessible only by tracks or footpaths. Each such bazaar has grown gradually into a town as market stalls turned into permanent shops and the shanties of wandering traders became dwellings. In India and most parts of the tropical world the climate permits a very tiny stall to be a dwelling as well. Each small Indian town in the great plain is a seething road for trade and traffic without distinguishing architectural or other dominant features to create a separate urban personality. Leisurely travellers in Europe before the age of the car learned the distinctions between the towns of a region and remembered them as personalities in stone. The writers of guide books about little towns in any part of Europe diligently describe ancient artifacts to which, very properly, they attribute the character of each. The modern visitor by car, grinding his way through a dozen exquisite towns in, say, the landscape of Var in Provence, still carries away an image of yellowing limestone, tiles of ochre in sunlight, tall, massive dwellings in shuttered tranquillity, a clock tower above a murmuring market, a fountain of clear water with geraniums about its feet, yet cannot in retrospect distinguish Vidauban from Cogolin, Les Arcs from Plan de la Tour. The emergent image, nurtured from antiquity, moves the heart. I do not believe the bazaar towns of North Bihar can be recalled or loved by the visitor in that way, because no lasting forms distinguish them, no antiquity. One can hardly treasure the windows of Bata's shoeshop or of Patel's hardware store – unless, perhaps, one happens to be not a visitor but an Indian youth, leaning upon his bicycle, in love at such a spot.

The plain itself has yielded its own eternity in Indian living. Its visible features, of cultivation, villages sheltered secretly by trees upon the horizon, have spread outwards through the haze of time. It was forested, impenetrable except by primitive hunters, until the age of iron when, with axes and knives and the power of elephants, more and more areas could be cleared for cultivation, each phase of extension conducted under the aegis of a princely power. Each such extension, as I understand it, was an achievement in an economy of command, of princely rule. The land, once cleared, very fertile, seemed to extend into infinite distance, a resource apparently limitless. And this limitless quality is the impression still made upon the modern traveller. Each dynasty of dominance was vulnerable to the hazards of fortune, temperament, war, murder and disease – all the ingredients of Shakespearean history, quite apart from the intrinsically Gangetic dread of drought, flood and devastating storm. Yet the immense fertility of each area cleared implied great speed of population growth. And so, I suspect, rapidity in the succession of crises afforded corresponding frequency of situations demanding the authority, the opportunity, of fresh command for their solution. These, I believe, are the main features in the enduring history of India's caste structure, her adulatory mythology, her gods and goddesses, her deepest values. All are rooted in the great plain through which I was moving. The modern bazaar towns, unlike the holy cities of the Ganges itself, with their temples and holy death, have emerged into their present shapelessness only during the past century and a half, perhaps a little longer, since the clearance of virtually the entire region and the end of all possible extension of the customary mode of rural life. The towns represent, therefore, the emergence of new living, by trade and manufacture, of a new economy, not yet customary but bounded to the horizon by the rural world of the past. *

We arrived at Purnea in moonlight. At a crossing in the middle of the bazaar stood a khaki-clad policeman on a circular platform beneath a concrete canopy, directing traffic with his cane. We called out to him 'Circuit house? Circuit house?' and he pointed the way. Traffic policemen in Bihar tend to cultivate an air of rather terrifying authority, and rightly. The smart drill and rigid postures are forbidding, but did not surprise me. My first thought was of sympathy with any man responsible for containing a sudden crowd in the middle of an Indian town. For him disorder and riot are more to be feared than mere crime, which is bad enough. The police forces of India at least know what they are up against, and their faces show it. It may take years to concert a policy. It should take only minutes to crush a riot.

Within minutes of our arrival at the circuit house I had visitors. My diary records it:

. . . I received a visit of welcome from three men – Mr Phani Bhushan Prasad, District and Sessions Judge, Purnea; Yogendra Prasad, Munsiff of Purnea; and S. N. Das, Personal Assistant to the District Magistrate who has had to go to Darbhanga, so that I shall not be able to see him. Programme: Start for Araria soon after nine o'clock this morning, accompanied by K. B. Lal, District Panchayat Officer, who, it seems, can speak English.

The sessions judge, Prasad, is a man of about forty-five, a Brahminical face, smooth, pale, balding, but very fit and spruce-looking. Das is large with a dignified manner. I have just read in a local paper that Darbhanga is stinking after the month-old strike of sweepers – sounds dangerous but I cannot miss Darbhanga.

This house, Das told me, became the circuit house in 1942 but was formerly the British District Magistrate's (Collector) house. It is a building of lovely proportions with a large portico

* For some of the ideas in this paragraph I am indebted to Sir John Hicks's stimulating book *A Theory of Economic History* (Clarendon Press, 1969; Oxford Paperback) and Romila Thapar's *A History of India*, vol. 1 (Penguin Books, 1966). The ideas are not explicitly developed by either author, but each, in his or her own way, has sparked them off.

and Greek pillars extending right across the front, forming a
deep verandah – a large garden, servants' quarters at the rear, a
stone guard house with armed police at the end of the drive,
and a big empty building that must have housed the car and
would have held the carriage in the last century. I have been
trying to squash a large brown cockroach in my room and a rat
ran round the skirting and scampered out – the place is silent.
Standing outside in the moonlight, whose gleam fell upon the
blackened, fungus-covered columns and the lost, wasted
garden, the straggling grass, I could see the life of fifty years
ago.

Yesterday's journey. Alternating areas of straggling
townships and open land. In the townships similar scenes are
repeated – a street lined with little brown, dark booths. The
brownness is that of old dried thatch, innumerable awnings
against sun and rain, palm fronds, banana leaves, propped up
by rough poles or boards – the whole darkened by the smoke
and fumes of cooking, the darkness of shade itself against the
burning sun. There are other, more solid shops and buildings,
too, some tall, ornamented and painted in brilliant colours, but
most are of rough, unpointed brick, some with balconies. The
streets of the little towns all seem battered, flimsy, as though
eternally makeshift – the haphazard makeshift of refugees from
sun and limitless land, dust and earth. Every street is crammed
with people, grossly burdened by traffic – shining painted
lorries, rickshaws, cows, cycles, chickens, dogs, children and,
suddenly, a garish temple or a white mosque. The land is so
rural that each town has the aspect of an intrusion, an
incrustation of metallic grime, oil and din. Perhaps it does not
have this character in the imagery of the young but, more
likely, in that of the old holy man who strides with his staff and
his bundle, on and on through the din about him – or the old
scholar, the pandit in his sandals, his sacred thread limp about
his body. The thousands of young men, most in trousers and
loose coloured shirts, express and belong to this world. The
scene in New Oxford Street would, for them, be only Purnea,
Beguserai or Kursela writ large. The women, standing,
walking upright, most beautifully so, seem only of India – their
dress and deportment seems to be more careful, more sensitive
than that of the young men. It is as though the confinement of

their lives within the rigid frame of communal rules – their subordination – cannot defeat their power.

The road we took runs along embankments standing some ten or fifteen feet above the fields. The excavation required to build it has left along both sides of the road levels of water (diminishing daily now that the monsoon is virtually ended). The line of vision to the horizon is wonderfully clear – rice and sugar, millet and pulses. The rice is vivid green. Some, however, has been cut now and ploughing and weeding, in preparation for another crop, wheat, are in progress. The great plain, seen from the elevation of the road, sometimes reminded me of a huge children's toy, with pairs of bullocks ploughing, a hundred yards or so apart, moving at right angles to each other, looking as though they had been put down by the hand of a child upon the rectangles of paddy fields: each pair driven by a peasant with a loose cloth upon his head to wipe off sweat or flick away flies, his dhoti about his loins leaving his legs bare for work in the soft earth. His brown skin has the same hue as the bark of the tree into whose shade he moves to rest. And here, too, in the fields, women work in their vivid colours – a sheen of brass balanced upon heads by bangled arms and small hands. Or the women squat, six or seven of them in a line across ploughed land, pulling weeds, not to throw away but to gather in little baskets, fodder for cattle in a land too tilled for grazing.

Far towards the horizon can be seen the reddish forms of a village built upon slightly higher land. In the centre a bigger shape, usually white, a mosque or, set apart from the village, the stupa-like form of a little shrine or temple, also white. Villages are made of mud and brick, mostly single-storey buildings with sheds, thatched barns and enclosures for goats and cows often beneath the shade of mango trees, peepul or banyan.

Everywhere there are cows, not in great herds but small groups, most of them white, humped beasts with horns, their forms still those chiselled in granite or sandstone behind glass in the archaeology of Mesopotamia before the Flood. Black buffaloes, heavy, stooping, backward-horned with coarse wrinkled skin, are seen in the fields among the cattle, their strong milk providing much of the cooking fat of the country, *ghi*. Buffaloes are often led by small children along the roadsides to water where they bask with inner lids grey over unseeing eyes. Sometimes a child lies naked, asleep along the hollowed back of a buffalo as it pads the dusty roadside, ears and tail flipping at biting flies. Often near a village women can be seen moulding with their hands the dung of cattle into small round pats about six inches in diameter. Such pats are laid neatly in rows along the roadside to dry in the hot sun. They are stored and used for fuel in the windowless, rectangular peasants' huts which are dark and often smoke-filled within. They are built to afford protection against the sun, against sandflies and against the cold of winter, the great drop in temperature when the sun goes down during the later dry weather.

The circuit house seemed silently to breathe decades of Indo-British history and, in a wider context, the history of British administration in rural settings in Africa, Malaya, Fiji and the West Indies. Just as the façade of an old country house murmurs with the voices of an age to the witness who stands before it, the house at Purnea murmured of something I had known, a grace once glimpsed but shared more keenly now that death had left it grey. The administrator's residence, flagpole above the entrance or centrally upon a lawn, was built, almost invariably, upon a site some distance from the bazaar or town, a situation hidden yet commanding, a little remote, to which petitioners must make their way. It must be dignified, its form, its garden, its exotic trees, the curve of the little drive, must engender attitudes of gravity in the minds of all who may approach the flag, the portico and the desk within. And yet, especially since the building of the Suez Canal, after which senior officers in India were usually accompanied by their wives and children for many months of the year, the official residence had also to be seen as a gracious family home. The petitioner approaching would be aware of the memsahib, of white children who, at times, may play with his own, a Royal Family in miniature within the visible world of authority, justice, order and decision.

The form of the circuit house at Purnea exactly embodies such features. Standing alone in a wide clearing of grassland several hundred yards in diameter, edged by trees, it is a single-storeyed rectangular structure. In the house itself is a wide central hall, with a dining room behind it from which doors led to other rooms, one of which was allotted to myself.

The building is evidently administered on what might be called by the British Treasury a 'care and maintenance' basis, which implies a sustained condition of decay – broken gutters, dripping taps, paint peeling and faded, ceilings and walls streaked with the damp and fungus of thirty monsoons. The garden is almost completely abandoned – a few straggly zinnias among weeds. In the entrance hall are several cream-coloured upholstered armchairs in synthetic fabric, chairs in which it is possible only to loll, but not to sit. The furniture in the rooms is of reasonable quality but all the items – chairs, beds, cupboards – look as though they had been ordered in triplicate from some central public warehouse, any object available for any room. The love of no memsahib had been bestowed upon a single feature. No sahib had said: 'This room shall be cream; that one green – the table there, my desk across that corner, flowers over there.' Many of the circuit houses in Bihar made me think of country homes in England in wartime, commandeered for troops or, in peace, converted into youth hostels or conference centres.

In such a setting I would sometimes be waited upon by an old servant who, able to speak a little English, was proud to remember from a distant past some of the ingredients of an English breakfast – orange marmalade perhaps, or a small spoon with which to eat an egg. As a general rule, however, the smaller the egg the larger the available spoon, or possibly the knife. Most of the servants at circuit houses are too young for such recollections, and the environment of universal drabness is all they have ever known of the world. Yet even they were kindly, as well as vacant. As everywhere in Bihar there were several power cuts in the course of the day, the shortest about five minutes, the longest about twenty. Standing under the shower or lifting a spoonful of dahl to my lips, I would find myself in blinding darkness. Within seconds a servant would scamper into my room, or into the shower area, to light a candle for me and withdraw with smiles and a little laughter.

Most of the next day was taken up by a visit to Araria, further north, a drive of about two hours through deeply rural scenes.

But first, immediately after breakfast, I received another visit from P. B. Prasad, the district and sessions judge, who wanted to show me his court in the middle of a big building in cream wash. The British, confident in the overwhelming rightness of their mission, built everywhere in India imposing buildings in which to establish the rule of law. The building opened long ago by my father at Purnea had been destroyed in the earthquake of 1934, the present one replacing it. The original district court had been established as long ago as 1840. Prasad showed me three large varnished boards on the wall of the courtroom with the names of all the district judges, and their dates, since 1840, including his own at the end. During the years from about 1928 onwards until after 1947, the names of British and Indian judges alternated, but soon after independence only Indian names appeared. I recognised several names mentioned in my father's letters, including those of his successors as Chief Justice. India's principles of jurisprudence are derived deviously from Rome, from Normandy, from England, from Indian tradition and from the Raj. Now, in the structure of the courtroom, I noticed that provision for a jury had been abolished, and that the dock for prisoners and accused, instead of being a small affair at one side of the court, consisted of a long railed enclosure at the back into which many prisoners could be put to stand trial together. This, presumably, is suitable for dealing with dacoities or gang robberies, common offences in rural India.

On the drive to Araria I had with me as guide a young man who spoke quite good English, Mr Anjum, District Welfare Officer, Purnea. He was helpful in explaining for me the operations of the so-called Ceiling Acts, which provide for the limitation of land holdings of various kinds, legislation which makes it necessary for the government to classify all land into various categories of potential yield and quality, each with its own maximum holding. I asked him many questions about his own work, the administration of welfare funds and the nature of the case work involved. As in all such work everywhere in the world, the job is inescapably frustrating. Financial and all other means are for ever limited. Needs are infinite and eternal. Decision is cruel. The drive was a two-man seminar with rice and buffaloes for background.

The land between Purnea and Araria is very low-lying. Floods

during the monsoon had severely damaged long sections of the
road and the alternating quality of the surface puts a great strain
upon drivers and upon vehicles themselves. In the bad stretches,
the road embankments above the paddy fields had been broken
away by flood water and large holes, several feet across, were still
part filled with water. Lorries with people perched on top of their
loads could be seen swaying, pitching and swerving around them
like ancient ships in a storm. Mohamed was very skilful at
zigzagging to avoid potholes, steering down the sides of broken
embankments and edging gently up again. Sometimes we got
out to push, but his judgment and deftness with the wheel and
gears was remarkable. Modern Western cars are slicker, but the
derided Ambassador of India revealed a vocational sturdiness it is
rather gratifying to record.

Often we passed large groups of workers, men and women,
repairing the surface of the road, and I was able to see something
of its construction. The engineering problem, throughout the
great plain, is that of making a roadway capable of supporting
heavy vehicles in a terrain of very soft alluvial earth containing no
rock at all. Broken stones suitable for macadamised surfacing are
brought from the foothills of the Himalayas, and piles of them
can be seen along the roadways. The road bed (most commonly)
is dug out by hand in the embankment, to a depth of, say, ten
inches. Along the flat earth bed are laid bricks in a zigzag pattern
similar to the blocks of wood used in parquet flooring. No
cement or concrete is used, but broken stones are spread evenly
over the bricks and rolled down hard with a heavy machine
roller. On top of the broken, rolled and partly crushed stones is
spread a thin layer of earth which forms a sidewalk for barefooted
pedestrians and animals. The centre of the road is asphalted for
vehicular traffic.

In memory I cannot distinguish the bazaar of Araria from
many others, but it is smaller than most. I do, however, recall the
aspect of the government area of the place with such buildings as
the district magistrate's office, the relatively small court building,
police lines, public works depot, a school, and an attractive,
all-purpose 'inspection bungalow' which served as a hostel for
officials and others requiring a meal or a night's accommodation,
with a pleasant little garden, cleanliness and good simple service.
Araria, as a minor rural administrative headquarters, reminded

me very vividly of a district headquarters anywhere in the middle belt of Nigeria thirty years ago.

Outside the district magistrate's office I was greeted by his deputy, Mr Ayodhya Nath Prasad, who introduced me at once to a remarkable old man, Shayam Sundar Prasad, who, before his retirement a few years before, had been an advocate at the Patna High Court. A very cheerful, beaming, talkative figure, he had been a law student in my father's day and remembered him clearly. He had travelled from some distant village especially to meet me. These men – all of us sitting in the district magistrate's office – took great pains to answer my many questions about land tenure, the reforms and the problems of rural development connected with them. The old man talked incessantly which made the whole business needlessly confusing for me, though I managed to grasp something of it.

The party led me over to the 'inspection bungalow' where I was given a meal of rice, dahl, cauliflower curry, fruit and water to drink. This I ate in solitary silence in the dining room, Kishore and Mohamed taking their food elsewhere. It was not fitting for me to inquire about them. In India one's antennae discern from moment to moment whether any question about etiquette is likely to receive an answer or be turned or evaded by a sensitive host. The whole atmosphere of Araria, more than any other small administrative centre that I saw in rural India, reminded me of the kind of station to which a young assistant district officer could have been posted long ago in the African bush. Such centres persisted there, and no doubt still persist, less upon the authority of power than upon a wide acceptance of their role, their links with the world beyond the rural scene about them. If, in the government area, one stands for a second and listens, one can hear a dove, a cock crowing upon a roof of thatch, the little flick of a cow's tail beyond a hedge.

Back at Purnea that evening, after a meal, I received several visitors, including the deputy district magistrate Prasad, the sessions judge and Dr Mohesh Narayan, a retired government medical officer, now living and practising near Purnea. He had travelled to meet me because he remembered my father, who had befriended him and given him encouragement during his days as a student. He wanted to tell me about this.

As we sat on the verandah with glasses of soft drink, talk was frequently interrupted by power cuts and the scamperings of candle lighters. This led naturally to discussion of the condition of India, the seemingly endless series of breakdowns and crises, economic, administrative and political. In a little while, however, I was questioned about Britain. The images of Britain with which these men had been brought up years ago were not those of the urban wastes described by relatives and friends who had visited 'UK', nor those of journalists and reporters on the media. The British past had vanished and the new Britain of which they were becoming aware was disturbing to them. Their deepest anxiety was about the frequent reports of the ill-treatment of Indians in the inner cities of Britain by gangs of skinheads, or by subordinate immigration officials. Indians have a predisposition to project into the future ominous trends discerned in the news. I said I did not believe any of this doom. In economic matters we would continue to slop along somehow. In politics nothing would ever happen completely, and in race relations occasional horrors would continue indefinitely. In short we should do quite well, on the whole.

Next morning, early, we left for the long drive back to Barauni and then turned northwards to Darbhanga. Before departing, however, we stopped at the court building where I bade farewell to Mr Prasad and his genial colleagues.

From my diary:

26 October. Circuit House, Darbhanga . . . A long, all-day drive yesterday. Somewhere near Beguserai the off back tyre burst – sudden explosion and bumping halt. I was interested to watch the imperturbable deftness of Mohamed, who changed the wheel in ten minutes. The spare tyre is so worn that I am determined not to leave Darbhanga until we have somehow equipped ourselves with a new one – we have hundreds of miles to go before we get back to Patna. Every now and then small defects appear, particularly with the wiring system. On each occasion Mohamed opens the bonnet and somehow improvises a remedy with bits of wire, scraps of wood, even a matchstick, always with evident success, and drives on.

When we turned north towards Darbhanga the appearance of the landscape changed quite quickly, becoming more wooded, more closed in, more densely populated too – a prettier, more European-like scene, with more villages. I think we had moved into the terrain of the Maharajadhiraj of Darbhanga who in the past was one of the greatest zamindars and landlords of British India.* But, after about twenty kilometres, the scene opened wide again into rice land, very low-lying, and we crossed several wooden bridges over deep banked rivers lined with mud, perhaps sixty feet below. Some of these bridges seemed most insecure, giving a feeling of imminent disaster; and so to this excellent circuit house at Darbhanga. A good night's sleep – a civilised place.

Darbhanga. After a shower and change and some tea on a very pleasant verandah - but troublesome mosquitoes – I was collected by car and taken to see Mr G. M. Kunandi, the district and sessions judge, at his residence. He is a man of about fifty-six who looks older. I was introduced to several other men, on Kunandi's verandah, who had been assembled to meet me – a tax inspector, various government officers – and offered a large dish containing various kinds of sweets, to which we helped ourselves with spoons, and tea. Among the sweets was an interesting nut-like thing, *makhana* – lotus seed, dried and toasted: very good – looks something like a small mushroom top, but crisp. I was introduced also to Dr S. M. Nawab, retired Principal of Darbhanga Medical College who, graduating in 1935, had known my father well. Curiously, Nawab much resembled my father in build, features and even haircut. He speaks very good English and has visited Britain and America several times.

There was talk for an hour or so. In discussing land and poverty in Bihar, Nawab said he attributed the backwardness of the plain to three main causes. First, the floods and low-lying

* The Maharajas of Darbhanga, who bore the ancient Rajput title of Maharajadhiraj, were descended from Manesh Thakur who had obtained the title of Raja and the grant of the Darbhanga Raj (a huge territory including many parts of north Bihar) from Akbar the Great early in the sixteenth century. One of the most distinguished representatives of the family was Maharaja Sir Lachhmeswar Singh Bahadur, KCIE (1856–98). He appointed British managers to administer vast funds in very good local causes, including the provision of hundreds of schools, dispensaries, the building of roads, the planting of thousands of trees along the roadsides to afford shade, the improvement of breeds of cattle and horses and many important works to prevent floods and by way of famine prevention and relief. After the earthquake of 1934, the Maharajadhiraj established the Darbhanga Improvement Trust for the reconstruction of devastated areas. The public spirited tradition continued until the end of the zamindari system in the early 1950s.

nature of the land. A large proportion of the rice crop is lost every year. The introduction of complex mechanical aids is difficult when floods are so massive and unpredictable. Second, the dry season arrives later here than further west and north. This makes the planting of wheat after the rice hazardous. Third, because of flooding, excessive water etc. insect pests are more dangerous here than further west, and the health of the people is inferior. Bihar has a much harsher climate than, say, the Punjab. He thought these physical factors were of more importance than any questions of land tenure or reform. All this confirmed the views of Dr Manik Singh of Patna.★

Long discussion of Britain. Kunandi very suspicious of the Thatcher Government – believes the British Government is heading towards a 'racialist' policy of repatriating Indians etc. I declared forcibly that all this was nonsense. I was glad to find myself supported by Nawab, who has had the advantage of long visits to Britain.

At about 9 a.m. this morning I was taken by Kunandi in his car to the residence of Mr Pillai, the Collector and District Magistrate and introduced to him, his wife and children – much smiling and greetings with hands pressed together. Pillai, about forty-four, baldish with a strong face and thick moustache. I described my mission – to visit scenes mentioned by my father in his letters. He listened intently with evident interest. Fixed a programme for my stay.

This morning I went for a short walk with Kishore. I like him more as time goes on. He helps me usefully as my interpreter. Discussed caste. As I had surmised, he is a Kyasth, of the writer caste. He appreciates my concern for his welfare and that of Mohamed. I let him use my shower at the circuit house – otherwise it would be difficult for him to get clean or shaved. He tells me he has friends here with whom he is staying – I wonder about them. One cannot ask. Mohamed sleeps in the car. He gets himself clean somehow in the servants' quarters at the back of the circuit house. Mohamed is a highly skilled driver and a resourceful mechanic, but in this society his calling is regarded as low and grubby. Kishore has the mastery of a clerk.

★ The Principal of Patna Medical College.

Caste and skill – knowing one's place. Men know their places in the social hierarchy of caste. Women know their place in the sexual, functional divides. I doubt if caste impinges upon the consciousness of women so powerfully as upon that of men – but they know and accept their power, expressed in the images of the goddess.

26 October, 1950 hrs. This morning, just as I had finished writing the above, I was collected by the district judge, Kunandi, and, together with his little boy son, Farukh Arshad, a very bright child, was taken to see his court. In structure the rural courts are all very much alike, almost unchanged since British times – a very English atmosphere. Perhaps the distinction lies in the visual importance of the court within the complex of public buildings. In an English town the court is not conspicuous. In India it is always dominant. This, I believe, is an immensely important historical factor in the social values of modern India. We returned to his residence, where he got me to take a photograph of him with his three sons and the family car in the background. Kunandi is a simple man. His little son of fifteen, doing science at school, is very intelligent. For some reason father and son both wanted to know whether French or German was the easier language to learn. This led to my telling them about German, and then about the Germanic and Latin roots of English. The boy took notes carefully, as though I were delivering a lecture. His elder brother has just qualified as a doctor but not yet begun to practise. On land Kunandi gave me the impression that, in his purely personal view, much of the land reform policy was ineffective, basically because many people who own more than the ceiling prescriptions of land are determined not to surrender any part of their holdings, and will fight legal battles right up to the Supreme Court to defend their interests. The administration of the reforms on the ground is left to the administration (district magistrates) but appeals lie to the judiciary with its chain of appellate courts.

In the afternoon of my first day I was escorted by one of Pillai's assistants, C. S. Roy Divakar. He took me somewhat out of the town to see the Chandrahari Museum and the various buildings that had formerly been palaces of the family of the Maharajadhiraj.

Scattered over several square miles, there are actually four large palaces, each in its own grounds of ornamental gardens, each in a distinct architectural style. The oldest has a long, low frontage and heavily ornamental façade, with a big archway at the entrance to the drive – the ornamentation being a strange concoction of late Victorianism and Hindu mythological themes – elephants and coats of arms all mixed up. The palace was occupied, until her death seventeen years ago, by the mother of the last Maharajadhiraj, Kumar Subeshwar Singh, but is now empty and obviously falling into ruin. The grounds are partially enclosed by enormously tall brick walls, massive like those of the Red Fort in Delhi, surmounted at corners and over a gateway by ornamental turrets in red sandstone, in the style of the Moghul period. This gives the place a majestic appearance, evidently designed to evoke the princely ethos of old Rajputana in the very different landscape of the plain of north Bihar. To my astonishment I was told the walls were not built until after the earthquake of 1934.

Near the gateway, as we walked towards the old palace, we were greeted by one of the advocates of the Patna High Court, Vijay Kumar Bhagat, whose home is in Darbhanga. He had seen me at the ceremony and tea party at the High Court on my first day in Patna over a month before. On an area of rough grassland in front of the ruined palace – an area which, in my father's day, would have been a large smooth lawn suitable for garden parties and fêtes – a game of cricket was going on. All the players were in white; it was a strange scene of Indo-Sussex. As we walked forward the players stopped and one of them, a stout young man, stepped forward to greet Mr Bhagat, who introduced me. The young man was a nephew of the late Maharajadhiraj. In polished English he told me he had got together a group of 'lads' who liked to play in the afternoons – I expect they were students at the university. His smile was amiable, showing lips and teeth stained by betel, his moustache Edwardian and his hair pleasantly floppy; he presented a cheerful rotundity. It was melancholy, I felt, that India was not able to have a real prince, a real university and a real palace all at once.

The largest, most impressive of the palaces, built entirely of red brick and sandstone, is a huge British Edwardian mass surmounted by cupolas of the Moghul form. It covers a great area, with a tall clocktower over the main entrance, and several big wings. A complex of buildings to one side of the main block had once been the European guest house – its splendour was mentioned in one of my father's letters, written from his room there when he had been a guest for a few days. He did not actually describe the building (he never did that) but he did indicate his feeling of being a humble nobody in the palace of so illustrious a prince as Darbhanga. The buildings themselves, as well as the ornamental grounds, white statuary, flower beds and fountains, seemed well maintained. Everywhere could be seen groups of students, strolling or cycling about, many with books. It is rather as though buildings of the size of Sandringham (similar in certain ways) had been converted into a university with 40,000 students. I did not see any women students, but it seems likely that some could be rounded up if required. The students come to Darbhanga from all over India. An attractive, quite modern palace in white stone, dating from the late 1930s, is now used as a residential college for postgraduate students, and yet another attractive white building is used as a training centre for senior personnel in the postal services of India.

Roy Divakar took me to the Chandrahari Museum, somewhere on the outskirts of the town. This is a large two-storey concrete building with a miscellaneous collection of exhibits, many, perhaps most of them, having been removed from the various palaces before they were converted for use by the university. There were many bronze and stone figures of gods and goddesses in mythical situations, and amusing little terracotta figurines from very ancient times. Their arrangement, however, lacked expertise – there seemed little appreciation of their didactic value. I suspect that Indian visitors to such a museum recognise the mythological themes but their interest in chronology and historical analysis is scant.

Among the exhibits were many personal relics of social occasions in the later decades of the Raj – little piles of valueless European coins and notes, photographs, things collected from drawers and dressing tables, reminders of visits to England and to the South of France where, one can imagine, the princely family would have occupied suites of rooms in grand hotels, taking with them their personal Indian servants.

I took a special interest in a number of paintings and discovered that the artist responsible for several of them was a member of the museum staff, Rajendra Prasad. He was introduced to me by the curator. His paintings were all large rectangles several feet across and as many deep. They depicted vast mythological scenes executed with immense care and beauty with minuscule brush strokes. The scenes contain great numbers of human figures, every face clearly depicted in delicacy of line and colour. One picture showed a mythical scene in a royal court. The background took the form of several rows of female figures standing upon tiered balconies, looking downward with varied expressions and gestures upon a magical scene in the foreground. In the centre, on a throne, sat a king in his robes. On the left stood a magician, scantily clad like a holy man. On the right was a figure in flowing robes, evidently a 'baddie'. The magician, with a sudden gesture of eyes and hands and the utterance of a horrendous curse, had caused the head of the baddie to be sliced off by a keen-edged but entirely invisible scimitar. Streams of blood were gushing from the severed neck down over the robes of the still-standing figure. The bearded head lay back, eyes and features full of the surprise of intercepted utterance. The huge scene, with its communication of horror, of acceptance and a strange tranquillity, was most impressive.

Within the Darbhanga estate Divakar took me to see two big adjoining temples to Lakshmi and Kali respectively. The light was failing and a power cut prevented me from seeing the figure of Lakshmi, but light was restored by the time I reached the Kali temple, and I was able to see the strange goddess with her wildly strained features, long black tongue sticking out and bloody hands outstretched. There was a long queue of devotees waiting before the image, which stood in a deep but brightly illuminated recess within the pyramidical building of black stone. There seemed to be as many men as women and most were young (an indication perhaps of the religion's vitality), all neatly dressed for the occasion, the women especially having made themselves attractive, both to the goddess and to the crowd about them. The ritual gestures are varied – kneeling, bowing, going down on all fours, touching or dabbing the forehead with yellowish dye – small actions quickly made. I find all religious ritual very puzzling, because it is impossible to discover what is happening in the heads of the participants. It is never practicable to bend down and whisper into the ear of someone engaged in the ritual of any religion: 'Would you be so kind as to tell me what is going on in your mind as you do this?' Even if such conduct were quite acceptable, to do such a thing would break the spell.

One evening I was collected by Kunandi and his young son and taken to his residence for an excellent meal and a great deal of talk on the verandah. It was an entirely Muslim gathering, with no women even remotely glimpsed. I was introduced to his eldest son, the newly qualified doctor, Aftab Faiz, to another – younger – son, Khurshed Garami, and to a business man from Pakistan whose name I did not catch. He owned property in London and had been selling flats to Arabs at fancy prices. Much of the talk was of Britain, which Kunandi had not visited but in which he was very interested. He told me that he kept himself abreast of British affairs by resorting regularly to *Titbits.*. The business man's notions seemed to be derived primarily from the Soho of striptease, and I was at some pains to appear less bewildered than I felt. Our talk, meanwhile was punctuated by power cuts and blackouts and this led to a discussion of India's industrial development which, conducted behind massive protective barriers, is frustrated by shortage of electric power and the cost of imported fuel. Whilst such factors are evident, there was a tendency to attribute these misfortunes to enemies and other people's wickedness.

When asked about my experience of India I mentioned religious festivals. Kunandi asked me gravely what I thought of Hinduism. Before I could settle upon some sort of reply he said, with an air of having deliberated the matter for half a lifetime: 'It is a religion, you know, of hero and heroine worship.' His gravity made me reflect on this.

On the following day, in the early afternoon, Divakar once more collected me and took me on a long drive to the north-east.

2025 hrs. Set off at 1430 hrs. for Madhubani – a large urban area of Darbhanga to cross before we emerged into the open country. The wide expanse of rice, brilliant green – spring in our English sense – reaching away to the distant horizon, is to me always wonderfully refreshing after hours in any bazaar, with the dense pressure of humanity, din and grit. Beyond

Madhubani, a small bazaar town, we visited a village – little fawn huts of mud, bamboo and thatch, with smooth, neat earthy floors and alleys, all very clean, in which a few women devote themselves to a style of very primitive painting on large sheets of paper. It is a style copied from something almost identical from the ancient past. In 1962 a central government body, Vhashkar Kulkami Handloom Handicrafts Export Corporation, New Delhi, began to subsidise women painters in this and similar villages by buying their pictures for export. I was told that over 700 women in several villages in the area of Madhubani were now producing similar work. I bought two examples from the village of Jitwar Pur Ranti. I did not buy them because I admired them but to avoid being churlish when the kindly old woman in one of the huts held them up for me to see. The work, however, seemed to me very crude indeed. In most of the pictures, for example, the human body was furnished with two left feet, or two right feet, not one of each, and all facial features were quite childishly represented. Some of the pictures showed more skill than others and commanded higher prices, and the products are now being exploited for their foreign exchange value in easing India's balance of payments. The pictures, I suspect, are bought by American and European dawdlers in search of bogus sophistication. Whilst such people may deserve to be fleeced, the encouragement by subsidy of large numbers of women in modern India merely to perpetuate the achievements of more primitive forbears may be considered cynical. In the meantime, whatever the merits of the policy, it must presumably be allowed to continue, merely to avoid distress. That is the trouble with subsidies.

27 October, 1155 hrs. Muzaffapur. Before starting from Darbhanga early this morning – equipped with a new tyre – I decided to call on Mr Pillai, the Collector, for a courtesy farewell and to thank him for all the sightseeing and for arranging for me to have the tyre. I sat in his office for about ten minutes whilst he finished his breakfast. It was a nice, efficient-looking office, reminding me very much of the office of a British resident in a province of Northern Nigeria long ago – files all carefully flagged for his attention in a pile on a clean, orderly desk. When he appeared he was gracious and spruce, with the demeanour of non-hurry that indicates the man more

busy than he looks. I asked him the name of the Collector and
District Magistrate at Muzaffapur – it is Mr G. S. Dutt. I said I
should like to talk with him, especially about land matters.
Pillai promised to telephone Dutt and warn him of my
impending arrival.

The road from Darbhanga to Muzaffapur is narrower and
more rural, with less traffic than the other roads along which
we have travelled. Within a few seconds of reaching the
outskirts, we found ourselves in the midst of Muzaffapur,
much bigger, denser than Darbhanga, with seething traffic and
crowds. Arrived at this attractive circuit house in gardens
adjoining a big open space, the Maidan, at about 1120 hrs. It is
now just after two o'clock – I have had a light sandwich lunch.
The additional Collector, F. Hazra, called on me about
1145 hrs. and stayed talking with me until 1315 hrs. – and
about that time K. B. Sekhar, the young district judge, also
arrived. I arranged to visit him at the court building at
1600 hrs. this afternoon. Will see Dutt tomorrow morning
before we set off for Motihari.

Talk with Hazra most helpful, not so much because he told
me anything very new but because he seemed convincing. He
emphasised that the abolition of the zamindari system itself
implied only the loss of their special functions as tax collectors.
It did not abolish them as owners, and other owners, not
previously zamindars, also remained. The Ceiling Acts had had
the effect of causing former zamindars and other large land-
owners to split up their estates into multiple holdings which
remained large, however, as collective holdings with family
linkages. He stressed, too, that the policy of combining small
scattered units of land into holdings of viable size was
proceeding, and how such combinations (*chakbandi*) were
being arranged and administered by *chakbandi* courts, administrative tribunals operated by the land revenue department.
Their functions included the arrangement of *chakbandi* deals or
settlements among holders, making surveys and plans and all
the procedures of publication, giving notice of time for
objections from interested parties etc. etc. The legal procedures
included a chain of appeals from *chakbandi* courts to the High
Court at Patna and thence to the Supreme Court – all very
time-consuming. However, despite such delays, the policies

are indeed working themselves out. I asked Hazra if it would be true to say that, as such schemes succeeded and public and private funds were actually invested in improvements in holdings of optimum size under the ceiling acts, the examples thus established could grow cumulatively. He agreed that it could. I found this encouraging.

It is, I think, significant that the kinds of people who had been asssuring me that the Government's policies of land reform were all 'eyewash', or had been declaring with knowing looks that all officials concerned with it were 'corrupt', had had nothing whatever to do with the subject in the course of their otherwise distinguished careers, though they were perfectly sincere and dignified individuals.

The layout of the government area of Muzaffapur is very reminiscent of the Raj, with dignified houses partly hidden by trees, flowering shrubs and little drives leading to pillared verandahs. On boards at the entrances the names of residents and their offices were painted in white block capital letters. Such dwellings are ranged round the Maidan with views across its great expanse of grass, now becoming dry. I walked several times across it and, from the centre, could gain a good perspective of the old place whose image must still be clear in the memories of long-retired British officers of Bihar. At one end of the Maidan stands a hill perhaps sixty to eighty feet high which seemed at first a strange feature in the midst of the rockless Gangetic plain. I realised suddenly that it had been the butts of an old shooting range, constructed no doubt many decades ago by British and Indian soldiers. It must have been used for firing practice when the Maidan had been primarily a military camp site, training and parade ground.

On one of my walks, about the middle of the Maidan, I saw three small boys playing together. One of them was white with blue eyes and yellow, thick, Scandinavian hair flopping over his face. Although talking in Hindi and dressed like his fellows he was evidently of European descent – a strange sight now in Bihar, but perhaps not so strange in a former garrison town like Muzaffapur.

29 October – Circuit house, Motihari. 2125 hrs. Before leaving

Muzaffapur I called on G. S. Dutt. He is a very young man, small, round features, keenly intelligent. His demeanour and appearance resembled that of a young Principal in Whitehall. He confirmed what his assistant, Hazra, had told me – that the land reforms *were* proceeding, despite difficulties – and mentioned also various measures to increase employment, especially inter-village road construction to promote mobility and commerce, and small manufacturing ventures, large water control schemes, the use of fertilisers, etc. I said I would like to see some statistics of all this development. He told me that figures could no doubt be given to me by the Planning Department at Patna, of which Mr Mulkund Prasad was the senior administrative officer concerned.

The aspect of Motihari differs pleasingly from that of other bazaar towns of north Bihar. We approached the government area through a wide avenue shaded by trees, lined on either side with well-spaced shops, traders' stalls and market booths. I was already aware of the reason for this relatively open layout of the town. In the earthquake of 1934, in my father's time, the place had been almost entirely destroyed. The new town which replaced it had been carefully planned to provide for a much bigger population in the future. I was thus able to see into the real future of the planners' work and wondered if any of those who had been responsible might still be living.*

The circuit house, probably a converted residence, is a pleasantly appointed one. There was nothing to eat in the place, however, and the man in charge was away on leave. A sleepy subordinate told me he would have to buy food for me in the market. This was done and I did get some sort of meal. The room and the washing area were full of mosquitoes and I asked if he could spray the place for me. He said there was no spray, because

---

* Responsibility for reconstruction plans after the earthquake would presumably have been shared by a few senior officers. J. E. Scott, OBE, ICS, was Commissioner for the Tirhut Division which includes the locality of Motihari and the District of Champaran. S. L. Marwood, ICS, was District Magistrate of Champaran District and the British predecessor of Kulpati Sharma who looked after me during my visit (see the following pages). N. G. Tanbar was Chief Engineer of Bihar and Orissa, and A. S. T. G. Lyster was Superintending Engineer, North Bihar. I am grateful to Mr Justice S. S. Hasan of the Patna High Court for his kindness in ascertaining these details and sending them to me in London.

sprays had always been pinched by visitors in the past; so I prepared to smother myself in insect repellant for the night.

From my diary:

At about 1800 hrs. I was collected by the driver of the District Magistrate and taken to his residence – to his office within it, that is. He, Kulpati Sharma, rose to greet me. In his late fifties he stoops a little with back trouble similar to that of Arun Pathak, the Home Commissioner in Patna – and they are, I think, rather similar men. Sharma has aristocratic light features and a sensitive, intellectual look in his lined face. He rather resembles the late Prime Minister, Jawarharlal Nehru. I think we took to each other easily – an enjoyable talk. After a few minutes he told me that, ever since his youth, he had wondered if a strange story about my father was really true.

'Your father, as you know, was determined to put down corruption among the judges and magistrates in this still very corrupt part of the world. Is it true that, in his study at Chhaju Bagh, he once took a revolver from his pocket and threatened to shoot one of the judges on the spot unless he submitted his resignation immediately?'

I had not heard such a story before but was aware of the general circumstances from which it must have emerged. Aware of strong indications that one of the puisne judges had been involved in some kind of bribery, my father had requested the man to call at his office at Chhaju Bagh. When the judge was seated, my father handed him a sheet of paper upon which, in his own hand, he had set out the circumstances of the suspected bribery and invited the judge to read it. When the judge looked up from the paper my father said to him: 'That is part of the draft of a private letter to the Viceroy. However, should you decide to take the opportunity to resign your office *at once*, no such letter will be sent to His Excellency, and I shall take no further action.' The judge resigned immediately. He subsequently made a fortune as an advocate, no doubt appearing in many cases before my father who, perhaps, could have been suspected of holding a pistol, as it were, to the good man's head.

I questioned Sharma about land reforms. He was pessimistic. He said there had been practically no headway with *chakbandi* deals for years. People with land in excess of the permitted holdings disposed of the surplus to fictitious persons. When I commented that such conduct was presumably unlawful, he said, in effect, that the whole administrative and legal system simply ignored such matters. He attributed this to what he called 'our dishonesty'. I asked if it would be true to say that if he, as District Magistrate, were to insist on a drive in the area for land reform in accordance with the ostensible policy of government, life for him could be made unendurable. He assented quietly.

This talk with Sharma, so soon after my talks with Hazra and Dutt in a neighbouring district, illustrates the difficulty encountered by anyone seeking the truth about a social, religious, economic or political matter merely by talking with people supposed to be concerned with such things. I do not believe that the seeming inconsistencies show that anybody was trying to deceive me. A young man hard at work on difficult problems will identify the satisfaction of his task with real development. An older man, more aware of human frailty, will be less confident.

Sharma took me in his car to meet the District and Sessions Judge, A. N. Sinha, an agreeable man of about forty-five who lives in a large house which, long ago, had been the local indigo planters' club. His large sitting room had been the ballroom. Indigo had been widely grown in this northern part of Bihar until the manufacture of chemical dyes completely superseded it. All the planters had gone (most had been British), and all that remained of their way of life was what was left of their bungalows, little overgrown areas that had been tennis courts, abandoned driveways and silence.

As Sharma drove me about Motihari we talked continually, he answering my many questions. I noticed that everywhere people recognised him and saluted him most respectfully. He told me he knew everyone in Motihari, where most of his service had been spent. He is, I think, one of those increasingly rare field officers (it does not matter whether we are considering the colonial past or the present decades) who do not aspire to the promotion within an official hierarchy that would make them merely more important bureaucrats, but seek the appreciation of the people for whose welfare they are partly responsible. Such men treasure the visible world in which their work is found. Yet on general matters Sharma was instructive. Thus, when I asked him about finance, he explained that the industrial and commercial development of India since 1947 implied that land revenue formed a smaller and smaller proportion of the total revenues of government. More and more of the revenue was now derived from indirect taxes on trade. The nationalised industries did not contribute much to revenue. Inflation was due to the huge growth of the public sector which could not be financed either by taxation or by borrowing. This in itself generated an ever-expanding money supply. The forcing up of particular costs, whether by trade union pressure or, say, the higher cost of imported oil, meant that plans could not be carried out without ever greater financial provision. All this seemed pretty familiar. In such a situation all attempts to control prices created black markets and widespread discontent.

I asked him what *good* things about Motihari could be reported. He at once mentioned technical advances in agriculture, the increased use of fertilisers, irrigation schemes and water control, and the growth of trade following improved road communications between villages. He took me back to the circuit house. There, as we sat briefly on the verandah over lemonade, I asked him what aspects of his work as focal administrator of the district gave him the most satisfaction. Before replying he explained that since my father's day various factors had caused a considerable reduction in the area for which a district magistrate or 'collector' was responsible. The abolition of the zamindari system of tax collection had meant that the whole burden of revenue collection from the land now fell directly upon government. The growth of population, trade and industry, the organisation of the 'block' areas for community development and increasing pressures due to the telephone had made it necessary to increase the number of administrators and courts. As for himself, he told me in a quiet, most sincere voice, that he found his greatest satisfaction in seeing some project through to completion – getting some much needed road built or repaired, a school or a bridge made, finding money for something against tremendous odds, for something good to be done, so that he could feel 'I helped with that – it will last a little while at least.'

He asked me if all was well at the circuit house and I mentioned a few small difficulties. He sent for the servant and questioned him in Hindi. As the man muttered his excuses, fingering his grubby dhoti, I watched Sharma's face. Listening in silence, he put his head sideways, his eyes almost closed, stroking his chin gently with the fingers of one hand. Understanding nothing, I sensed the meaning of his posture, which might have been expressed thus: 'As you see, I am listening. And, as you know, I am able to detect what part of your explanation consists of lies and what part is the truth.' Anyway, within moments of Sharma's departure a spray for mosquitoes was produced and put to good use, and my supper was not bad.

I had companions at the circuit house that evening. S. N. Sinha the District and Sessions Judge of Palamau, a district in the south-west of Bihar, was on tour here in the north, taking the vacation courts, accompanied by his wife, daughter and one of his sons. I had already encountered the family very briefly at Muzaffapur, but we now became friendly and he invited me to spend a weekend with him at Daltonganj, the administrative centre of Palamau, explaining that I could get there by bus from Patna – an all-day drive.

I was about to eat a greasy omelette for lunch on the circuit house verandah when I was greeted by a bright-looking young man with a notebook who introduced himself as representing *The Times of India*. After asking questions about the circumstances of my visit to India he wanted to know my impressions of the country, and I gave him a form of words. I believe they published some kind of report but I never saw a copy. I told him I had been impressed by the tremendous development of industry and commerce in India. It was easy to be critical but my basic impression had been one of enduring strength in the forces of unity and stability, and by the strength of the stratified structure of Indian society.

Since the road from Motihari to Bettiah, our next destination, is quite short, I decided to make a detour to Birganj, just over the Nepalese border. I did so only because the Chief Justice had urged me to visit the place, merely to enable me to say that I had been to Nepal. This meant going to the Bihari frontier at Raxaul, a rough bazaar town with a few modern buildings and a depressing police station concerned primarily with smuggling. There we sat on a wooden first-floor balcony for about three-quarters of an hour drinking tea in the company of three or four police officers, none of whom knew a single syllable of English. They were big men in khaki uniforms and peaked caps. Their features seemed to me exceedingly ferocious, though perhaps they were merely glum and in that milieu of total inarticulacy I was mistaken. I was not exactly frightened of them but could not avoid the feeling that, unlike my own soft and sheltered self, they were hardened to the sight of pain and desperation in the faces of the dacoits and drug pedlars who came their way. I wondered how such men fared with their wives and children, if any, after their constabulary duties had been done.

One imagines it to be impossible to visit Nepal without going uphill, but I recall no hills – merely a continuation of the plain and the negotiation of an old wooden bridge over a muddy river before entering the quite large town of Birganj. Our two police officers sitting in front were evidently frequent visitors and at the frontier post we were waved through without formalities. The bazaar town is dominated by a tall, recently built pagoda-like structure at a main crossroads, which seems to declare that this is Nepal. In India you can see nothing like this pagoda. The structure evokes at once architectural features of the Far East and something from Hindu mythology, and I suppose that similar things can be seen quite plentifully over a vast area between Thailand and Java. Despite this cultural message, Birganj is basically an Indian town. Most of the people in the streets look like Biharis but a few with mongoloid features belonging to the Himalayas can be seen among them. I noticed well-stocked shops containing goods from many parts of the world, and it was clearly not the policy of the Nepalese Government to protect local manufacturing against foreign competition. Some of my companions in the car made purchases of Japanese textiles, unobtainable in India, to take home to their wives. I, on the other hand, kept quiet in the back of the car and made no purchases, feeling that the diversion had been rather a waste of time. The afternoon sun was very hot and we were held up for ages in the Birganj traffic jams. Also, I did not much like the prospect of arriving at Bettiah after dark, for dacoits had been active in the area and were said to be a danger to travellers by night.

It was indeed quite dark and late when we drove into Bettiah,

Mohamed and Kishore shouting out 'Circuit house? Circuit house' until, in the customary way, a policeman on traffic duty stepped down from his rostrum and pointed the way smartly with his cane. The circuit house was a large, two-storeyed building of brick and stucco that had once been the planters' club, now crumbling and fusty. One entered a bare hall from which a black-timbered stairway led to a landing and several large rooms. After waiting in the hall for some minutes I was greeted sleepily by a dishevelled steward who ushered me up the stairs to a front room with two pairs of French windows overlooking the flat roof of the porch. In the room was a seedy-looking bed with a worn counterpane and no apparent likelihood of sheets, a bedside lamp with tangled heaps of flex and a scurry of cockroaches round the skirting.

After a shower and change of clothes I went downstairs to the dining room. It was a big hall with a heavy black carved table, a matching sideboard and tall carved chairs – relics of long-departed splendour. Everything in the building was sad, upholstery ragged, cobwebs moving gently in draughty corners, marks of fungus damp stretching down the walls, and little to eat. The staff had sent out to the bazaar to fetch me something – the usual watery curried cauliflower, tepid rice and leathery chapatti, glass of water and fruit. By now, having consumed so many meals of this calibre, I was losing my appetite and had to force myself to eat.

I am much indebted to the administrative and judicial services of Bettiah district for the programme they arranged for me the next day – one of the best in my tour of the north. It was all arranged quickly over the telephone with an excellent man, Shambu Sharan, sub-divisional magistrate (administrative, that is) of the district.

At about 8.30 a.m., whilst I was considering how best to advance upon two very tiny eggs with a very large spoon, Shambu Sharan called to introduce himself. I liked him at once – he was an outward-looking intellectual, smart, thirtyish. Observing my preoccupation with the spoon, Sharan said he would return in half an hour with transport and another fellow to show me the main features of Bettiah, have a picnic lunch on a lake nearby and bring me back later to meet the Bar Association for tea. They would be laying on something for me. He apologised for the melancholy state of the circuit house. 'It is far too big for us to maintain. We have not the money or the staff for it. This place – the whole district – was founded upon indigo, and there is no indigo now.' I said I was all right, and thanked him.

He duly returned in a Land-Rover with a driver and a companion who was a local advocate. This man, aware of my father's reputation, wanted to meet me. I forget his name. He was big and tall, thick-set and strong, about thirty-five, an agreeable, kindly character with two somewhat off-putting traits. As a committed pan chewer, he had allowed the whole inside of his mouth and his lips to become horribly stained with the bright red dye, and he spoke persistently in a very loud rasping voice, as if he had trained himself to converse exclusively with the seriously deaf. The simple frankness of his questions about Britain, bawled into my ear amid the traffic of Bettiah, I attempted to answer as we rolled through the dust. He had a powerful desire to go to Britain and thought that I must surely be able to pull wires to make his dream come true. I could only steer him towards the British High Commission in Calcutta and say that I would have no objection if he mentioned that I had done so. If something could be done about the condition of his mouth and the rasp of his voice, his prospects in the world could be transformed, but I could mention to him nothing so personal. It is sometimes easier to be tactless in theory than in practice.

Among the advocate's questions about Britain was one something like this: 'In India we owe our whole administrative and judicial system to your country. Tell me how the collectors and district magistrates function in the countryside of Britain nowadays?' I had just begun to frame a reply when he asked me, at the top of his voice at a traffic jam, how the morality of British women compared with that of Indian women. It seemed that he viewed the affairs of the planet in a broad shifting perspective.

Our first call was at the Khrist Raja High School. This, run by an American Jesuit mission known as the Catholic Mission, Bettiah, is one of the finest privately endowed boarding schools in India. The school was founded in 1927 and its present buildings date from 1930. There were about 1,000 boys between five and seventeen years of age. I recalled that the Chief Justice had told me that he had been a pupil there. I was introduced to the headmaster, Father K. T. Thomas, a tall American in grey robes who conducted us round the school, introduced us to his colleagues and gave us coffee and biscuits in the canteen. The classrooms, beautiful gardens and general form of the school, together with its fine church with classical façade and lovely interior, recalled a dignity and grace of the past that still clings to an élite of Indian youth today. The school itself was on vacation.

Father Thomas explained that, whilst in the past the school had drawn pupils from all over India, its field was now restricted to Bihar. At the school, in addition to full-time tuition in all the usual school subjects for its own pupils, the Khrist Raja Educational Association, assisted by public funds, provided informal education in its classrooms after regular hours for about 350 'under-privileged' children from Bettiah, teaching them Hindi, mathematics and English and providing a certificate for those who kept it up for five years. Also, the school conducted adult education classes and various projects in local community development. The Projects Officer responsible for this valuable work was an Indian, Father K. M. Joseph, who was introduced to me. On the outer wall of the church was a plaque indicating that the benefactor, a woman, wished to remain anonymous.

I was shown over another large Catholic school, St Stanislaus, which provided primary education for about 800 local pupils of between four and a half and fourteen years of age. This school, too, had a most beautiful church attached to it, built after the great earthquake of 1934. Its inner walls are surrounded by well-made relief mouldings, each of about fifteen by eight feet, depicting about twenty events in the life of Jesus – didactically most effective. There was an American headmaster who showed us over the school. He had been there over thirty years, a most dedicated, excellent man.

At Bettiah we visited the Kalibagh temple, contained in a large rectangular space surrounded by walls, with images of Kali and Hanuman and many objects associated with Shaivite ritual arranged round the cloisters. The temple contains a collection of sculptured figures in stone and marble – many of them figures of goddesses, some probably of great antiquity – a museum and temple combined. Shambu Sharan was helpful in trying to explain to me the significance of the ritual (in which I took part together with my companions) and the relations between intellectual and popular interpretations of the symbolism. An old

priest seemed grateful when I performed a ritual gesture and
allowed him to sprinkle a little water on my hands and touch my
forehead with some holy liquid.

Looking closely at the images and the attitudes of their
devotees, I recalled the view of the Muslim judge Kunandi at
Darbhanga that Hinduism is a religion of hero worship. One
cloister contains a long row of figures of a goddess, each showing
her grasping in one of her several hands a different object
representing some specific power, faculty or activity – a spear, an
agricultural tool, a musical instrument, some unrecognisable
object probably well known in the distant past. Many of the
figures in popular Hindu imagery symbolise particular faculties,
powers or arrangements of attributes associated with myths. A
devotee selects among the images heroes and heroines of whose
specific powers he would avail himself in his own humble
predicament on earth. Ritual is the attempt to tap transcendent
sources of needed power and authority. The qualities of 'gods'
and 'goddesses' are heroic, in the sense of being superlative
manifestations of attributes desired by men and women in the
world.

After leaving the temple we called at the police station where
we were joined by two armed officers who, in the Land-Rover,
accompanied us to the lakeside a few miles away. To get there we
drove along a country road through a forest in which dacoits
were said to be hiding – hence the precautions. One of the police
officers told me that they knew how many dacoits were in the
forest and that 'one of these days' they would mount an offensive
and round up the lot. My own small experience of trying to deal
with an enemy in the middle of a forest was enough to persuade
me how difficult the task can be.

The lake, Saraya Man, is a lovely stretch of clear water several
square miles in extent, surrounded by trees whose branches
overhang the rocky edges. We drove to a small brick rest house in
a clearing, with a little jetty; the place belonged to the forestry
department. Here we climbed into a boat equipped with oars and
an awning against the sun. A pair of oarsmen rowed us out on the
lake for half an hour whilst a light lunch was prepared for us in the
kitchen of the rest house.

My companions told me that the trees surrounding the lake
were called *jamun* which yielded a small black berry, ripening in

May and June. The berry is edible, promotes digestion and is supposed to purify the water of the lake. The water looked wonderfully translucent though May was still a long way off. I mentioned that it looked most tempting for a swim. 'Then you certainly should,' Sharan said. One of the men quickly handed to me a long piece of cloth which I was supposed to wrap about my loins. However, in the half second before diving in I dropped the cloth into the boat behind me and swam in the nude. In such inviting water, the cloth seemed an encumbrance and I felt that if my companions were going to be shocked at the spectacle of a nude European – then let them be shocked. The swim was delightful, a sudden exhilarating liberation, and I swam in a wide arc, far from the boat, for about twenty minutes. Eventually they heaved me aboard, laughing, and the cloth was put to use as a towel. We returned to the jetty where servants with brass containers brought omelettes, chapattis, salad, fruit and orange juice, and we set out again on the lake to consume them.

Adjoining the rest house was a small plant for generating gas for cooking purposes and perhaps also for lighting. This was achieved by the fermentation of cowdung in water by subjecting the mixture to solar heat. The plant was very simple and its use is spreading steadily in rural India. A cylindrical drum-like container of cast iron, about three metres in diameter and a little less in depth, with an open base and covered top, was lowered over a large copper-like vessel containing the mixture of water and cowdung. The weight of the heavy iron cover imposed pressure upon the air contained between the inside of the cover and the mixture below. Gas in the mixture was released through a tube leading from the top of the cover into the kitchen of the rest house. With the aid of a tap at the end of the tube the gas could be turned on and lit with a match. The device, known as the Indian Gobar Gas Plant, had been developed by a public body called the Khadi Gramodyog Board, and persons wishing to install such plants could apply for a subsidy from the Government. Whatever the economics of the device, the flame produced is at least smokeless.

We got back to Bettiah about tea time and drove straight to the district court building where, much to my surprise, a gathering of fifty or sixty lawyers, magistrates and judges had assembled outside to greet me. They were the district Bar Association. The

senior advocate, Mr M. Obaidullah, a man in his seventies with a
clear memory of my father, greeted and introduced me to his
colleagues, and then showed me quickly over the courts. The
whole gathering (smartly dressed, many in black legal garb) then
moved into the assembly hall of the Association within the court
building, where long tables were set out for tea.

Obaidullah, very much in charge of the proceedings, was a
slenderly built, athletic-looking man, much younger than his
years, with thick, barely greying hair, keenly lined features and a
short moustache. I was presented with a shiny tinsel garland,
which was hung round my neck. Obaidullah then made quite a
long speech in which I was accredited with the lustre of my
father's image. (This transfer of qualities from the departed to the
living is accomplished with eager readiness everywhere in India.)
He caused delight by recalling a remark of my father in response
to the flattery of some young advocate who had referred in court
to 'the learned Chief Justice'. 'Learning,' said my father, 'con-
notes neither wisdom nor courage.'

During the laughter I took a sip of tea and a bisuit and then
stood up to reply. I spoke of my happiness to be greeted in
Bettiah by so delightful a gathering, including people who
actually remembered my father, and promised to take the garland
back with me to my home in London, where it would be
treasured most carefully – for England was not, all things
considered, a place much given to garlands. They clapped and
cheered. One's reserve does not easily withstand the emotional
impact of such occasions.

On the way back to the circuit house we passed through a part
of Bettiah where most inhabitants are Christians, their culture,
no doubt, influenced by the Catholic schools and their beautiful
churches. The appearance of the streets and houses was quite
unlike those in the other parts of the town. As in a village in
Spain, Provence or Southern Italy, many of the houses were quite
tall, with balconies, painted doors and window frames, and a few
steps leading down from front doors to small pavements or into
the street. Although many of the women wore saris and the
general appearance of the people was as Indian as it was in any
other part of the town, the style of life seemed to resemble that of
Catholic Europe. The streets themselves were very much cleaner
than in the ordinary bazaar.

Long stretches of the road from Bettiah back to Muzaffapur
being reportedly good, I felt that we could safely cover the
distance that evening without staying another night among the
hunting scenes and cockroaches of the planters' club at Bettiah;
and this we did, arriving at Muzaffapur well after dark but in time
for a shower and a greasy omelette at the superior circuit house
there. I was glad we did so, for I met again S. N. Sinha, the
District and Sessions Judge of Palamau, with his wife and
beautiful daughter. Sinha at once renewed his invitation for me to
visit the family at Daltonganj, and I much looked forward to that
diversion.

We had a long way to go next morning, for I wanted to visit
Vaishali, where an ancient city had once stood, and to see the
pillar erected there by Ashoka, the great ruler of the Mauryan
empire, to mark the conversion of his people to Buddhism. To
reach Vaishali we turned off the main road at about midday and
travelled for several miles along a winding country road through
a fresh green landscape of rice fields and small villages, a scene
probably unchanged for centuries. Nothing is left of Vaishali
except the Ashoka pillar itself and a partially excavated mound
quite close to it. The interior of the mound consists of brickwork
whose purpose is not evident. The pillar, perhaps sixty feet high,
is surmounted by a squatting stone lion which, gazing in
tranquillity over the plain, has had a remarkable view of the
landscape over the past 2,000 years. The pillar stands upon a
brickwork base and is itself made of bricks covered over with
very strong cement to form a smooth, slightly tapering cylinder.
All round are scrawled the names of visitors going back at least to
the time of the Napoleonic Wars and all through the nineteenth
century. Most of the names are written in various Indian scripts
but there are many British names among them, usually with
dates. The British names could have belonged to soldiers or
clerks employed by the East India Company, and I wondered
how some had managed to chip or scratch their names with such
elegance a long way above the present ground level.

An undulating area of grassland nearby must conceal the
unexcavated remains of Vaishali. I walked over this area, a
few hundred yards in diameter, and found in the grass many
fragments of terracotta which, for all I could tell, could have been
of great antiquity. The experience reminded me of a walk in the

Alban hills near Frascati, a few miles from Rome, where, at every other step, one disturbs with one's feet small fragments of Roman mosaic or little coins, bits of broken marble. Near the pillar is a small museum with fragments of pottery, photographs of traces of the ancient town, and a pleasant little guest house .where we were able to get a simple meal.

We reached Hajipur by mid-afternoon but had to wait about three hours for the ferry to arrive. We drank tea and ate biscuits at a stall on the rough track leading down to the river's edge, a dozen huge lorries standing about us, all waiting to cross. When the big new bridge to the east of Patna is opened, its impact upon economic development of the great plain to the north will be considerable.

When at last we moved off, the sun was setting beyond the other bank, a red ball in the sky whose fading colours were reflected in the water. A great silence, on the river, was broken only by the gentle rumble of the engine. We passed several boats with large, limp sails, drifting slowly to the east, each with its pile of goods, jute, textiles, sacks and boxes. The expanse of moving water extends far to the northern horizon, bounded by a fine rim of land upon which no more than the tiny form of a palm tree and a little sand can be distinguished in the failing light. The hugeness of the river, coming and going mysteriously, its origins and its destination unknown to the people of the plain, implied an ineffable cosmic power, bringing life, destroying it, unknown in all but the massive impact of itself – the Ganges of India's millions.

8

Patna and Daltonganj

It was dark when we reached the landing stage at Patna and drove up the steep ramp with its slanting row of lights reflected in the water. We reached the Hotel Republic within a few minutes and there I parted from my good friends Mohamed and Kishore. In the hotel I was greeted by the staff with a kind of warmth that belongs especially to India. It is expressed in little gestures, glances and thoughtful acts – that of the steward who brings me the newspaper of my choice without being requested for it, the waiter who brings to my table some item of food or drink which, he remembers, I appear to enjoy, the manager who says: 'I am putting you in Room 52 this time. I thought you would probably like it better.' The hotel is actually quite a rough place, as hotels go, and the food needlessly boring, but in human relationships with guests all the staff make charming amends.

There followed some days in Patna when I was entertained by various people and had much talk with them. It seems now remarkable that, with whatever intemperance certain views were expressed to me, I do not recall a single occasion when anybody said: 'Please keep this to yourself. I am telling you this in the strictest confidence.' I never found myself in the position of those who, during visits to the Soviet Union, encounter people who, craving to unburden themselves, live in fear of any Big Brother in their midst. On the contrary I became aware of a prevailing intellectual liberalism which seemed to stem from two mutually independent cultural roots. The deepest is the multiplicity of values inherent in the Hindu tradition. Whatever the Hindu may believe, whatever the ritual or *modus vivendi* he observes, his commitment is still a matter of personal decision. Unlike the citizen of a theocracy or under a communist oligarchy, he is beholden to no organised authority over his intellectual life. The other cultural root is European and secular, derived from such exemplars as David Hume, John Stuart Mill,

A. V. Dicey and British constitutional tradition of the nine-teenth century. It derives, too, from pre-French Revolutionary notions of the popular 'will', but I suspect that dangers from that source are not greatly to be feared. Indian society is stratified too powerfully to be shaken by any such supposedly 'democratic' attitudes.

As in Bombay and New Delhi, I met in Patna people who were very gloomy about the condition of India, who seemed to be awaiting some awful disaster. But when I asked them to tell me precisely what shape catastrophe might be expected to assume, their replies never implied anything that we in Europe would regard as 'revolution'. This, perhaps, is because India has never experienced the kinds of upheavals which have characterised much of European history. Catastrophe, for Indians, meant increasing momentum in the growth of breakdowns and crises – in law and order especially, and by the workings of the public sector. Such breakdowns could be expected to accompany natural calamities, failures of monsoons, floods, tidal waves. And underlying all is the ever-growing pressure of population in the great Gangetic plain by which Patna is surrounded.

In their replies to my questions Indians seemed to take for granted (and thus to leave out of account) the enormous strength of their own stratified society. At the bottom are many tens of millions of exceedingly poor human beings who constitute the 'scheduled castes', very large numbers of whom subsist as sweepers and scavengers on the edges of cities. At Patna their wretched, flimsy habitations can be seen along the railway embankments, devoid of drainage or sanitary facilities, stinking. Unlike the poorest people in Europe, these Indian poor are al-most entirely endogamous, chained for ever to certain vocations and spurned by virtually the whole of the rest of the population, and almost wholly illiterate. A great deal has in fact been done to improve the status of these people, both in law and in material ways, but such improvements are much more likely to be the consequences of administrative and financial measures taken on their behalf by members of higher castes than of any likely conduct of their own. I do not believe that ameliorative forces in India can be expected to emerge from below.

Making arrangements for my visits to Daltonganj and other parts of the south of Bihar involved several visits to the secretariat, to banks and to the High Court. In all such offices the scene is the same. The senior officers work in privacy, dignity and seclusion; the congested dusty corridors are piled high with old files. The working atmosphere is almost exclusively male. Although women work on the land almost as frequently as men, and in the towns, as in Russia, women 'harijans' do labouring jobs, middle-class women, down to the level of the humblest clerks, are seldom seen in offices, at least in this part of India.

5 November, 1800 hrs. Went for a walk across the Maidan in the setting sunlight. The road leading northwards to the Maidan is now full of choking dust, and the sweepers are still on strike. The dust stinks vaguely of unfresh spiced vegetables and urine. I feel an awareness of germs, as though the dust, breathed into my lungs and swallowed in saliva, must eventually sicken me with appalling microbes. Yet a vast humanity survives in this atmosphere and many people appear actually to be old.

Ever since I have been in the hotel both sides of the road have had upon them large piles of broken stones. I had assumed that they were building materials. Today, however, their purpose became clear. Coolies, including many women, have been digging out large areas of dusty earth, rectangular in shape, along one side of the asphalted area in the centre. It is clear that the stones are to be tipped into such areas, each about ten inches deep, to form a macadamised base that will be less dusty and more easily drainable in the future. This is good.

6 November, 0725 hrs. I have been reading André Béteille's valuable book *Castes: Old and New*. In a chapter on India's élites he writes (p. 226): 'There is in fact a view, widely held among Western-educated Indians, that the new type of political leader is ignorant, semi-literate and crafty in the arts of manipulating the loyalties of caste and community, in other words, obscurantist and reactionary: whereas the planner and administrator are seen as representing reasonableness, intellectual clarity and modernity.' I have met educated men, both within the administration and outside it, who have expressed these views very strongly.

At 1515 hrs. I had an appointment to see Mr X., a deputy secretary in the Land Revenue Department, to discuss land reform. The rank of deputy secretary sounds important, but in

India it is a lowly executive rank, and to get to his office I was led by a messenger through several dark corridors into a small, stuffy area with three or four deal desks and several chattering clerks and chaprassis – an area whose evolution had been arrested somewhere between the stages of passage way and office. The messenger pointed to a deal chair facing Mr X. across one of the desks, and I sat down. He is a small man in his middle forties, smooth thinning hair brushed straight back, regular features and a somewhat rigid, straight mouth. He did not look up but continued to deal with a pile of papers, glancing through forms, writing a word or two or his initials with a red ballpoint pen. A chaprassi stood waiting to collect the papers as he finished with them, holding another pile in his hand, ready to place them on the desk as soon as Mr X. had finished with the others. After some minutes, without lifting his eyes from his work, Mr X. said severely: 'Yes?' To which I replied: 'I'll wait till you can spare a moment.' He evidently wished me to know that, whatever I wanted, I was wasting his valuable time, a view with which I felt myself in agreement. He went on working and there was no pause in the general hubbub of activity about him. Then, still not looking at me, he said: 'What can I do for you, Mr Taylor?' In the African continent, the Caribbean and the Indian Ocean my name is commonly rendered as Taylor or Tiller by otherwise masterful persons. However, the silences of Mr X. put me at a certain advantage for, whilst he was preoccupied, I was at leisure to consider how to deal with such a man.

I said I was anxious to be properly informed about land questions, and should therefore be most grateful if he would tell me briefly about any aspect of land reform with which he was especially concerned. He nodded seriously and at once went into an account of a part of the subject of which he had clearly had years of experience. He described an act of the newly independent Government of Bihar in 1947, The Bihar Privileged Persons' Homestead Tenancy Act. Before that, he said, a landless labourer who occupied a house on the holding of a landowner for whom he worked could be driven off the land at will and the house destroyed. The Act provided procedures for giving him security on administrative decision. Down to 1980 as many as 900,000 families in Bihar had

benefited – about sixty per cent of all the homesteads potentially affected by the legislation. I felt much rewarded by this
helpful information. Just as Mr X. concluded, however, we
were interrupted.

Mr Lakhman, private secretary to the minister, entered and
greeted me by my correct name. He said he had met me at
Purnea. He seemed a very pleasant, strong character. When I
told him I was trying to get some statistics or other evidence
about the progress of land reform, he picked up the telephone
and arranged for me to see J. L. Arya, Special Secretary, Land
Reform, and took me straight to his room. Arya, a young and
senior member of the Indian Administrative Service, was at the
moment engaged at a meeting with half-a-dozen departmental
colleagues, but I was at once introduced to them all and Arya,
for my benefit, delivered an excellent verbal summary of the
position. It seems that the administration of the Ceiling Acts
and other legislation had been in the doldrums till about 1972,
but since then much progress had been made. The present
Chief Minister, Mr Jagannath Misra, had recently announced a
policy for the completion of the land reforms in Bihar in five
years under the new plan. Also, legislation was pending to put
an end to fictitious disposals of land ostensibly to comply with
the law. Arya confirmed my impression that *chakbandi* deals,
although they might present some legal and administrative
difficulties, advertised themselves whenever there was a successful development project involving them; and this had a
snowball effect. I expect to hear more from Arya, who
impressed me warmly.

7 November, 0750 hrs. I had been invited to dine at Chhaju
Bagh last night but, on my return to the hotel from Arya's
office, I found a note postponing the invitation till today. This
morning the Divali festival is on and there are new images to
see in the streets. Loudspeakers are already blaring outside, as
loud as ever.

The chewing of pan seems a revolting habit. Indians who do
it have usually never been away from India. I understand that
Indians with European wives abstain from the habit because
their wives are so put off by it. The other day I sat in an office
with an extremely senior person who chewed pan continually,
occasionally interrupting his own most interesting talk to reach

under his desk for a long chromium-plated spittoon into which he would direct a fierce-looking gobbet of red liquid and small bits of betel nut, turn again in my direction and continue his exposition with equable poise. I do not suppose such an intelligent man would dream of so conducting himself during any visit abroad. Much of the unpopularity of Indians in the world could well be explained by the persistence of habits, gestures and expressions native to a social milieu so physically separated from the rest of the world. I doubt if even the complex caste system could have persisted in any other large territory through which neighbours could easily pass by land. The successive penetrations of India over the centuries by foreigners was always achieved by groups too small ever to affect fundamentally the society in which they found themselves. However, Indians have essentially European features. They are roasted Europeans. Real Europeans are a bit undercooked.

1315 hrs. I telephoned Professor T. and asked if I might call for a talk with him. I walked across the Maidan to his house overlooking the Ganges, and sat with this excellent man in his garden for one and a half hours – a useful discussion. Here are some of his views:

In the past few decades there has been a growing economic strength of the middle peasantry (Prasad's articles, which I had read).

Sanskritisation (Srinivas) of the political leadership of the middle peasantry is important in the long-term development of the country.

An important political motive of ministers and politicians is to steal the thunder of the Marxist left-wing factions by raising the status of the landless, the scheduled castes and tribes, by pressing on with land reform. This seems to support what Arya had told me.

On inflation and the size of the public sector, he emphasised that the central government was now cracking down on deficit financing by the states and trying to provide inducements to private investment. It is interesting to find how Indian and British problems seem to evolve in parallel from such different bases

1715 hrs. Walked across the Maidan. Sat reading Narayan's

My Days and looking about me between paragraphs – lovely clear air (strange, with so much dust). On the way back to the hotel I passed an image of Lakshmi with loudspeakers going full blast – a big crowd, a few people making devotional grestures, cycle and rickshaw bells ringing, dust rising in clouds. I watched a modern-looking young man, about twenty, who crossed himself devoutly, with eyes closed, before the image.

The dinner party at Chhaju Bagh was most enjoyable. On the verandah were several small children, some of them nephews and nieces of the Chief, being entertained for Divali with fireworks – small harmless ones with no loud bangs. Over dinner I mentioned the young man who had made the sign of the cross before the image of Lakshmi and I wondered if the gesture could actually have been a Hindu ritual rather similar to the gesture of Roman Catholics. The Chief Justice said no. He added, however, that it would have been quite natural for a young man who had been educated at one of the many Catholic schools in Bihar, but remained a Hindu, to make the Christian sign of the cross before a Hindu image.

We talked about land. All those who expressed themselves on this seemed to accept my own tentative suggestion that the Ceiling Acts, as yet, had probably adversely affected private investment in improvements leading to increased productivity, by frustrating the profit motive. I was glad, however, to find that *chakbandi* was considered a good thing. The Ceiling Acts were a politically motivated measure to silence the Left. It has obliged government to furnish a great proportion of the capital required for the development of smallholdings.

The Divali festival in Patna seems a rather dreary business. Electronics have vulgarised Durga and rendered Divali dull. In 1945, during Divali in the little princely state of Bhavnagar, there had of course been no loudspeakers and no festoons of tiny electric bulbs to hang over the façades of buildings. On a charming maidan women and girls had danced gracefully, each carrying a little lamp of burning neem oil. No doubt such grace still persists somewhere in rural Bihar, but in Patna I saw only buildings draped with electric bulbs, entirely without grace or ingenuity and the half-empty streets were full of the thumpings

of pop from loudspeakers. Perhaps the people had had enough of
the Durga shindy and could now spare little enthusiasm for
Divali so soon afterwards. If Europe has too little festivity, India
may have too much of it. It is a hot country for too much of
anything whatever.

On the morning after the dinner party I walked back to Chhaju
Bagh to collect some travellers' cheques from the private safe of
the Chief Justice, who was kindly looking after them for me. On
the way I heard suddenly a noise of drums and bugles and in a few
minutes was overtaken by a large band of uniformed men, a
group in front bearing a banner with the words 'Punjabi Band'.
Behind the musicians followed a lorry supporting a huge image
of the goddess Lakshmi and many young people and children
marching, or rather straggling along vaguely in time with the
band. In the marching years of my more ostensible imperialism
we used to make a point of putting down our left and right feet in
unison and swinging our arms all together. Such together-
ness created an agreeable crunch of boots and some hopefully
visible stagecraft. In religious festivals in India young people also
march, but each follows the rhythm according to his own private
prescription – a swing up of his left arm may roughly coincide
with an upswing of his neighbour's right, each pair of legs
likewise independent of each other pair.

At Chhaju Bagh I found that the Chief Justice had gone to the
maternity hospital where his sister-in-law had just had a baby by
Caesarean section. The poor woman, who already had diabetes,
had now, in the hospital itself, caught tetanus and was near to
death, though the child had survived. There was great anxiety for
her.

Anu, the Chief's sweet younger daughter, invited me to sit in a
basket chair on the verandah and went to fetch me some coffee.
As I was sitting there a woman servant approached softly and
knelt before me, holding my sandalled foot between her hands.
Pressing her hands about my instep she bowed her head, raised
her eyes to look up at my face with a faintly perceptible smile,
gathered up her red sari and moved away swiftly. Her movement, so tender, was not so swift as to deprive me of my own
returning smile. Hers was the smile of timidity overcome; my
own that of bewildered pleasure. It was some time before I
became aware of the probable explanation.

The Chief Justice returned from the hospital and I moved into the large sitting room where I sat with his elder brother. Outside on the verandah, at one end of it, was a bed in which an elderly woman lay. Next to her, combing the old lady's long hair, sat the woman servant who had held my foot in her hands. The old lady was the wife of my companion, and she was ill. I said to the old man: 'You have many troubles in this house – sickness.' 'Yes,' he replied, 'she is over eighty years old.' After a pause he added: 'We pray God for his mercy.' There was a silence, after which I said to him: 'You say: *his* mercy. That is surely not a Hindu expression?' He replied: 'Oh yes, it is Hindu. All of us, in all religions, pray for *his* mercy.' The old man's reply may indicate that a personal notion of divinity is a stronger concept in the minds of Hindus than I had been assuming. I apprehend very puzzling features of the religion: the relative strength and, indeed, the meanings of personal and impersonal cosmic powers – the relative strength and meanings of the symbolic and the personal in the *puja* associated with individual 'gods' and 'goddesses'. It seems likely that, if I were myself a devotee of any particular religion, I should be less aware of such questions than I am. It may be that a Western man such as myself who attempts to understand these matters in any depth must find himself exposed to the intellectual danger of adopting a definitive view of something that is essentially quite shapeless. Hinduism may be so vast that no individual Hindu can ever be confident of understanding his own faith.

8 November 1845 hrs. I called at the Morrisons – had tea with them – very delightful. *A propos* gestures of puja, etc., Hazel said that, during the past few days she had seen an image of Lakshmi with small figures of Jimmy Carter and Ronald Reagan at its feet – with film music blaring over loudspeakers and *puja* going on at the same time. Consider this. [The presidential election campaign in the United States was in full swing at the time.]

When I mentioned to Hazel the gesture of the woman at Chhaju Bagh who had held my foot in her hands, she said that the gesture would probably have been made on account of my age and would have nothing to do with my personal identity. She is probably right. However, the woman, who was perhaps in her late forties, could have been a child in the house during my father's time, and the old lady might have told her who I was. I shall never know the truth, unless someone at Chhaju Bagh reads this book one day and is prompted to ascertain the meaning of that little event.

I was expecting to be collected by car this evening and taken to another programme of Indian music, as a guest of the Chief Justice, but have now been informed by telephone that his sister-in-law has died in the hospital. It is very sad.

9 November, 1500 hrs. On my walk through miles of filthy streets this morning, passing many old colonial houses set back from the roadways in areas that had once been gardens and were now slimy and stinking, I saw a white cow whose face, legs and tail had been painted light mauve. The animal was grazing upon a piece of filth in the roadway, indifferent to its own visible impact upon observers who, in turn, treated it with the indifference it did not perhaps deserve. As I was observing the sacred cow I was addressed softly by an elderly man in a dhoti who said: 'From what country are you coming?' 'England,' I said smiling. 'For what purpose are you coming?' 'Why do you want to know?' I replied. 'I want to know because I like your people and can remember the past.' He smiled, looking into my face with earnest intensity in his eyes. I told him who I was and he at once told me that he remembered my father well. He had been a student in the 1930s and was now a supervisor in some obscure department of the railways. He wrote down his name in bold block capitals, and his address, on a page in my notebook, and wanted me to visit him. I said I should never be able to find his address in a rickshaw and invited him to come and have coffee with me on the 13th, after my return from Daltonganj.

I never saw the old man again, but waited half an hour for him.

On 10 November I set off on the day-long bus journey to Daltonganj to stay there over a weekend with S. N. Sinha, the District and Sessions Judge of Palamau, and his family. This adventure was a diversion, for my father had not mentioned the place or that part of south-west Bihar in his letters, though he had probably visited it. I looked forward to the break from the hotel and a change from circuit house food, though by now I had little appetite at all after so many tepid makeshift meals. The journey involved crossing the whole width of the Gangetic plain from the river to the beginnings of the Deccan hills in the south, and I wanted to compare the scenery of the two sides of the plain. I knew, too, that near Daltonganj was the Bethla National Park, and there was a prospect of wild animals.

The Department of Tourism of the state of Bihar runs a bus service between Patna and Daltonganj. Indians do a good deal of travelling as tourists within India, and the overwhelming major-'ity of tourists are Indians from other states of the union. Such foreign tourists as exist are very much concentrated at such attractions as the Taj Mahal, the Ajanta caves and Kashmir. I think I was the only tourist of any kind on the bus, which seemed to be full of ordinary passengers travelling between Patna and the sizeable towns and villages through which we passed.

I arrived at the tourist office in a rickshaw only to find that I had lost the ticket I had bought a few days earlier. Before being allowed to travel I was therefore required to sign a solemn statement that I had indeed bought a ticket. At the same time I had to deal with a young man who, I understood, was a paid official of Mrs Gandhi's Congress Party. A few days before, he had called at the hotel to see me and had spent half an hour trying to persuade me to address some political group or meeting in Patna. The young man's calibre and tactics as an active 'entryist' were evident to me, and my problem was that of evading his clutches without revealing my awareness of his mental condi-tion. Now here he was again. He was going to Daltonganj as part of his job connected with a by-election for the state legislature. Unless I was very firm I saw I should have to sit next to him on the bus all day, an impossible prospect. For his brains were covered by a heavy helmet of Marxism, impenetrable by argument. He had the burning eyes of the politically slumberless. Fortunately the driver of the bus ushered me to a special seat by myself, right in front on the left of the hot engine. I much preferred that kind of heat to the other.

The most important place through which we passed was Dinapore. This consists, in the main, of a military cantonment and training centre which must have expanded greatly since its establishment by the British long ago. Imagery associated with it had formed in my mind from various flashes – personal experience of Indian camps during the Second World War, references to it in some of my father's letters ('It is late – your sister has gone off to Dinapore to dance with the regiment'); the names of other places rich in military history – Poona, Deolali, Rawalpindi, Dehra Dun, Barrackpore, Meerut; the evocative words 'cantonment' and 'maidan', and, of course, an irrelevant song about a girl called Dinah. From all this I had imagined line upon line of white marquees, roofs sloping together in the sun, bell tents in diagonals, parade grounds of hardened earth and dried grasses, bugle calls, tasselled scarlet lanyards, a flag, dark cannon pointing up before the steps of regimental headquarters – the penumbra of antiquated war and older peace.

The real Dinapore impressed me by its massive look of permanence, its strong, solid buildings of brick and stone, its well-painted cleanliness. On a wide parade ground I saw troops drilling, smart and deft in their movements. Everywhere were noticeboards with regimental signs, directions and information inscribed boldly (and correctly) in English. Although the bus did not stop anywhere in the cantonment itself, moving slowly through the immense area of it, I felt at every turn an awareness of the strong frame of India's unity, and a spirit to sustain it. Whatever may be the logistical problems of defending the vast expanses of India against external attack or internal disruption (and perhaps India's real defence is that it would be a liability to the aggressor), the aspect of Dinapore most evidently proclaims: 'Try it on..'

Shortly after leaving Dinapore the road turns southwards into a long stretch of low-lying paddy fields and mixed cultivation in which the only substantial towns whose names I can recall are Bhita and the much larger Aurangabad. There the minor road on which we travelled crosses the main highway from north-western India to Ranchi and Jamshedpur to the south-east. Every now and then we could see the irrigation canal which runs roughly parallel to the Son river – a great feat of engineering going back to the middle of the last century. We crossed the canal and various rivers, tributaries of the Son, by long bridges. Now, in November, early in the dry season, the flow of the rivers was diminishing and great areas of sand and clear shallow water were visible. Occasionally a long line of black buffaloes or cattle could be seen stretching across the sand to the water's edge. During the monsoon months such rivers are wide, fast-moving, full of silt and turbulent. Now they were gentle and enticing for a swim.

Whilst the landscape itself does not differ much from that on the northern side of the Ganges, there is a noticeable difference in the appearance of villages and towns to the south. Buildings are more solid, with thicker walls, more tiled roofs can be seen, more paintwork, cream, white or pink, greens and blues. Solid-looking shops are located in permanent buildings, stone steps sometimes lead down to real pavements – the whole aspect of village and town life is more salubrious and aesthetically pleasing. The difference is that whereas in the north the tributaries flowing southwards from the Himalayas cause appalling floods, the rivers flowing northwards from the hills of Chota Nagpur are far less temperamental. Buildings in the north tend more often to be made of light materials merely to prevent people from being killed if they collapse. Bamboo and thatch are seldom lethal in their fall. Stone walls and tiled roofs generally are.

We reached Aurangabad as it was getting dark. Shortly before doing so I had become aware of a slight upward slope in the land and had caught sight of a horizon of rugged hills ahead. In the semi-darkness I could distinguish little of the town except the outlines of several big buildings and quite wide thoroughfares. In a little while the lights of the bus showed that we were passing through jungle and that the road was twisting a good deal, always upward. Sometimes an outline of mountainous granite rocks, similar to many that can be seen in Africa, appeared against a starlit sky.

The stopping place for the bus at Daltonganj (of which I could see little but the familiar aspect of a bazaar town) was very close to the residence of my host the judge. The bus, which had been delayed by very bad stretches of road and by long traffic jams of bullock carts and lorries, arrived about an hour late. I found Mr Sinha and his three sons waiting in the street to greet me. We climbed into the family car and were driven into the small driveway of their home. On the verandah I was greeted by Mrs Sinha and their daughter, Mrs Sinha in a large flowing red sari, Nita in a dark blue one, slightly spangled. All the members of the younger generation were larger and taller than their parents. The only member of the family able to speak English with any fluency was the judge himself. In modern India the

career prospects of young people whose command of English is
negligible is severely limited, however intensive their education
in other ways may be. Nevertheless, Nita was a student of law
and all the sons, too, were entering professional careers, in
teaching and other parts of the public service.

I had eaten only a few scraps since breakfast and was tired after
the heat of the day-long bus ride, but I still had no appetite. This
made me an awkward guest. Unfortunately the family, being
strict Hindus, were observing dietary rules in anticipation of the
Chhat festival on 13 and 14 November. After a shower I sat with
the family on the verandah for a meal which was not supposed to
involve much cooking. It consisted of some curried vegetables
and rice which, though of perfectly good quality, I found
difficult to digest, and I must have looked miserable. I went to
bed almost immediately afterwards in a big room from which
members of the family must have been expelled in my honour.
Breakfast next morning was, for me, more like some other meal,
consisting of a kind of chapatti, rice, fried potato, mango and
lemon pickle, a banana, and water to drink. I forced myself to
consume this at about eight o'clock in the morning, for an
expedition lay ahead of us and there would be nothing more to eat
till we got back in the late afternoon.

That day, 11 November, was a full one. At about nine o'clock
Sinha took me to pay a courtesy call on the commissioner,
Mr Varma. His residence was secluded by a wide garden
area and a small drive. It was a very fine old colonial
bungalow which, many decades ago, had been the residence of
the first Commissioner, Colonel Dalton, after whom the present
town is named.★ Varma was a tall, athletic, intellectual figure,
whose presence and manner reminded me of the kind of British
officer who would once have been a Resident at one of the bigger
provincial capitals in Nigeria. He seemed alone in the house,
apart from evanescent servants. In a large, well-furnished
drawing-room with watercolours on the walls he chatted with us
over coffee for about twenty minutes.

★ Edward Tuite Dalton (1815–80). Entered the Army in 1835 and served the whole
of his career in eastern India, mostly in Bengal which of course then included Bihar
and Orissa. He took part in campaigns in Assam and Nepal and in the suppression of
rebels in Palamau district in 1858–9. Author of *The Descriptive Ethnology of Bengal*,
1872. Promoted to major-general in 1877.

We then drove for about two and a half hours through undulating country (Chota Nagpur) to a very old market town, Nagar Untari, not far from the border of the state of Uttar Pradesh. At this place is a temple containing images of Lord Krishna Bansidhar – that is, playing the flute – and his love Radha. Both figures, I was told, were made of solid gold. If that is really true they must be of immense value, for the figures are about five feet and three feet tall respectively. They were certainly covered in gold or some surface material resembling it, and were elaborately dressed in shimmering, spangled fabrics. The story of their origin is not known but that of their discovery and arrival at the temple has become semi-mythical.

The *Bengal District Gazetteer of Palamau* by L. S. O'Malley, dated 1907, contains this: 'The Untari estate extends over 48 square miles. There is a handsome temple in the village dedicated to the god Bansidhar, a title of Krishna, which contains a golden idol said to have been found lying in the jungle in the time of the great grandfather of the present Bhaya.' Bhaya is the family name of the zamindari family whose estate was derived from a feudal *jagir* (title to land) granted by a Moghul emperor at the end of the seventeenth century.

The *District Gazetteer of Palamau* by P. C. Roy Chaudhury, dated 1961, contains this: 'There is a temple behind the garh of Bhaya Saheb containing the idol of Shri Bansidharjee. Rani Saheba Shrimati Sheomani Kuar of Nagar estate is said to have brought this idol from village Manuli . . . The idol is made of "Ashta Dhatu" [eight metals] and is one of the most beautiful of its kind in Northern India . . . The idol weighs about 30 maunds [about one and half tons].'

A descendant of the former Rajah is at present a minister in the state government of Bihar. In view of my interest in the idols of Krishna and Radha, my friend Romesh Pande of Patna questioned the minister closely about their history and was given the following story by Shri Bhaya himself:

'The present Rajah's great-great-great-grandmother was a devotee of Krishna. The god appeared to her in a dream one night and asked her what she wanted. She replied that all she wanted was that he should always be with her. He directed her to Manuli village, where there was a hill known as Shiv Pahari, and told her to dig there and then install him where she wished. The Rani, whose name was Shivani, told her husband Rajah Bhagwan Deo of her dream and with great reluctance (as he found the story incredible) he ordered that the instructions be carried out. After digging to a depth of seven feet the image of Krishna was found. The other image is of Krishna's consort, Radha, and was made on the Rajah's orders at Benares.

'At this point the story gets confused and for some reason the East India Company enters the picture. To sort out matters, it would appear that the image was left where it was, along with the second one. Later on, during the East India Company period, the image was claimed by the Rajah of Singrauli and the East India Company ruled that the image belonged to him whose elephant could lift it. So the enormous elephant of Singrauli tried, but could not budge the idol. Then a much smaller elephant of Nagar Untari lifted the idol effortlessly, placed it on its howdah and walked away to a place where it sat down and died. The temple is built where the elephant died.

'This is what I could piece together from the Rajah's account.'

It seems that the present Rajah stated that the idol of Krishna is indeed made of solid gold. It is remarkable, I feel, that so valuable an object can rest safely in a village temple without a permanent and very strong armed guard.

To continue the diary:

Both figures are of elaborate workmanship but stylised and stiff, with staring eyes. In the museum at Patna the simple little terracotta figurines from ancient Pataliputra (much older than these figures of Krishna and Rhada), are entirely naturalistic and delightful. Perhaps it is true to say that individuality of expression and naturalistic realism belong more to decorative or secular art than to art associated with *puja* and ritual, in which a sort of hypnotism is involved.

The scenery is rugged with outcrops of reddish granite and steep dried-up hillsides, interspersed with great flat stretches of cultivation, with a good deal of millet as well as rice. Eroded gullies, stretches of sand and rock blackened and split in the burning sun show that drought is often severe. In this part of the country, as in many parts of Africa, rainfall is not only irregular but the water sinks deep below the frail soil. Wells are often difficult to make.

It was market day in Nagar Untari and the wide, gravelly market place was full of peasants and the bright colours of textiles for sale. We walked through the market and I inquired the names and uses of spices, herbs, odd-looking vegetables and objects. Over fruit and sweet stalls hovered some of the great wasps of Hajipur. Beyond the market are the remains of the Rajah's palace, approached through a crumbling archway standing by an old watch tower. The palace did not look as though it could ever have been quite so grand as the word seems to imply, but certainly a large country house had been there for generations, the present remains looking more like an old barn somewhere in Europe. At one end a few rooms are still inhabited by the family. Sinha told me that, when he was a boy, the Rajah used to entertain much at the palace, arranging shooting parties and grand dinners for his Indian and European guests, some of whom were government officers on tour in the area. In those days administrative officers, British and Indian, spent several months in every year on tour, under canvas, moving from village to village on horseback accompanied by their office staff. The peasants of today see and know very little of the human beings whose government, far beyond the horizon, is supposed to be their own.

We got back to Daltonganj for a very late lunch, but again I could eat little and rested for an hour until, after four o'clock, we set off again in an open Land-Rover type of vehicle (obtained by Sinha from the Public Works Department), together with a driver, a civil engineer and another man, on a visit to the Bethla National Park of the state of Bihar – a large undulating area of forest reserve for wild life a few miles to the west.

The park is well arranged as an attraction for visitors, who come mostly from other parts of India. We sat in a vestibule for almost an hour, consuming tea and biscuits, waiting for darkness to gather sufficiently for animals to be seen to advantage by means of a searchlight. The light, powered by the car's batteries, was carried in the Land-Rover by a man who stood in the back behind the driver's seat. We also stood in the back, holding the front rail of the hood (removed) for support, and gazed into the jungle from left to right, following the sweep of the searchlight. Thus we travelled for many miles in an undulating circuitous track, repeating the journey several times in the course of about two hours. Every now and then we would see the eyes of deer reflected back to us. It was always exciting to discern these lights before the forms of the creatures became visible in the searching ray. Watching, one sensed the magic delicacy of the surface of an eye, liquid, silent, wild and vanishing. Once, at close quarters, we saw several slowly moving lights, the eyes of a family of bison, the adults massive, heavy, turning their heads and great horns towards us, standing motionless as we passed.

We got back to the house at Daltonganj at about 9.15 in the evening. At the suggestion of her father, Nita prepared for me in a few minutes a warm milky dish of rice, soft nuts, sugar and raisins, flavoured, I think, with cinnamon – delicious food for my condition, and I slept well that last night.

On the return journey I was again given the hot seat on the left in front. It was a wonderful position from which to see the country, especially during the descent to the plain through jungle-covered hills, and to get a clear impression of the commercial centre of Aurangabad. Over long stretches of the plain – on either side of the river – one can sleep for half an hour without discerning any significant change of scene on opening one's eyes. Yet the landscape, however uniform, seemed always lovely to me.

As darkness was falling the driver stopped at a road junction in Patna, especially for my benefit. He got down from his seat, hailed a rickshaw for me and paid the man in advance to take me to the hotel. I have no doubt that Sinha had especially briefed him to look after me. However, I paid the man again, when he requested it, pretending not to have noticed.

Back at the hotel I was given yet another room, in a newly built wing, all in white with bright new chromium fittings, new fan and telephone. The room faced a side street overlooking a forgotten rooftop with broken brickwork, part of an old bicycle, a rusty enamelled bowl and some weeds protruding comfortably. For the first time in my experience of the city no religious festival was in electronic blast.

13 November, 1300 hrs. This morning I went to Chhaju Bagh to collect mail. The Chief Justice and his family are all in deep mourning for his sister-in-law. He is unshaven and sits in the vestibule with two or three men guests – he looks twenty years older. His son Jitendra sits on a mat beneath the verandah, bowing his head to the ground, a book of scriptures in one hand. The old woman, his elder sister-in-law, lies on a charpoy in another corner, stony-eyed, waiting for death. A group of silent women sit by her. In India people show their feelings at every change in the human situation, the manifestation always prescribed.

9

Last Days in Patna

I had planned the visit to Daltonganj in time to be back in Patna for the Chhat festival on the bank of the Ganges in the late afternoon of 13 November. This was a glorious business, for reasons overwhelmingly aesthetic. The main feature of the event is the worship of the setting sun and then of the rising sun the following day. It is a very localised festival which, I was told, only occurs in Bihar. For some hours beforehand vast numbers of people, most of them women and children from villages for many miles about, gather on the sloping brickwork of the river bank. Peasants carry on their heads round baskets of fruit and vegetables, each at least two feet or more in diameter and each containing three or four little burning lamps of neem oil, like night lights among the produce. To reach the river bank long columns of people, the women in saris of the brightest colours, advance across the great width of the Maidan. All the lanes and garden approaches to the river are crammed with excited people dressed in their best, the great baskets borne aloft.

Standing to their waists in the river are a number of especially holy women whose task it is to pray, with palms together and eyes closed, facing the huge disc of the sun as it declines over the river to the west. Each has fasted for forty-eight hours before immersing herself wholly in the water. She stands cold, dripping, her hair hanging down her back, her sari clinging to her form like the draperies on the marble of a Greek sculpture. Families of peasants lower their baskets of produce carefully to the waterside and the holy women sprinkle a few drops of the water over the fruit and vegetables before turning to the west to pray. When the baskets have been thus blessed the people carry them back into the town or even back to their villages, but return again to the river before dawn for the second ceremony. I watched and photographed the first ceremony, at which I was accompanied by Mr Tewari of the Home Department.

I never saw such a display of colour and grace as at the Chhat festival at Patna, the slanting light causing all the reds and yellows to glow wonderfully, reflected in the glassy Ganges. I felt some concern, however, for the holy women; whatever their devotional ecstasy, they all seemed to me due for chills on their kidneys and other invisibles. The faces of some seemed blue with cold, however warm the temperature of the air itself. I wondered how they fared overnight before a second empty-bellied immersion at dawn the next day.

I did not think it wise to walk alone across the Maidan before dawn on the 14th and it would not have been fair to Tewari to request him to get up to join me at such an hour before going to his office. And, as it was, I had had a small purse stolen. I lost little, but the key of my suitcase was in the purse, and the case was locked in my room. I mentioned my loss to the manager who, within ten minutes produced from his cornucopia a living locksmith, a smiling youth with a small wooden box, a pink shirt, natty trousers and gleaming plastic shoes. Kneeling on the floor of my room he took from his box a large bunch of keys all roughly similar to that of my case, and tried a few of them without success. After a few tentative experiments, feeling gently to discover how far each key would turn in the lock, he selected one of them and fixed it into a small vice, also taken from the box. With a file he worked at the key for about ten minutes, then inserted it carefully into the lock, which worked perfectly. As a final professional gesture, similar to that of the barber who insists on spraying the back of one's neck with powder after cutting one's hair, he put a drop of oil into the lock from a small can, wagged his perspiring face with a smile of satisfaction and stood up before me, teeth and moustache glistening. It was a joy to return his smile and meet his modest charge.

Contrary to a very common Western view, India's many castes of minor artisans are of great value to their society. The caste system, with all its ills, sustains not only the élites of authority and direction, but the values of India's artisans throughout the country.

I was due to leave Patna on 16 November on the final stages of of the 13th, after the Chhat ceremony, I had invited Romesh and Sita to a meal with me at the Rajasthan restaurant. It was a comforting experience to talk with this couple who, despite the confines of the Indian world about them, seemed in their attitudes to belong to the West.

I asked Romesh about the flooding of the northern plain. I suggested that, if over the millennia of Indian history, the plain received each year an addition of silt from the Himalayas deposited on the river beds, would not the gravitational movement of water towards the Bay of Bengal cause the area of land to be extended ever outwards to the south-east? Also, would not the areas of flooding be gradually extended eastwards whilst floods would diminish in the relatively western reaches of the plain as more soil was accumulated? Romesh told me that there was certainly evidence that the level of the plain was steadily rising and extending forward into the Bay of Bengal. Having regard to the vast volume of silt carried annually by the rivers from the Himalayas and the Deccan, the extension of the plain seems very slow, but eventually the plain of north Bihar could be as relatively free of floods as that of Uttar Pradesh further to the west.

After dinner they took me to the Bankipore Club on the river bank, about two hundred yards from Chhaju Bagh. This was a place I had hoped to visit and had been a little surprised that the Chief Justice had never mentioned it to me, for my father had often referred to it in his letters. Romesh suspected that the Chief was not a member at all, and perhaps for his taste the club was too much of a resort for the commercial and Westernised strata of local society. We arrived too late to see any members about and there were no lights in the bar area. The evidence of age, emptiness and decay made the place look haunted. The membership must by now be wholly Indian and representative of middle-caste strata, but in my father's time the whole British community and many senior Indians used it as a centre of social activity and gossip.

Leaving the club we drove along Main Road to a bazaar area to the north-east of the Maidan. Here the streets were gaily illuminated and men were cleaning the asphalted centre of the roadway with hoses. Romesh and Sita explained that before dawn on the following morning (the second Chhat ceremony) people would proceed along the area of cleaned roadway in a strange manner. Each would lie down at full length on the ground and move forwards towards the river bank, some two hundred yards perhaps, by successive stages, each accomplished in a prone position. This imposes a self-inflicted suffering intended to 'appease the gods' and to secure the grant of wishes, such as the recovery of sick relatives or friends.

Loudspeakers were now blaring again. I went to the window and peered round the side street into Exhibition Road after trying to sleep for two or three hours. Nobody was in sight. Yet, from amplifiers above the figures of Lakshmi along the street the screaming, howling, thumping din, whose meanings – musical, commercial or devotional – I could not begin to surmise, was deafening and continuous. Presumably Indians, lying on their charpoys all over the city, are able to endure the shindy because they know what it is intended to communicate.

My last two days in Patna were very busy. On the 14th I went to meet officers of the Bihar Industries Association and the Chamber of Commerce in a big white building not far from the museum. These men, sitting round a table, were affable but, like so many of their kind elsewhere, unwilling to express personal views concerned with the economy or public affairs of their own country. They preferred to utilise the occasion to pump me about Britain. They – most of them – had clearly been reading journalistic reports about Mrs Thatcher's 'anti-Indianism', her 'cold' Toryism, and so on. I defended her, insisting that her concern with the nationality law and immigration was intended to provide against damage to racial tolerance in Britain which could be expected to follow any large and sudden increase in the number of immigrants. I agreed that subordinate immigration authorities had sometimes behaved badly in their attempts to detect illegal immigrants, and that there was a ghastly hooligan element in our cities. It was not right to blame Mrs Thatcher for such things. On 'monetarism' I also defended her generally. Inflation during the past half century had been the main cause of the low confidence of investors in the capital equipment of British industry in the private sector. Those who, in all sincerity, minimised the importance of inflation neither understood nor cared about the private sector, and many of them assumed that a state-run economy could sustain the intellectual and personal liberties to which they had become accustomed. I said I did not think there was any evidence in the world to support such optimism.

In the eyes of some of the men round the table, I could see a glint of approval. In the downward looks of others was something else. But no one expressed anything but affability, and they handed me some glossy material about industry in Bihar, to read in London. Their tea was twice born.

On the afternoon of the 15th I went to see Mr Mulkund Prasad, Secretary of the Planning Department, whom I had been advised to meet by G. S. Dutt. With this young senior civil servant I had a rewarding talk, mainly about land. Prasad told me that the long-term policy of the Government of Bihar was to sponsor and assist labour-intensive agriculture in small holdings, noting the success of the Japanese experience. This, with an ever-growing population in the rural plain, was preferable to large-scale holdings with their implication of ever more proletarianisation of rural labour. In all my talks about land in Bihar, nobody, except Prasad himself, had expressly advanced this view of the matter. Others had contented themselves with expressing contempt for politicians who were seeking the votes of a semi-literate peasantry by promising them land at the expense of the rich. Prasad was now giving me a logical argument for the policies of the Government of Bihar. He gave me material to read about the next development plan – then still in draft form.

On that day, too, I went to Chhaju Bagh in the morning to say goodbye to the Chief Justice and his family. Despite the sadness of mourning, he embraced me with a warmth to remember – against the background of my father's house, his young daughter Anu standing on the verandah, smiling to me with hands pressed together.

I had lunch with Frank and Hazel Morrison. Frank suggested to me a number of important rural and industrial projects to see on my journey through south Bihar to Jamshedpur. Unfortunately I was not able to take his advice, but his suggestions were instructive. Good, warm, kind people.

In the evening I went to dinner at the house of Nripendra Narayan Singh, a businessman and grandson of a close friend of my father who had been President of the Legislative Council of Bihar and eventually a member of the Governor's Executive Council. He is a cousin of K. B. Narayan Singh, the Chief Justice. The house, in the middle of Patna, had been built by his grandfather in 1924 and was full of relics from the past. At dinner, too, was a Muslim merchant, Khaja Aftab Noor, grandson of Sir Khaja Mohammed Noor, a judge of the High Court appointed by my father, and another man, Ravi Shankar Singh, grandson of a well-known landowner of my father's day. It was thus an occasion for some nostalgia. An entirely European meal of roast chicken had been prepared with silver and cut glass, but I was extremely tired and had no appetite.

After dinner Nripendra showed me the original letter patent from the King Emperor George V appointing Nripendra's grandfather to be a member of the Executive Council, signed by the Secretary of State for India, Sir Samuel Hoare, in the early 1930s; and a large photograph of Sir James Sifton and his wife. Sifton, Governor of Bihar in the middle 1930s, was a character about whom my father had written in his letters to me; Lady Sifton in a long white dress, white gloves, looked suitably severe for the occasion. Nripendra also gave me a few old copper coins bearing the image of the King Emperor – coins with dulled, tarnished surfaces from an old mahogany drawer.

During those last days in Patna I had read in the local press reports of robberies by armed gangs, use of violence at elections and shocking murders. In my long road journeys in Bihar I had encountered no such happenings, but the newspapers gave an impression of a state of near anarchy in the country, with more crime than the police, the courts or the prisons could contend with. Prisons were (and are) crammed with people awaiting trial for months, even years, on end, and vicious corruption was depicted as common throughout the public service. Buses and trains were held up by dacoits, often at night. I had travelled far enough in the state without incident to feel that ordinary dacoits were less to be feared than editors, with their eyes on copy, seemed to hope. However, the many reports of violence at polling booths affected the viability of India's Constitution itself, curdling to the intellect as well as to the blood.

At elections the procedure at polling booths, I understand, is that the voter, often illiterate, is given a rubber stamp with which to record his vote against the pictorial symbol of the party he favours. The staff at the polling booth are supposed to check the name of the voter against an electoral roll and indicate when a vote has been cast. Apart from the personation of voters, multiple voting and the bribery of officials, much violence and the threat of it is reported. A political (or not so political) boss, for example, will bribe the police to stay away from the area of the booth, which will then be seized by a gang of his minions, genuine polling staff being gagged and suitably disposed of. When illiterate voters arrive they will be ordered, under threat, to vote for the boss or some stooge in his pay or under his protection. If a voter resists, one of the gang will seize the voting stamp from his hand, record the vote required by the boss and tell the would-be voter to clear off. Voters who protest may be beaten up or knifed mysteriously in the night. Many people are too scared to go anywhere near a polling station during an election at which they have a right to vote. I was told of people who had arrived to vote only to be told by grim-looking individuals that their votes had already been recorded, so they had better buzz off. I was told that the Government of India, in order to reduce personation and multiple voting, was considering the practicability of issuing identity cards to registered voters. The problems involved, especially in dealing with illiterate and virtually homeless members of the scheduled castes (who number millions); must be very considerable. Reading and listening to reports of all this I could not resist a feeling that, in view of the problems of operating a franchise with universal suffrage in such a country as India, the original makers of the Constitution were a bit starry-eyed. Democracy might perhaps have been less dishonest if it had developed by stages of extension of the franchise over several decades, as in Britain in the past. I mentioned this thought to several intelligent Indians. Every one of them agreed with me. However, the possible consequences of attempting to restrict the franchise at the present stage of India's history are perhaps a bit off-putting.

However sensational the press and other reports of electoral violence may be, their importance depends on their incidence. How often do such things occur? During my last days in Patna I put the same question quite independently to three Indian friends. 'Suppose there were to be a general election in Bihar a couple of months hence, can you give me a guess as to the proportion of the polling booths at which you would expect the rigging of elections by violence or threats of it to occur? Each man, with a strange promptness, gave me the same reply: 'Seventy per cent.' Such a figure was bewildering.

One of these friends gave me a painstaking account of the structural basis, as it were, of political corruption in India. Senior, literate politicians, men of ministerial or potentially ministerial status, especially in state governments, will make promises to less literate and less intelligent political candidates. They offer them a share in the inducements forthcoming from private firms in exchange for contracts for miscellaneous public undertakings. In exchange for political support for ministers in legislatures, such candidates will receive financial assistance for their campaigns, including funds with which to bribe the police, engage gangs of thugs to seize polling booths, and so on. The state legislatures were said to contain many members described as contemptible riff-raff, lacking the education required for any serious responsibility. Such people form the voting fodder required to sustain an appearance of parliamentary support for whatever group is in power.

I have reported the above account because it is representative of the kinds of stories to which one can listen at social gatherings in India where intelligent people exchange views about the world they inhabit. There is no way of discovering how widespread corruption and political violence actually are. A particular story may perhaps be unravelled at a formal inquiry, but no inquiry into the subject as a whole is likely to be fruitful. How corrupt were politics in Britain in the age of the first two Georges? How corrupt was the regime of Louis Napoleon and the Second Empire? *

During and since my stay with the district judge at Daltonganj, and especially after seeing the old town of Nagar Untari, whose Rajah had in the past entertained British and Indian touring officers, I had discussed with various people the question of administrative touring in modern India. In our own country

---

* In his *Clive of India* (p. 122) Nirad Chaudhuri writes: 'With respect to all methods of money-making, fair or foul, England and India stood at opposite poles. To consider corruption alone, there was in England a recognised and accepted form of it – which was to use money to gain or keep political power and position; in India, on the contrary, it lay in using political power for personal monetary gain. Far from being regarded as corruption, monetary gain from political position was universally regarded in India as the main use of political power . . . To have political power and not to use it for making money was inconceivable in India.'

Chaudhuri is writing, of course, of the eighteenth century. My impression is that his description of Indian corruption continues to be true of modern India.

it is not thought necessary for local officials to spend any of their valuable time on tour, with or without tents and camp beds, to enable their features to be known to the humble masses of the countryside. It is not absolutely *de rigueur* for them to establish their presence upon village greens, interviewing petitioners beneath a spreading tree with a Union Jack aloft. The importance of touring, of 'public relations', depends upon the social distance between ruler and ruled.

In modern India the social distances between the peasantry and the district administration are less than they were during the Raj, but they are still vast, and will remain so as far ahead as one can imagine, whatever parties may come to power and by whatever means they do so. Yet touring in the old sense has almost wholly ceased; in a car, in a country with more and more roads, the district administrator can get round his district quickly, his face and figure hidden. Besides, ever-increasing paperwork and the ubiquity of the telephone keep men in their offices. I was told, however, that paperwork was a poor excuse for the neglect of touring and that the commonest real cause was its discomfort, especially today when officers can be accompanied by wives and children but with far fewer servants and provisions than long ago. I was interested to learn that the Chief Minister of Bihar, Mr Jagannath Misra, had recently issued a directive that all district magistrates must devote at least ten days in every month to touring their districts. But long periods under canvas, moving from village to village, are now distant memories. The diminution of touring must have an alienating effect upon the peasantry, fewer and fewer of whom can be expected to associate the authority of government with the necessary feelings of awe, loyalty and affection. This does not mean that I foresee any basic change in the broad stratification of rural society in India by caste and gradations of authority. It does, I think, imply a more inert, inward-looking society, perhaps less adulatory, less warm in the cohesion of its hierarchy than in the past. Faceless rule, too, may be more readily corruptible.

10

By Road to Jamshedpur

My tour of the southern part of Bihar was much too short, and there were various reasons for this. I had been stuck in Patna for long stretches by religious festivals during which public offices were often closed. This made it difficult to talk with officials and seek their help. I was determined not to waste landscape by air travel. But my comprehensive rail ticket was due to expire on 24 November and it was already the 16th. Finally, I wanted to visit Cuttack and other places in northern Orissa including the great temples at Konarak, Bhubaneswar and Puri on the coast, each of which had been endowed by my father with imagery framed in the best of his letters. There was, however, another cause which almost completely deprived my visits to Hazaribagh and Ranchi (two of the most important towns in the south) of the kinds of social contacts that had been so valuable in the north. For some reason the teleprinter messages that were supposed to have been sent by the Home Department and by the Chief Justice to the administrative and judicial authorities in those places, warning them of my arrival, were never received at all. So at Hazaribagh and Ranchi I arrived at the circuit houses unannounced and could make few arrangements to meet people or have meals prepared for me.

For the drive to the south the Government kindly provided me with a practically new car hired for the occasion. I paid a substantial sum in advance to cover the estimated cost of fuel plus the hiring charge but, as a special concession, the charge for the fuel that had been consumed on the northern tour was waived. Kishore Kumar of the tourist office was again my companion and interpreter but we had a new driver, a man of such effective taciturnity that I began to suspect that his name or nickname was either non-existent or undisclosable. We left the hotel soon after breakfast on the 16th.

To reach Hazaribagh we drove along the main road to the east

already familiar from the journey to Purnea, roughly parallel
with the Ganges. Apart from sudden glimpses of the river to the
north, the road is lined for some miles with crumbling suburbs,
market gardening land and villages, occasional factories, many
brickfields – a generally sprawling region. The road turns south
after about fifty miles into a well-made highway, and for a long
distance we were once more in the midst of the great plain. Then
we rose from the plain into an area of jungled hills and rocky
ridges, ochre, rust, yellow, green, in which the most remarkable
feature was an artificial lake, Talaya, forming a reservoir. The
lake has a wonderfully irregular coastline among the hills, with
reaches of clear, deep blue water, part hidden by promontories,
and deserted beaches of sand or gravel.

The circuit house at Hazaribagh, was being redecorated and
renovated in preparation for a visit by Dr Kidwai, the Governor
of Bihar. I was introduced to the district magistrate in the circuit
house where he was personally supervising workmen. He was a
very young man, apparently in his twenties. His teeth, lips and
tongue were stained red from chewing pan and his sartorial
appearance was, as it were, somewhat sanskritised. He said he
had received no message whatever about me from Patna and
regretted that the place was in such a state. Plaster and dust
covered the carpet of the room in which I was to sleep, there was a
ladder against one wall, and everywhere tangles of electric cables
and pots of paint. The steward was away on leave and the only
available servant was a dishevelled, greying figure in a dirty dhoti
whose lugubrious voice seemed only to indicate: 'I'm no use.
Don't bother me.' No food or drink was available but a mosquito
net, somewhat torn, was eventually fixed over the bed. The tap
worked at the shower.

After we had changed I asked Kishore to make inquiries and
take me to the nearest catering place for something to eat. At a
distance of only a couple of hundred yards or so we found a
restaurant called The Prince, a modest but reasonably attractive
building with a classical frontage of white pillars and a pleasant
verandah. Here I accepted the risk of settling for 'non-vegetarian'
food and was given a dish of smashed mutton bone fragments
and a little meat, accompanied by tepid rice, weak dahl and
weaker cauliflower, the business terminating with a banana and a

glass of water. Kishore selected some sort of vegetable patty and I envied his discretion. We arranged to return for breakfast at 7.30 and to get away from Hazaribagh at speed.

At The Prince next morning I made friends over breakfast with a middle-aged businessman sitting with his newspaper. He was anxious to talk, which he did affably in atrocious English. He offered a broad sociological analysis of Indian society. Indians, he declared, could be grouped into three categories: 1 in politics; 2 in business; 3 in service (in the sense of 'naukari').* He said that in other parts of the world, but especially in Britain, the very best people were in category no. 1. The next best were in no. 2 and the worst in no. 3. In India things were different. There the best people were no. 3; the worst, politicians of all descriptions, were unquestionably no. 1. This, I suspect, is a very common Indian opinion today, and I heard various versions of it, though nobody put it so succinctly as my man in Hazaribagh. British politicians, it would seem, have a reputation to sustain.

The drive from Hazaribagh to Ranchi, about three hours, was completed before midday. The road passes first through jungle-covered hills, teak, acacia and palm, with clearings for crops ripening in the hot sun. Then, about half way, we came to the open-cast coal-mining district of Ramgarh, a struggling region of grey dumps, corrugated iron, smoke and the dust of coal and granite clinging to every visible thing. This industrial environment, like many others, is grimly isolated, both from the rural scene and from any alternatives for the men and women who live in the shanties, working and dying in the heat, noise and dust.

At Ranchi we drove through the scruffy bazaar town directly to the government area and to the office of the Deputy Commissioner, D. S. Mukhopadhyay. I was ushered directly into his darkened office which, at midday, was lit only by a solitary green shaded lamp over a big desk. There I sat for about eight minutes watching him dictate letters or minutes to a male stenographer whilst a woman assistant or secretary sat at the telephone the other side. He was a distinguished-looking man,

---

Naukari is used of service either to a government or to an individual. It would apply equally to the Chief Justice, the Army Chief of Staff and the humblest servant in what we call private service. There is a feeling that it is preferable to trade.

strong-featured, with thinning hair, about forty-three. His expression had an air of rather severe command. His manner seemed to represent the prestige of the Indian Administrative Service and that of caste distinction. In a pause he looked at me, unsmiling, and said 'Yes?' I introduced myself. He nodded. Still with no smile he said he had read something about me in *The Searchlight* a few weeks before but had received no message or instructions about me from the Home or any other Department in Patna. Nor did he think the Judicial Commissioner had received any communication from the Chief Justice, or he would have mentioned it. However, relaxing a little, he kindly invited me to meet him at 8.30 in the evening at his home for a talk, and, on the telephone, his secretary spoke to the circuit house and made arrangements for me to stay overnight. He said I would be given a room at the new circuit house (the old one was being prepared for a visit by two ministers of the Bihar Government) and this turned out to be a pleasant bungalow with a verandah and rough garden area separating it from a wide roadway. I had a light meal and was promised 'roast' chicken for supper, and wondered what roasting might imply.

My first task was to go back to Mukhopadhyay's office, where I asked his secretary if she would kindly telephone the district magistrate at Jamshedpur and request him to book a room for me at the circuit house there for the following night and explain that I should welcome assistance in getting a berth on the train for Cuttack, in Orissa, as soon as possible. I was a bit apprehensive, for Kishore and my driver would not be able to accompany me beyond Jamshedpur, our last stop in Bihar, and I should also lose the car. Thenceforth I should be alone and unable to speak a word of any Indian language.

From my diary:

17 November, 1715 hrs. Took photographs of urban scenes – the bazaar of Ranchi is bigger but very similar in its general aspect of congestion, dust and clatter to the other towns in Bihar – then drove out a few miles to look at the enormous mass of the Soviet-built steel plant. Very few human beings were visible. Nearby is a big area of flats for staff. A notice forbids any photography. I had no authority to visit the works and no wish to incur the suspicions of vigilant 'anti-imperialists' of any description, so departed very properly impressed with the importance of the vast investment in the economy of India which the works represent. People told me that the difficulties of management, of spare parts, of labour and efficiency were great, but I am in no position to assess the relative importance of these factors. If the plant is indeed inefficient it is conceivable that it will not remain so forever.

At the circuit house the 'roast' chicken, awash in a vague watery juice with a little curry, presented problems of mastication. I then went across to keep my appointment with Mr Mukhopadhyay. In the sitting room the secretary came to apologise for her chief who was still at his office on business. I wrote out a chit for him to say that I fully understood his difficulty and would not wait to see him after he had had so long a day at his office. Whilst waiting for a few moments I had been able to glance round the room. The house was of the colonial period, graciously proportioned; it had the feel of repose and orderly domesticity – a child's tricycle, a verandah in lamplight, clean, attentive servants.

The night sky was beautiful. I strolled on the dry grassy area in front of the circuit house with Kishore, watching the stars. It surprised me to find that Kishore, though possessing an ostensibly good secondary education, knew nothing whatever about the stars or the moon. I have no doubt, however, that as a respectable Hindu he would have been quite at home with the semantics of astrology and that his parents had committed him to marriage with the advice of astrological soothsayers. I told him about the Pole star and how to find it by means of Cassiopeia and how the apparent positions of the stars, relatively to the Pole star, would move during the rest of the night. He said he had had no knowledge of 'anything like that' before.

During the night I decided that I would not simply abandon Ranchi as I had abandoned Hazaribagh, but would at least try to meet the Judicial Commissioner of Chota Nagpur, whose court was at Ranchi, and also drive out to see an old hospital for tubercular patients at Itki, a few miles to the west of Ranchi. I would do both of those things before returning for the long drive to Jamshedpur to the south-east.

After the usual nasty breakfast I got Kishore to telephone the residence of the Judicial Commissioner, Mr Anand Prasad Sinha He was at home and invited me to see him immediately, his house being only a few yards from the circuit house. He said he had a holiday that day on account of the Muslim festival of Mohurram, and would be able to show me over his court.

The Judicial Commissioner of Chota Nagpur, a very large area of wild, jungle-clad country with many villages, but including Ranchi itself and other towns, must be one of the most senior judges of Bihar. I was ushered into the sitting room of his neat, smallish but pleasing house and he appeared within seconds to greet me. He was a round-faced, strongly built man in his late fifties or early sixties, balding a little. Whilst shaking hands he told me I reminded him of my father – though I am smaller – whom he had known personally during his student days at Patna. He had been one of the many young men whom my father had befriended. He ordered a tray of excellent tea, with biscuits, for Kishore and myself, and after a little talk took us in his car to the court buildings a mile or so away.

By modern Western standards the decor and furnishings of the judge's sitting room were elaborate. I mention them because I feel that they are characteristic of the *modus vivendi* of an important section of India's intelligentsia. The walls were covered in bright pink emulsion paint, with many ornaments and several pictures. I remember tinselled models of elephants, carefully stitched dolls, very colourful figures of goddesses and processions, all hand made, I believe, by the judge's wife and daughters, rather similar to those I had seen in the house of Arun Pathak in Patna. There were many family photographs on polished tables and shelves, several glass cases containing shining objects of china or metal, and everything seemed to gleam.

The court building was a massive, two-storeyed structure of brick and cream-washed cement, of the standard pattern common to law courts in India. Devoid of architectural frills, by its size and weight it expressed the authority of law and government. All the old, battered, dusty-looking doors of the building were locked for the holiday and it took a long time for a custodian to discover the key of the Judicial Commissioner's court. Inside I was much impressed by the size and dignity of the court and stood with Mr Sinha at his desk, looking down at the courtroom below and over to the gallery at the back. As in the much smaller court at Motihari the most interesting features were the big varnished boards on the wall behind the judge's desk showing the names and dates of all the judges, British and Indian, since the establishment of the court in 1862. I was aware of all the British names for the twenties and thirties mentioned in my father's letters. It was moving to see the names of three men, Macpherson, Saunders and Meredith, each of whom had been a close friend. Meredith, after succeeding my father as Chief Justice, had once distinguished himself by swimming the vast width of the Ganges without encountering a single crocodile.

We took the main road to the west for perhaps a dozen miles, then turned off along a small roadway to the hospital at Itki, very isolated in the rural scene. Gently undulating, with granite outcrops in eroded land, the country to the west of Ranchi has a plateau-like character. In the monsoon months such areas will be lush and vivid; in late November they seemed harsh indeed. At lower levels, however, there is a good deal of cultivation, and I saw millet and rice almost white in the sun. In the lower areas the water table is close to the surface and there are many shallow wells operated by the same simple methods that I had seen far to the north. Occasionally, part of the green revolution, could be seen a motorised pump, usually of a mobile kind, transportable on a bullock cart and sunk quickly and anywhere at will. There are numerous tube wells and a few tractors.

I was sometimes surprised to discover the real appearance of a building mentioned by my father in his letters. He had exhorted Indian university and school teachers to train students and pupils to *observe and describe* their physical environment, instead of looking eternally inwards into their own minds, or into the inward-looking literature of their own tradition – the Indian disease, as he felt it to be. Only by cultivating a pragmatic extroversion could Indian educators ever hope to bring their country to an effective apprehension of the planet in which they were obliged to live. And only thus could India ever hope to produce a literature meaningful to the rest of the world. Yet I had now discovered, by travelling in his footsteps, that, whilst writing vividly of people, animals, insects and the Indian climate, he never once described the appearance of a building – his own house, the High Court, a circuit house, Government House, a street or even a landscape. His mind in India seemed to have been fixed constantly upon human relationships and attitudes or, in the world of things, small objects close at hand – his cameras, photographs, flowers, a woman's hat. He always wore bi-focal spectacles in which the lens of the left eye was much thicker than that of the right, and I suspect that the general effect of his natural eyesight was to make him much more short- than long-sighted. The effect of his unconscious neglect of description of the physical was to cause me to imagine for myself the physical settings of his letters by drawing upon my own experience of other parts of the world, and, of course, developing a powerful curiosity as to their real nature. His account of the pathetic story of Mohinia's small sister who died in the hospital at Itki includes not a single word about the building except that the little girl, to her astonishment and delight, found herself in a European style bed, with sheets, a fan above her and European food – all of which my father had arranged for her because she was one of the children of his compound, suffering from the dreaded tuberculosis of the country. In my mind had developed somehow the image of a three-storeyed, gabled house such as might be seen in Highgate, say, standing alone in a jungled landscape of hills with palm trees and acacia similar to that of the bush in parts of West Africa. The real Itki was nothing like that, but several long bungalows of strong red brick, with deep verandahs.

The brickwork of the buildings is of good quality, not the poor crumbling bricks so common in India, and the buildings are spread tastefully over a considerable area with many flower beds and flowering shrubs interspersed among them. Compared with public hospital buildings in Patna, which look ill-kempt, truly alarming places in which to entertain the smallest prospect of illness, those of Itki are actually welcoming to the sick. They go back to a time when pulmonary tuberculosis was one of the cruellest diseases of the country. It is nowadays treated quickly and much more effectively, and I got the impression that the wards at Itki now have more empty beds than patients. Such patients as there are seem isolated in this rural place miles from Ranchi or any other densely inhabited town. I doubt if they receive many visitors.

At the reception office we were told that the superintendent, Dr M. P. Vaishya, and his medical staff were on their daily round of inspection but would no doubt be glad to see us in a few moments. They duly appeared, walking along a pathway towards us, the superintendent and another doctor in black suits with stethoscopes round their necks, the matron and nurses in white caps and blue skirts. They seemed very glad to see us and for twenty minutes or so I accompanied them during the inspection of a ward with half a dozen patients, women and girls. I mentioned the story of the little girl from Patna who had died in 1937, and the matron took me over to the now empty building that had formerly been reserved for European patients.*

To get to Jamshedpur we had first to return to Ranchi. About halfway we got involved with a very excited crowd of Muslim youths. To the sound of drumming and the blare of horns, two young men fiercely opposed each other in the middle of the road with quarter-staves. Each contestant, holding in both hands a strong, broomstick-like rod, seeks to score points by striking the body of his opponent with his rod. The contest was fast and strenuous, accompanied by loud cracks when the rods clashed. The crowd of youths watched with yells of enthusiasm, swinging their bodies and clapping to the rhythm of the drums.

Our driver drew up to the edge of the crowd and switched off. Whilst the contest and the drumming continued as vigorously as ever, a dozen angry youths swarmed about the car, thrusting heads through the open windows, cursing, clenching their fists and hitting the bodywork. Sitting with Kishore in the back whilst the driver and another man from the Bihar tourist office sat in front, I was convinced that we were now about to be assaulted. Three Hindus and a solitary white man shut in a car were helpless. I could understand nothing of their yells and there was no action that I could usefully take. I sat still, looking as impassive as possible.

After some seconds Kishore gently opened the off-side back door and got out. He spoke quietly to some of the youths, assuming a tone of polite appeal. Other youths, however, continued to menace us with their fists, shouting with anger, sweat streaming down their faces. The crash of drums went on.

Suddenly to the left I noticed a new commotion, a group of figures pressing through the crowd to reach us. The youths made

* The Itki Sanatorium for tubercular patients was established by the Government of the province of Bihar and Orissa in 1928. It is now run by the Department of Health of the state of Bihar.

way. A woman appeared with a child in her arms, with two men in attendance. Kishore spoke with them and nodded affirmatively. The left-side doors were opened and the party clambered into the car with us, the woman and child squeezed in front, the two men behind, very crushed. In a second the youths opened a way for us and we slid away towards Ranchi. Kishore whispered: 'The child is sick. They asked us to take them to the hospital in Ranchi. Good!' I looked at the child, an infant of about ten months. Its eyes were closed, its brow sweating. The mother wiped the sweat with a tissue and rocked the child, murmuring.

We reached a gaunt hospital building on the outskirts of Ranchi about half an hour later. The party descended, smiled wanly, thanked us with bows and hands pressed together, went up the steps into the building and disappeared.

We returned briefly to the circuit house to collect my suitcase and settle the bill, and then set off for Jamshedpur. Shortly after leaving the city we digressed to ascend an isolated hill rising several hundred feet above the immense plain, upon which stands an enormous white marble figure of the Buddha. This, only a few years ago, was presented to India by the Japanese as a gesture of goodwill. I admired the goodwill more than the Buddha which, to my inexpert eye, seemed a somewhat vulgar, clumsily executed and feebly inspired bit of showmanship.

As we sped along a well-surfaced highway, the land seemed to be gently descending from the plateau whilst a long range of jungle-clad hills, grey-blue, rose across our horizon to the south-east; and beyond those hills lay a different land with a moister climate. We stopped for an hour at a rough wayside stall where, sitting at a trestle table beneath a corrugated iron roof, we had vegetable curry patties, yoghurt, fruit and strong tea. In India I usually enjoyed such meals, simple, hot (in both senses), tasty and cooked over charcoal. Such is the food of lorry men, people descending from buses. The food available at such places is much preferable to that provided at most circuit houses, which are usually operated under remote public control. However, the circuit house is frequently the only place at which a European-style bed, with or without sheets, a shower, a fan and a towel, are obtainable. For such amenities one is prepared to nod to the cockroaches. The wayside café is the best place to eat, provided one avoids uncooked food and peels the apple.

Our first experience of Jamshedpur was a view across the eastern horizon of smoking factory chimneys and the outlines of industrial buildings silhouetted against the sky of late afternoon, and a pall of black-ochre dust which hung over the town. The black particles surge into the sky from the factory chimneys, the ochre ones arise from the arid soil in the dry months. The spectacle ahead, growing ever greater as we approached, seemed grim after our long rural drive, a massive purgatory for the soul of India. We reached the city at dusk and it was almost dark by the time we arrived at the circuit house in the part of the city traditionally known as Tatanagar, the town of Tata, perhaps the greatest industrial company in India.

I very soon became aware that Jamshedpur consists of two urban areas, a large crowded bazaar town similar to others in Bihar, and a substantial township administered by the Tata company itself, primarily for its own thousands of workers. The contrast between the two areas is interesting and, I believe, of great importance in relation to policy for urban government and development in the future. During the half hour it took us to reach the circuit house we passed through a good deal of both areas and later, when I returned to Jamshedpur from Orissa, I was able to see more. The bazaar town is as slummy as any I saw in Bihar, but more forbidding because of the choking industrial smog. The company-administered area of the city was, for me, an astonishing spectacle. It is full of wide, tree-lined avenues, broad streets with tall, well-proportioned buildings of brick and concrete in pretty good condition, and well cleaned. It was rather like finding myself suddenly in a largish industrial town in the Po valley of Italy. Here are schools, clinics, hospitals, technical colleges, research laboratories, crèches, sports grounds – the whole area looks clean and dignified, with thousands of purposeful-looking people in streets from which the familiar chaos of an Indian bazaar is almost wholly absent.

At the circuit house I was relieved to find myself expected, thanks to the telephone call of the secretary of the Deputy Commissioner at Ranchi. On the following day I hoped to get away by train to Cuttack, and knew that I should need help in obtaining a seat on any train. I felt, however, that I must in politeness wait till the next morning before seeking such assistance from the administration of Jamshedpur. I proposed to have a shower, a change of clothes (I was smothered in dust) and a simple meal before going to bed. I ordered the usual oniony omelette (in preference to smashed mutton bones or cardboard pullet), with bread and butter, squash and fruit.

I was about to pull off my impossibly filthy bush shirt when there was a smart rap at my door. Opening it I found a large, powerfully built young man with a moustache, who said: 'Mr Richard Terrell?' His name was Jyoti Kumar Sinha and he was the Superintendent of Police here at Jamshedpur. He had been informed of my arrival and was happy to make my acquaintance. I was the son of the late Sir Courtney Terrell, 'one of the most illustrious Chief Justices India ever had'. I might perhaps have heard of the Rhotas case, 'one of the most important cases in Indian legal history'?

'I'm afraid I don't know about it,' I replied. 'But I have heard people mention it and must somehow look it up.'

'Well,' said Mr Sinha, 'there was a special police inquiry into the case and my own father, A. K. P. Sinha, of the CID of the Imperial Police in your father's time, was in charge of it. As a boy I was brought up, as it were, on stories about the famous Sir Courtney Terrell, so it is an important event for me that his son is now in Jamshedpur. What are you doing this evening?'

'I have ordered an omelette here,' I said.

'Then cancel it. You cannot eat in this place. I will take you to my club, if you like, and you shall be my guest.'

I was, of course, extremely grateful and, after I had changed, he took me in his car to a substantial club building with an attractive dining room whose walls were panelled in brown timber. Here we had a European meal of fried fish and chips, squash and fruit salad.

After telling me about the Rhotas murder case,* Sinha wanted

---

* A man had been convicted of murder by the High Court and sentenced to death. He appealed against conviction to the Judicial Committee of the Privy Council in London, the final court of appeal in the empire. The Committee had rejected the appeal and the condemned man was awaiting execution in prison in Patna. Within a few days of the date set for his execution my father, from a private source, came to learn of what seemed to him disturbing evidence that the condemned man had been the victim of a conspiracy. Notwithstanding that his appeal had been rejected by the Privy Council, my father promptly ordered a stay of execution. The police inquiry by Sinha's father was ordered and its findings led in due course to the arrest and trial of the conspirators, followed by their conviction and punishment. The condemned man was set free.

to know my impressions of India and we had much talk about certain aspects of the country. I was impressed by the quality of his English, better than that of any other Indian I had met in the country, and felt that he could only have acquired such mastery after spending much of his youth in Britain. He assured me, however, that he had never left India. His achievement is very rare, especially for a man so young as he.

The reader may remember that, during my last days in Patna I had discussed with various people the question of violence at elections, including the seizure of polling stations by gangsters in the pay of politicians, the forcing of electors to cast their votes for particular parties and the bribery of the police on such occasions. I now felt that few people would be better placed to give me a useful opinion about the incidence of such occurrences as Jyoti Sinha. I asked him how credible it might be that as many as seventy per cent of the polling booths in Bihar could be expected to be affected by such things.

Sinha said that such things certainly did occur, but nobody could say just how frequently. If they occurred at no more than ten per cent of the polling booths, that would be very bad indeed. Seventy per cent, however, was an incredible estimate. The Constitution did work as it was intended to work, but with abuses which everybody recognized. He argued that if either the Government of the day or an opposition group of parties really did possess the money and the power to rig seventy per cent of the elections by violence or threats of it, it would not be likely that big changes of opinion would make themselves felt at the elections. But Mrs Gandhi's party had, in a few years, been swept into power, swept out of power and then returned to power by vast changes of opinion that had been expressed precisely by means of elections. He declared that when Mrs Gandhi lost the election Congress had no such power to prevent that from happening. In 1979, on her return to power, the Janata party had no such power to prevent her from doing so. He said that every kind of evil in India was reflected in the press, for its news value. This influenced the intellectuals and made them cynical. In any event, their opinions were based less upon observation of what really went on in the country than upon arguments with each other. The ordinary honest election did not make news. Then again, people lived most of their lives in towns, their own towns, with little opportunity to see any of the places they read about in the newspapers. Real happenings were fewer and less important than the press seemed to imply.

Looking at the broad arena of Indian politics, I asked him which forces seemed to him to present the greatest dangers to the social structure of the country and to the Constitution – the various 'Marxist' cliques or those of the extreme right. He thought that the right were more dangerous, for their roots in the stratified structure of Indian society were so much older and stronger.

Sinha was most helpful to me. After taking me back to the circuit house that evening he telephoned the railway police at the station and instructed them to meet me there early the next morning and ensure that a place was reserved for me on the train to Cuttack, all of which they did. He himself arrived to see me off. I said goodbye to Kishore and my driver, giving them presents which, I fear, were smaller than I should have wished, and they set off at once for the long return drive to Patna, hoping to reach there in one day.

A Little of Orissa

I sat in a depressing waiting room at Jamshedpur waiting for the train, which was very late. It was now about ten o'clock and I had had no breakfast. For some time I pondered how I could safely leave my suitcase whilst I went in search of sustenance. Eventually I befriended a fellow traveller who was able to speak English and who offered to guard my things. This reminded me of a long journey I made in the Soviet Union in 1936, in the days of my Bolshevism. Before starting off I went to see Beatrice and Sidney Webb whose simplistic volumes I had read with the enthusiasm of the naïve, and had a long talk with them at their home in Hampshire. They suggested that, if I should lose my way in the streets of any Soviet city, I should look out for any middle-aged man wearing spectacles and carrying a black briefcase. Persons of that description were able to speak American or German, both of which I could at least imitate. French and English were virtually unknown. All such persons would be eager to point me in the right direction. In India I followed the same advice but did not have to imitate German or American, but merely Welsh. How the intelligentsia of India have come to speak Welsh with greater fluency than the inhabitants of the Principality is one of the mysteries of science.

The coach on the train, air-conditioned, was a good deal cleaner and more comfortable than I expected. The only disadvantage was that the brilliance of the landscape was obscured by brown glass, so I spent most of the seven-hour journey to Cuttack standing in the passage at the end, where I could look through open windows on both sides. As I had expected, the scenery to the south beyond the hills of Chota Nagpur in northern Orissa, in late November, is greener and more rain-washed than in Bihar to the north-west. Rain had fallen recently, cumulus clouds were piled above the hills, and water could be seen among the paddy fields and below the rail embankments.

Villages of bamboo and thatch began to appear, though the train passes through some considerable towns too – the rail junction of Kharagpur in West Bengal, Balasore, not far from the coast, and Bhadrach.

In Cuttack there were two men I very much hoped to meet and, indeed, I could have been somewhat stranded had I not done so. The Chief Justice at Patna had written to his colleague the Chief Justice of Orissa at Cuttack, Mr Ranganath Misra, asking him to expect me. And, at a social event in London, I had been introduced to Mr Justice H. Mahapatra of the High Court at Cuttack, a much respected figure in Orissa. He remembered my father and told me amusing anecdotes about him. He had given me his address in Cuttack, though at the time of our meeting the prospect of my visit to India had not yet arisen. Neither of these men knew the date of my arrival and no arrangements had been made for me.

Although Cuttack is a considerable city there were no taxis at the station – I believe there was no fuel for them for reasons connected with the trouble in Assam and the blockage of supplies by Assamese nationalists. Only rickshaws were available and I had no idea of the whereabouts of the circuit house, except that it was near the river bank somewhere. Rickshaws in Cuttack are of a design different from those in Patna, being smaller and closer to the ground, the 'puller' sitting on his saddle much higher than his passenger behind. I hailed a young rickshaw man and we set off slowly into the hot sunshine.

Almost at once I became aware of being in a country different from Bihar. There were, I think, three reasons for this. First, in every direction along the streets could be seen shop signs and advertisements in the Oorya script of Orissa instead of the heavy Devanagari script in which Hindi appears in Bihar. Second, the streets were much cleaner than any I had seen in Bihar – no doubt the sweepers' strike in Bihar had much to do with this, though people in Orissa assured me that the Biharis were a dirty people anyway. Third, to reach the circuit house I was taken through part of the town which looked more like the Christian streets of Bettiah in the far north than those in an ordinary bazaar. After travelling a longish distance down a wide commercial roadway we turned to the right along a rather charming, winding street, almost devoid of the makeshift booths so common in Indian towns. Eventually we turned again to the right towards the bank of the Mahanadi river and drew up at a new concrete building of three storeys, the circuit house.

The manager was an intelligent man who spoke good English, the reception desk and staff suggested the atmosphere of a small hotel instead of the down-at-heel sloppiness to which I had become accustomed. After hearing my story the manager arranged a room for me, with tea and biscuits on a clean tray, and telephoned the homes both of the Chief Justice and Mr Justice Mahapatra. The former was not in but Mahapatra spoke to me personally. He promised to collect me an hour later and take me to his house, where I was to be his guest.

My first thought was to find the old circuit house which my father had mentioned often in his letters, though he never described it. The manager pointed it out to me, very close by, a large brick and stucco house in a dignified colonial style, with a wide curving frontage and a pillared portico. It was now used as a girls' school. My father used to stay in the circuit house occasionally for several weeks at a stretch to try cases on appeal from the district courts of Orissa. He liked the opportunity to visit Cuttack in December to escape the European social occasions at that time of year, which bored him to misery. Apart from the dinner parties, dances and theatricals, at which he was expected to keep late hours when his health was failing, he disliked the cold weather of north Bihar, with its dusty sunlight and cold nights. At Cuttack, after a day in court, he would return to the circuit house, take tea and sleep for an hour and then walk along a footpath by the river, watching the monkeys as they leaped from tree to tree on the other bank, the females carrying their babies with a deftness which delighted him. For the Christmas days he would go further south to Puri, on the coast, for sea bathing. I was now discovering the country which seemed especially to touch his heart. The footpath had disappeared, so I walked for some distance along a minor roadway on an embankment above the river. Lorries, bullock carts, bicycles, a buffalo, men and women washing clothes in the river – all showed that Cuttack must have become far more populous than it had been in my father's time. The monkeys had receded to distant hills and forests.

Mr Justice Mahapatra sent his driver to collect me and I was taken to his house a mile or so further along the attractive street I had seen from the rickshaw. It was a small, modern house with a large comfortable main room, one end of which could be made into a bedroom for a guest, separated by a curtain. In the centre part was a lounge with many books and paintings, and the far end formed a dining room. The paintings were landscapes, most of them in styles that seemed to me European. Adjoining the dining area was the judge's study, a small room with a large desk on which lay neatly arranged case papers and correspondence, as though handled by an efficient secretary. The lounge and study both opened into a small garden with a little verandah where the about the house an air of discipline, order and intellectual strength, personal attributes of my host himself.

When I had met Mahapatra in London a few weeks earlier, I had guessed him to be about fifty-six years of age, but had since learnt that he was actually seventy-two. This, of course, explained the vividness of his anecdotes about my father, whom he had known personally as a young man. He was a small, robust, slightly rotund figure with short, straight thinning hair, clean shaven. His features were very strong and firm, and he had excellent eyesight. Though still trying cases at the High Court, he was no longer a full-time judge and was able to devote much of his time to the chairmanship of various cultural organisations in Orissa. His daughter was married to Ranganath Misra, the Chief Justice.

We dined alone, a simple meal of curried vegetables, yoghurt and fruit. He wanted to know my impressions of India and I sought his assessment of the strength of Indian society, of caste, of the political system, and of the importance of corruption and violence.

On caste and the rigidities of Indian society, especially such institutions as arranged marriages and adulatory attitudes to authority and status, Mahapatra defended them. He argued that, in any society, attitudes, values and customs that have endured for very long periods – many hundreds, even thousands of years – are right. They must be accepted as right because they have contributed as much to the goodness in a society as to its evils. The older social and ethical values were, the less vulnerable they became. The less vulnerable they were, the more readily acceptable they must be.

I had mentioned the common view that Indians are generally inward-looking people, relatively disinclined to notice the visible, unable to describe the world about them, largely oblivious of chronology, happy with cobwebs and crooked pictures on their walls. On all this Mahapatra said that Indians were concerned to discriminate between the essential and the inessential. Their deeply religious experience of life disposed them to such discrimination, something quite alien both to the Americans and to the Japanese. If an Indian woman loses her most beautiful clothes or her jewellery, she will not reveal much distress, for her training since childhood will dispose her to decide that what she has lost was not essential. Basic values are not affected by mere loss. As to violence and corruption, I was interested to find that he supported the view that the ever-continuing expansion of education in India will cause such evils to diminish. This, of course, is a purely Western notion of progress.

As a widely travelled man who had served the judiciary in India during the last ten years of the Raj and for more than three decades since independence, Mahapatra seemed to me a most valuable contributor to the civilisation of modern India. His arguments supported tradition. Much of his *modus vivendi*, most of his books, were of the West. Whatever for him might be essential, his pictures hung straight on his own walls.

I slept well that night. At breakfast I was introduced to a nephew, Prasenjit Mukherjee, a tall, good-looking man in his middle or late twenties who was a lecturer in literary subjects at Ravenshaw College, the main centre of higher education.* I had asked Mahapatra if he could recommend some good Indian novels or other literature available in English. Overnight he had asked his nephew to assist with this, and at breakfast Mukherjee handed me a reading list of novels, poems and plays. He felt that the best of such works today had been written in Indian languages and later translated into English.

---

* After having been a high school since 1868, the school was raised to the status of a college affiliated to the University of Calcutta in 1876. It was named after Thomas Edward Ravenshaw, a member of the Indian Civil Service who was Commissioner of Revenue and Circuit at Cuttack from 1870 to 1878. He had arrived in Bengal in 1849 and had a long and distinguished career in the service of Bengal, according to the old records of personal service at the India Office Library and Records in London.

In the afternoon Mahapatra took me in his car to the High Court, a tall, very substantial red brick building which looked a bit like an Edwardian hospital, with a clocktower. Here I was introduced to the Chief Justice, Mr Ranganath Misra, his brother judges and many members of the local bar who had been assembled to meet me for tea. Misra was tall, athletic, with aristocratic features, in his middle forties. We drove back later to his residence, which was much smaller than the sort of house that was formerly provided for the head of a provincial judiciary. Here we found Mahapatra waiting for us, and we all dined together. I was glad to meet Mrs Misra, Mahapatra's daughter, at dinner with us, for it is rare in eastern India for a man's wife or daughter to dine with male guests.

Between them, Misra and Mahapatra helped me wonderfully with my travel plans. A car, driver and interpreter were mobilised for me as a guest of the state judiciary, to take me all the way to Puri. Misra telephoned the district judge there, K. P. Acharya, and requested him to meet me, book a room at the circuit house and see that a seat was reserved for me on the train back to Jamshedpur on the 23rd. He also telephoned his namesake, S. Misra, Registrar of the Civil Courts at Baripada, a district in the far north of Orissa, requesting him to travel to Jamshedpur (150 km.) to meet my train, arrange for me to be a guest of the Tata company, to have a sightseeing tour of Jamshedpur and, finally, to ensure that a seat was available for me on the night train to Bombay on the 24th. All these steps were taken with exhilarating efficiency and promptness. But then in Orissa the judiciary and the High Court are in Cuttack, physically separated from the capital, Bhubaneswar, by some thirty miles of open country. The more isolated a departmental authority the greater can be its freedom to act in matters of courtesy, minor expenditure and common sense. Distance confers responsibility for decision upon men prepared to accept it. My hosts took action.

Time did not permit us to do more than drive through Bhubaneswar which, so far as I could see, was likely to detain only those with practical business to attend to. We stopped for an hour, however, to wander about the area of the great temple beyond the new city. When I asked my guide and interpreter if I would be permitted to go in he shook his head, and in any case I was in no mood to make myself conspicuous by pursuing any inquiry. The temple buildings go back to the mid-twelfth century of the Christian era, so they are roughly contemporary with some of the Gothic cathedrals of northern Europe. It was the first great Hindu temple that I had glimpsed, for the plains of Bihar to the north are almost devoid of them. I understand that before the Muslim conquests of the north there were many in the region, but that certain of the conquerors destroyed them, presumably in indignation about their erotic decorations.

There is something rather forbidding about the physical structure of certain Hindu temple buildings – forbidding, that is, to the Western observer. For they are immensely solid, dark and utterly windowless. Windows signify openness. Walls that are impenetrably massive, shielding what must be a small dark space behind them, are architecturally mysterious. At Bhubaneswar, however, there is a complex of buildings, some of them beyond the shielding walls of the main structure and apparently not in much use for religious purposes, so that visitors are free to wander about and gaze at their decorative sculpture, as I did myself. The biggest building, in dark brown stone, has a fine rectangular tank of clear water adjacent to it, where people immerse themselves and rinse clothes. The clarity of the water is presumably explained by some inflow and outflow system. The building itself is decorated with stone figures of musicians and dancing girls, chiselled more than seven centuries ago. It seemed to me that, broadly speaking, whenever an erotic element appears in the representations of human figures, the expression-less stiffness so prevalent in the sculptures of ancient India is replaced by a most sensitive awareness of tenderness and sensual truth.

The road to the temple at Konarak, about a mile and a half from the sea, passes through a long stretch of very flat land. One does not see the temple itself from any distance because its tall tower collapsed long ago. A short walk from the site is a convenient hostel and canteen for tourists. There, over a simple lunch of rice and fish, I met three other visitors – a young German, his wife and another German girl, all of them senior students. After lunch I walked out with the unmarried German girl to see the temple.

The great temple of the sun god Surya has now become one of the coffee-table wonders of the world, so I do not propose to describe its structure at any length. The buildings, which date from the reign of the local king Narasimha Devi I (A.D. 1238–64), about a century after the temples of Bhubaneswar and Puri, are enclosed in a flat, sunken rectangular area surrounded by walls upon which are the remains of towers. They consist of three main structures, all standing upon a platform of heavy flat stone. The platform represents the base of a vast chariot upon what were originally twenty-four stone wheels, each about nine feet in diameter. The whole thing is drawn along by seven horses and two stone elephants, represented as trampling upon enemy figures, evils of one kind or another. The structure at the southern end was the great tower which, at least until the year 1838, could be seen by ships at sea and was known as the black pagoda. The tower is supposed to have stood 120 feet above ground level, the tallest temple structure in Orissa and similar in form to the main buildings at Bhubaneswar and Puri, which belong to the same dynasty. Much of the tower has fallen for reasons unknown, and fragments of it are scattered about the walled enclosure. The undamaged condition of the fragments has suggested to some authorities that the tower was never fully completed and that the building process was frustrated by some event, or that the task itself presented insuperable difficulties. The other two structures on the platform consist of rectangular stone pavilions, the middle one much larger and taller than the front one. At the side of the larger building is a huge, expressionless image of Surya himself.

For centuries, down to the early years of the present century, the whole temple, apart from the tower, was embedded in sand from the dunes along the coast and covered in wild vegetation. It was then excavated and partly restored for permanent preservation. The temple is supposed to have taken sixteen years to build and involved the labour of thousands of people. It is a work of extraordinary artistic and engineering skill, quite apart from the almost superhuman task of cutting and transporting the stone for many miles.

The smaller structure is decorated with stone sculptures of dancing girls and musicians. I noticed that the instruments illustrating a wide range of copulatory postures and sexual happenings between men and women. There are also some figures of humans having intercourse with animals. The sculptures vary greatly in size, some being small, eroded and commonplace, others more than life-size. In many of the larger ones there is great anatomical charm, moods expressed in tiny movements of limbs and facial muscles – in, for instance, the stone lips and eyes of a young girl as she looks up into the face of a smiling bearded man whilst amusing him and herself with his erect penis. Most of the smaller figures are sadly eroded by centuries of weathering, but the variety of sexual excitement on show is as clear as ever it was.

For me the erotica at Konarak were as pleasurable as I suspect the artists intended them to be. It is known that these Hindu temples afforded gathering places for many popular festivities and happenings not immediately associated with religion, though I am in no position to make an accurate list of them. The large rectangular space containing the structures at Konarak could clearly have been filled by hundreds of people from time to time. Did such gatherings consist mainly of men, with only a few women present? Did children join the throng? Did women see the sculptures as freely as men? Was there any restriction of entry at all? Presumably untouchables were prohibited, but not inevitably and not during the whole seven centuries since the structures were built. It is possible that some authorities will have provided answers to such questions. They are important if one is to consider the effects, if any, of the erotica upon the sexual conduct of the people in the region. I get the impression that the rules of conduct for daughters were probably not conspicuously permissive, whatever the decorations upon the outer walls of the temples might have been. But is that impression correct? The notion that a girl is always somebody's daughter is quite an odd one in the mental scheme of most men. The female form, less or more clad, descends directly upon us from heaven without any parentage or other encumbrance. And our intentions towards such descending femininities is always to find some method of conducting them back to heaven again.

If we suppose, for the sake of argument, that the lives of Hindus at the periods of greatest usage of the erotically decorated temples were indeed much more permissive than before or since, how would certain consequences have been dealt with? Would there have been a good deal of infanticide? If so, would such infanticide have been largely confined to girls of the lowest social strata? Or was it quite general? Did the permissiveness take the form of relatively wide freedom of sexual intercourse between willing couples inspired by the sculptures and other art forms, or a great amount of prostitution, whether sanctioned by religious formulae or frowned upon?

A. L. Basham, in his *The Wonder That Was India*, suggests that the erotica at Konarak were possibly intended to advertise the services of temple prostitutes or dancers. If this was so it seems to me a bit unlikely that much in the way of sexual gratification could have occurred actually inside the dark and constricted spaces behind the walls, but somehow elsewhere in the temple premises. Moreover, all the erotica seem to be on the outer walls – none whatever inside. In his good but somewhat gushy book *Konarak: The Sun-Temple of Love*, Rustam J. Mehta suggests that the inside spaces of the temple are austere because only the ritual of *puja* took place there. The erotica on the outer walls were intended to stimulate sexual excitement in order to prompt devotees to seek their sexual pleasures *before* going inside for a purely spiritual experience, by which time they would be in a condition described by Vladimir Nabokov in a somewhat different context – 'light of loin and clear of head'. The evidence for this theory may well exist in a literary form surviving from the thirteenth century, but I do not know.

Basham writes that in ancient India girls and women were generally considered to be relatively more libidinous than men and that many of the rules and conventions of social life were designed to shield females from dangers implicit in their very nature. If women were indeed especially libidinous one reason could perhaps have been that the sexual impulses of their menfolk were often less strong than women desired them to be. The intensity of lust in men has surely much to do with their physical environment, including diet, climate, working conditions and innumerable other factors. I suspect that such conditions during much of the year in India were, and still are, somewhat inhibiting to male sexual desire. Between about mid-April and mid-October India is hot, often exceedingly hot. The atmosphere, too, is often very moisture-laden and life is made miserable by biting mosquitoes and sandflies, especially in the region of Konarak. If I happened to have been an Ooryan peasant in the fourteenth century A.D., a married man with a wife and an occasional girl friend somewhere near the temple, I suspect that there would have been nocturnal occasions when, streaming with sweat and pestered by mosquitoes, I should have presented a disappointing prospect to either or both of the women in my otherwise worthy manner of life. It is not inconceivable that, weather permitting, a leisurely visit to the temple could have restored a little of my *joie de vivre*. And, if they had any sense, both women would have approved. For all I know one or other, or even both, might have been pleased to join me in a stroll towards the temple.

To reach Puri from Konarak we had to drive back a long way towards Bhubaneswar to a junction with the main road to the south, so that the journey was much longer than the apparent distance on the map. Soon the top of the temple of Juggernaut at Puri could be seen, black and mysterious, rising above a distant horizon of palms. Always I felt an awareness of mystery about the tall, seemingly solid, windowless mass of a great Hindu temple, so utterly different in its emotional meaning from that of a mosque, a synagogue or a church. It is more than a little forbidding, and the two qualities, mystery and repulsion, are facets of each other. For entry into big temples is usually denied to all who are not clearly intent upon religious observance. Mere curiosity, however deferential or sincere, is often not welcomed. The edifice thus literally forbids, and is mysterious because it does so. Hinduism and Judaism are religions whose social history has predisposed their adherents to the preservation of an identity, not the dissemination of a faith. The world of Hindustan was thrown upon the defensive long ago by the fanaticism of Islam, and Judaism by the savagery and fanaticism of Romans and Christians.

For years past I had felt a longing to visit Puri, for it was from here that some of my father's happiest letters to me had been written. It was the scene of his best holidays in India, just as, in England, his happiest memories had been associated with stretches of sand and shining sea in Devon and Cornwall. He usually travelled to Puri by train, sometimes spending a night or two in Calcutta on the way, and somehow he managed to have with him three or four of the children of the servants at Chhaju Bagh, including the little girl Mohinia, and some of their parents. His bearer Ghulam always accompanied him. He and his retinue would occupy the circuit house for ten days at a stretch, the children making castles on the sand until my father, in his beach

gown and topee, appeared to take them down to the sea to teach
them to swim. Then he would demonstrate his own considerable
aquatic powers to an assembled group of children, fishermen and
servants who stood on the sand to wonder and admire.

The city of Puri today has a resident population of about
150,000 but at times of religious festivals, when the temple
attracts throngs of visitors and pilgrims, the population, I was
told, can rise to half a million. It is a place, therefore, of greatly
changing seasons. There is a wide main bazaar thoroughfare with
shops and booths, the temple standing in a narrow street near a
corner of it. We drove through the town to the edge of the coastal
suburb where the circuit house of the 1920s still stood, on a
low-lying stretch of ground which, at the time of its construction, must have been no more than two or three feet above the
sand. It was built of bricks covered with cement, with a little
stone and concrete, a two-storey building with two big rooms on
the upper floor at the back, and french windows opening to a
large flat roof. At the front was a small reception office and a
flight of concrete steps leading up to a balcony from which doors
provided entry to the two upper rooms. The front, facing away
from the sea, looked out on a short sand-blown roadway on
either side of which were boarding houses and a few private
residences. I doubt if any of the buildings existed before the war
and there was a seedy, melancholy look about them. In my
father's time the circuit house must have seemed wonderfully
isolated on the beach. About a hundred yards to the south stood a
white coast-guard station and flagpole and beyond that something of a maritime promenade, rather battered, with bigger
buildings, small hotels or boarding houses facing the sea.

Between the water and the dunes, at mid-tide, was a great
stretch of hard sand extending far into blue haze in both
directions, and here people walked in family groups. The visitors
were mostly from Calcutta or the hot, dusty towns of the plains
to the north. Compared to the Western world few Indians are
able to swim, their homes being far from available water. Many
will stand in the sea half clothed, lowering themselves into the
holy liquid for a few seconds, whilst children splash and play with
little boats.

Within an hour or two of my arrival at the circuit house, the
District and Sessions Judge, K. P. Acharya, arrrived to greet me

and to see that the manager was attending to me properly.
Acharya was a powerful, rather formidable-looking man in his
fifties. Owing to a bereavement – he had lost his mother a few
days earlier – he had had his head shaved and was bare-headed, his
scalp grizzled, his features strong and very dark. The poor man
was also on a restricted diet, part of the ritual of mourning, so
that, with my own loss of appetite, our mutual relationship was
not without *angst*. He told me he had arranged for me to join him
and some friends for dinner at the nearby Railway Hotel that
evening and would call back to fetch me a little later. He also said
that he had arranged for two of his court messengers to attend me
at all times, and they would sleep in the concrete passage outside
my room at night. He was clearly gratified when I showed my
appreciation. In India one does not decline such courtesies,
for courtesy is a repository of values deeply felt.

When Acharya came to fetch me he said there was too little
petrol in his car to take us even the few hundred yards along the
coast to the Railway Hotel. The shortage was due to the trouble
in Assam. He would therefore take me first to his home, where
we could wait for the arrival of his friends' car to take us all to the
hotel. The house was only a short walk, and I sat alone on a settee
in his living room for about twenty minutes until the other car
arrived. I mention this only because I was able to look briefly
round the room of a man of Acharya's considerable status in the
society of Orissa. In its domestic feel, this living room reminded
me of the home of S. N. Sinha, his colleague of Daltonganj in
Bihar, indicating very similar economic status. The furnishings
and objects about me resembled the contents of a council flat for
an artisan on the edge of a British industrial town. I suspect that
the life style of a district and sessions judge is now relatively more
impoverished than that of his British or Indian counterpart half a
century ago. The change is explained, I think, less by market
forces, the inflation of the Indian currency or any kind of financial
stringency than by the impact of egalitarian attitudes in the
Congress-dominated India of the past three and a half decades. I
do not believe it reflects any important change in the mutual
relations of castes in Hindu society but it has occurred despite the
continuing values of castes and status. I cannot say whether or not
public reverence for the rule of law and for the judiciary as a
whole has been affected,

Acharya and I were collected in the other car and taken to the hotel adjoining the beach where, on a white verandah, I was introduced to other members of the party. They included N. K. Dash, a visiting judge from the High Court at Cuttack, Dr G. C. Kar, a young psychiatrist at a mental hospital there, and Dr N. K. Patnaik, an oral surgeon at the Cancer Institute of the Medical College of Orissa. These men were clearly intelligent, but I found that only the High Court judge could speak more than half a dozen words of English. This seemed strange since the literature of their vocations is itself written largely in English. It was unavoidable, therefore, that nearly all the talk was between the other guests in Oorya and Hindi. The food was entirely European – some sea fish *meunière*, followed by stewed chicken in a dark brown gravy with potato and cauliflower. This was the best food available in Puri (food for Europeans, that is), but the chicken was so tough that I could hardly dissect it at all, and the vegetables were tepid and oily. An ice cream followed. I ate the fish with pleasure and struggled with the chicken, the potato and the north-west corner of the ice.

Acharya accompanied me back to the circuit house where, after thanking him for his kindness, I mentioned that I should like to stroll down to the edge of the sea for a few moments before going to bed. I was glad to see that he appreciated so odd a wish. He at once summoned one of his messengers from the balcony outside my room and the man came down the concrete steps fastening his scarlet band about his body and the brass catch of his belt inscribed 'District Court'. Acharya ordered him to accompany me across the sand to the water's edge.

To reach the beach the man led me along the sandy roadway to the coastguard station and turned left into the soft sand, now cool, across which we walked. We had moved only a few yards when he cautioned me with gestures to be careful where I put my feet, and the reason for caution became clear. Like the wide, beautiful maidan at Patna, the stretch of dry sand above tide level at Puri is used by people in the city as a latrine, especially at night. As we moved further the stench of excrement became stronger and, after a little, I saw a dead dog, part covered by sand, the more powerful stink of the corpse now dominant, fading away as we reached the clean wet sand below.

I thrust back physical revulsion and gazed into the black,

unseen mass of the sea, listened to the crash of invisible breakers a hundred yards beyond.

I decided to seek no engagements on the following day. At Puri, virtually the last place for me to discover on this visit to India, I would ask no more questions, attempt to grasp no answers. I would swim in the sea, sit on the flat roof of the circuit house and write up my diary, walk along the sand, lie on a towel in sunglasses, read an Indian novel, explore the bazaar for bookshops, watch crowds at the temple and take a few photographs on the shore.

It is now 1000 hrs. I have been writing at a small table on the flat roof. This is the same room that my father used – the scene very little changed. Sitting in the blazing sun, which is now too hot for me. I shall lie on the bed for a while . . .

1230 hrs. I had an arrangement to swim at 1100 hrs and the two messengers were to accompany me to the sea, mainly to look after my things. They did not turn up – presumably they had duties at the court – so I went down to the desk dressed in swimming trunks and dressing gown, with a towel, and made it clear to a servant that I intended to swim. He understood and accompanied me down to the sand by a track through the casuarinas. Awful stink, lumps and sloshes of excrement all the way, then clear wet sand and lovely sea – long, low waves, warm, glistening. Swam for about fifteen minutes. Many people on the beach – a few men swimming, but no women. I am back in the circuit house – have had a shower and sit in the room by the open french window leading to the dazzling roof. A small breeze from the sand fills my room with the stink of excrement. Oh India! They cannot deal with their own filth, the filth of their own numbers.

For lunch I must eat 'omelette'. I know what it will be like – soggy, oily, oniony and half cold, with *sweet* bread. I cannot enjoy circuit house food – almost always prepared by low officials with no interest in the products of their labours. I asked if I could have some tea, hoping for a pot, but after a long interval was handed a cup half filled with lukewarm, purplish tea from a flask, saturated with sugar.

For some reason, perhaps a change in the direction of the breeze, the stink has now gone. All I can hear is the sound of the waves. Between the branches of the casuarinas I can see fishing boats with dark sails cruising down the coast, perhaps a quarter of a mile off shore. I am told that I can have no fish this evening because of some religious festival. It seems that most festivities in India imply self-deprivation of one kind or another. Mourning means fasting. The subjectivism of self-denial is usually boring to me. I go without food sometimes – especially in India – as a form of therapy, but never as a mystery. It seems to me that fasting does *not* enhance the power of consciousness unless the digestive apparatus requires rest for therapeutic reasons. It could well be that the spiced food eaten daily by Indians imposes such strains upon their metabolism that their many fasts indeed have a therapeutic value. Certainly much of the excrement on this beach is in a liquid form. Somewhere near the beach there is now a gabbling loudspeaker – blaring incessantly, probably a stream of political clichés and abuse of this or that enemy figure. That is what it sounds like, but it might be some kind of religious exhortation.

1315 hrs. Omelette as expected. I forced myself to eat half of it, followed by curd flavoured with some kind of seed, cardomom perhaps, a banana and some water to drink. I sit down again to this diary, to the beauty of the sea beyond the casuarinas and the warm air now stinking again. If this were a scene in any part of Europe, America or Japan, human power would have conquered. I wonder. I shall not in future deride the suburban values of coastal sanitation. Is India hopeless? Can there be only epidemics, death, failure and renewal in endless sequences? Maurya, Gupta, Konarak, each towering above its own filth. Nobody will look at India from her own standpoint. And that standpoint will not stand. This is the land of purity. But it is the purity of caste, and caste is crumbling.

If I were a young Indian I think I should wish to attach myself to some movement to revive something of the spirit of the early Congress – *outward*-looking modernism – and it would have to engage in anti-Sanskritic acts, deliberate breaches of caste, breaches of religious taboos, a deliberate study of English or any other globally spoken language, a powerful advocacy of more and more pragmatic education, and the participation in politics of people who could resist both bribery and violence.

To omit references to the stink would be to deceive readers, Indian and Western. But to include them without reflection would be to seem unreflective. The foreigner in India is exposed to powerful sensory impressions, some so repellent as to deprive him of the disposition to reflect at all.

In the tropical world of rural peasantry and fishermen, human beings commonly defecate on the land beyond their villages, or on the coast. The excrement is rapidly destroyed by insects, rain, the waves and tides of the sea. Such simplicity is accepted, as old as mankind, provided the density of population or other circumstances do not cause a problem of tolerance. The levels of tolerance at any time are those to which people have been obliged to accustom themselves.

In India a very high level of tolerance in the country as a whole is sustained, I believe, by three main factors. First, although the areas of open land immediately beyond villages (however large) are vast, the *urban* populations are enormous and within all township areas the cost of constructing latrines for all the people who would use them is far beyond the available resources, even if none were embezzled. People cannot escape the towns merely to avoid the proximity of stink. They are forced, therefore, to tolerate it. Second, the caste system has the effect of forcing millions of the scheduled castes, otherwise 'untouchables', to endure a much higher concentration of stink than the rest of society, thus confining it largely to a particular social level. Third, in all parts of India there are places of pilgrimage, such as Puri, which attract huge numbers of people for several days at a stretch, during which normally tolerated levels of endurance are exceeded. Such excess is only possible because, as Mahapatra could have pointed out, the people attach more importance to religious observance than to what goes on in their nostrils. In the time of Chaucer the same was perhaps true of pilgrims to Canterbury, and it is not irrelevant that insects in northern Europe are less serviceable than those of the tropical world. Some day, perhaps, much of the city of Puri will be transformed into a concreted system of resounding latrines. As for public sanitation in general, India puts me in mind of a tombstone in a corner of an English churchyard upon which are inscribed only the name of a woman buried long ago and the epitaph: 'She hath done what she could.'

The Way Back

The train for Jamshedpur was not due to leave Puri till 11 a.m. next day. After breakfast I did my packing and went down to the beach accompanied by one of the court *chaprassis* for a last swim in wonderful early sunshine. Few people were on the beach at that hour and sunlight from across the bay was sweetly clear. Eventually, after my swim, two cars arrived at the circuit house to deal with my departure, with Acharya himself, another magistrate and at least four other individuals, uniformed and haphazard, each handling some item of my moderate impedimenta. With smiles and handshakes for everybody I stepped into my compartment and the train pulled out at about midday, with a dragging journey of many hours ahead. I was on my way home. In a few seconds the blue sea vanished, left behind like love herself.

The train, like all the others except the Rajdahni Express from Bombay to Delhi, was old and rough, but clean at least at the start of the journey – though the dust gathered rapidly as we rumbled over embankments above the paddy fields of the coastal plain. It was a Sunday and I was told that no meals would be available until about 7.30 that evening, after leaving Kharagpur in Bengal. I felt sleepy and empty all day, though I did manage to buy some tea and bananas at Balasore, a large town whose lovely name, I fear, rhymes with the roar of the presiding fauna or divinity and not with the Italian *Salvadore* or even *trovatore*.

During most of the journey I had three companions. I occupied a right-facing corner seat. On my left, very close to me, was a thick-set man of about forty who sat cross-legged on the seat wearing a singlet and a striped sheetlike garment round his waist. His plump brown arms, strong face, excellent teeth, glossy hair of medium length, thick neck and torso all seemed to ripple with health. He was perhaps the owner of a garage, warehouse or cinema in Calcutta. He had a very loud voice, emphatic manner and great flow of words, raucous to a keen listener like myself with little notion of what he was on about except the broad drift when he spoke English. He went on for hour after hour with enormous, enviable vigour.

Opposite me in the corner, also sitting cross-legged (Indians seldom sit in trains with their feet on the floor like Europeans), was a lean man, a little older, a curiously flashy individual, but strong-looking. He had angular, pointed features and a recently shaved head (perhaps following a bereavement), thin lips, a very sensual face. His flashiness was expressed in his clothing and various oddments – much gold in his teeth, a glistening new watch and metal strap, at least four rings on his fingers with large stones. He wore a very clean white shirt and a brightly coloured cloth round his middle and legs, full of scarlet, gold and yellow stripes. I could envisage him as a theatrical *éminence* or perhaps the lord of a dozen brothels, the proprietor of a chain of jewellery shops on Chowringhee and probably homosexual. He spoke little but listened closely, without evident fatigue, to the vigorous bawling of my neighbour.

My third companion was a heavily built, egg-shaped figure in his early sixties, a balding, oval head, sallow face, droopy moustache and widening abdomen, feet on the floor in shoes and socks which looked appallingly hot for any man, whatever his shape. He wore an open-necked shirt, thin grey jacket and dark trousers with a belt, a conventional figure of retired officialdom. He spoke with the others in a thick-sounding English not easy for me to follow, though his gestures were curiously expressive. He was clearly a dominant personality, accustomed to arresting the attention of others at social gatherings, using rhetorical gestures and timely pauses, turning his palms outwards to demonstrate emptiness or totality, negatives or bland affirmatives, using facial expressions and finger-pointings in a wonderful emphasis of every nuance. As he spoke the virtuoso on his left would look sideways at him slyly, wagging his head in affirmation, flashing his rings, flicking his coloured skirt or *lungi*. If, as a trio, these men were to be reassembled and put down anywhere in the Western world, their cultural isolation would silence them. Their mannerisms, modes of self-expression, belong exclusively to India. Such expressiveness can seem irritating to Westerners because it appears somehow to indicate unclarity of thought, an undrilled profusion of impulse, like the ornamentation on the façade of one of their own temples.

The talk of all three hovered between a smattered English *lingua franca* and Bengali. I think my neighbour and the virtuoso were Bengalis and the oval man a Bihari whose own language was Hindi. Listening a little I gathered that the older man was probably a retired senior police officer or civil servant in the Home Department at Patna. Much of the conversation was about crime, dacoities, burglaries and thefts of ingenuity – about busloads of people on country roads being relieved of their possessions which reappeared on the stalls of local markets. This concern with problems of law and order I had seen reflected repeatedly in the local press. My neighbour was all for drastic punishments, the egg-shaped man told most of the stories, shrugging his unshruggable shoulders sadly and moving his moustache from side to side. The man with the gold teeth uttered clucks of distress but suggested no audible remedies.

As the train ground its way slowly across the long bridge over the Mahanadi river at Cuttack I thought of the old circuit house there, of my father's letters, of the spot on the river bank from which I had seen the bridge, the long barrage and weir and, just there somewhere, Mahapatra's house in the late afternoon sun, where he would perhaps be sitting in his basket chair, dozing a little, his newspaper on his knees. The train slid away to an embankment, the vanished scene leaving me with the still images of memory.

Shortly after leaving Kharagpur in darkness trays of food under sheet metal covers were brought along by ununiformed stewards. As in Britain and elsewhere, one of the manifestations of 'alienation' is the abandonment of uniforms by persons performing services – postmen, stewards, conductors, drivers, etc., though others engaged in basically authoritarian pursuits such as policemen and soldiers wear uniforms with more or less demonstrative minority consciousness.

From my diary:

At last – Jamshedpur, about 10 p.m. by which time my companions were all stretched out asleep, the oval and the stout above, the impresario down below, and I left them quietly. On the platform, badly lit and very noisy, I could hear my own name being announced over the loudspeaker. I was being asked to report to some office, but could not distinguish which. However, I saw a notice – 'Inquiries' – and advanced to a grille below, caught the eye of the clerk and announced myself. I was asked to go to the railway police office and there, only a few yards away, I found Mr S. Misra, Registrar of the Civil Courts, Baripada, whom the Chief Justice at Cuttack had instructed to deal with me. Misra, a slender, intelligent-looking man in his late forties, was accompanied by Mr Bhattacharya, a stout man from the public relations office of the Tata company – indeed, he was in charge of it – and, a third man whose name I did not catch, a legal colleague of Misra of the judicature at Baripada. They took me by car at once to the special guest house of the company, a drive of about ten kilometres. Here I found myself in a well-appointed hostel – the atmosphere rather like that of an officers' mess in peacetime – for use by members of the firm from all over India, guests, and other visitors on business. I was ushered into a comfortable room with a tiled modern, bathroom, good fans, flowing hot water, telephone, writing desk – as in a decent hotel. A steward asked courteously if he could bring me anything to eat, so I asked for some soup, bread and butter and hot milk, all of which I found when I got out of the bath. Thus administered, I slept.

Next morning, by appointment, I went to Bhattacharya's office – a short walk – on the first floor of the big new building that was the headquarters of the company. Here I found a group of men, some visitors like myself, others young departmental officers of the firm. Bhattacharya himself sat at a large desk, the others, including myself, in chairs facing him. The central chair opposite Bhattacharya had been left vacant for me and he waved me towards it as I entered the room. I got the impression that he had assumed, from whatever he had gathered about me from the Chief Justice at Cuttack, that I intended to conduct an inquiry into the operations of the Tata company, as though I were some authority from, say, the Massachusetts Institute of Technology or possibly the Department of Trade in London. The gathering had apparently been assembled to deal with the searching questions that I was expected to raise, covering anything between the technology of fibrous materials and the minutiae of wage differentials. My momentary condition as a VIP was not something anybody intended to question.

After a brief exchange of greetings and bowings I felt that I must properly establish an identity for myself, which I did. I said that, whilst most grateful for the kindness of the Tata management, I was in no position to trouble the company with any technical questions, though I was much aware of its great importance in the industrial development of India, both in the past, in the history of the railways, and now in heavy motor transport, and in innumerable other fields. I should be very happy simply to be treated as an ordinary tourist and to receive any literature which they might allow me to see. I think there was general relief. After a little discussion Bhattacharya invited me to join him in his car on a brief visit to the plant where they assemble lorries, and I watched the assembly line from the early stages to the end, when the vehicles (that is, chassis, cabs and engines) are driven off, all painted a shining yellow like splendid toys. Then he took me out to the testing ground, consisting of an oval, steeply cambered concrete trackway where we watched the testing of one of the vehicles by a dashing Sikh. Bhattacharya told me how the buses and lorries of Tata could be seen all over India, the Middle East and South-East Asia.

The industrial estate, extending for miles, includes impressive-looking welfare facilities of many kinds, as well as vast areas of housing and flats. People were everywhere, the ordinary people of India who, in costume, style and manner, differ little from those in the streets of towns I had seen elsewhere, except that they are even younger and the extremes of age, weakness and beggary are hardly visible at all. There is about their faces the look of people whose lives are more secure, more fortunate, than those of others in an environment less massively afforded to them. In the vast land beyond, whence they have come, each from some tiny part over the horizon, power remains that of the eternal cosmos. In Tatanagar power is that of man's decision, unseen, unknown, built and done about the workforce. Reflecting on this in retrospect I feel that a valuable study might be undertaken to try to discover how the new industrial world of Tatanagar may have affected the meanings of religious symbolism in the minds of those who live and work there. Can Siva, Durga, Parvati, Kali, Hanuman, Ganesh mean to these people what they still mean to fisherfolk in their huts upon sand during the storms of the monsoon, or to distant villagers in the plains of Bihar and Bengal?

When we got back to Bhattacharya's office we found a demonstration going on. Outside the main gates of the factory area, about eighty yards away, a crowd of several dozen men, mostly very young, were shouting slogans and raising their fists in the communist style. Bhattacharya said they were a group of casual workers who were demanding recognition of a trade union. It would not be wise to open the gates to allow anybody to pass out or in, so I found myself immobilised on the asphalted area for about forty minutes. I noticed that the yelping of the same few words and the raising of arms in vaguely threatening gestures was orchestrated by three agitators who were obviously themselves not casual workers – their hair styles, spectacles, jackets, all their movements, suggested that they were 'students', members of higher castes, activists doing their best to 'alienate' the 'working class' from the 'system'. There were two or three policemen and various officials of the firm standing about like myself in the area before the buildings, but nobody took any notice of the demonstrators who melted away eventually as throats became sore and other engagements more pressing.

As soon as the affair had subsided the gates were opened and Bhattacharya drove me back to the guest house and left me there for the lunch break. I felt most grateful to him and to the firm. He is one of those valuable personalities who, after a lifetime in the service of a great concern, is re-employed after retirement to assume responsibility for dealing with the public at large.

It had been arranged that Misra and his companions would collect me at four o'clock to take me sightseeing before seeing me off on the evening train to Bombay. I had time, therefore, for a pleasantly sociable curry lunch, a rest afterwards and the task of packing. On the drive they took me round the fine suburban area of Tatanagar, a bit reminiscent of New Delhi, but on more undulating land. We drove through Jubilee Park at dusk when there was a view of the distant hills of the Santal Parganas, dark grey against the reddening sky, their outline reflected on the surface of a lake. In another direction, also silhouetted against the sky, could be seen the angled shapes and vertical thrust of chimneys from which smoke never ceased to swell in blackening curves. Over the entire region, but especially the bazaar, hung the dense smog, now augmented by hundreds of charcoal and kerosene cooking fires in the streets and alleys of the city and by the wicks of dim lanterns. The smog blackens the mucus of nose and throat and smarts a little in the eyes. I was conscious of a good deal of coughing, especially during a period when I walked in the bazaar in search of bookshops. I wondered what life must be like in Jamshedpur during the hottest months, between mid-April and mid-June.

The superiority of the amenities of urban life in those parts of the city of Jamshedpur that are administered by the Tata company over those of most other towns in India must, I think, have two main causes. The first is sheer efficiency. The second must be the superiority of the financial resources available for investment by the company for the benefit of the people – derived, in one way or another, from the company's sales. The resources for such investment must be vastly greater than those of most municipal authorities responsible for populations of comparable size.

The reader who has followed me so far may have noticed that, whilst I have sometimes been critical of conditions in India, I have generally avoided attempting to prescribe remedies. I know that all government is vastly more difficult than most people realise. The more ignorant people are, the stronger their convictions, indignations and protests. From a standpoint of ignorant non-responsibility, but with some humility, I now make a few suggestions about the philosophy of town government in those towns of India, mostly in Bihar, that I have actually seen. For the sake of public health, greater industrial efficiency and in order to improve conditions for the lowest social orders in the towns, I suggest that the two main factors implied by the Tata company's achievement in Jamshedpur should be applied over a long period of years to other towns. Over, say, a thirty-year stretch, the levels of grants in aid from state or federal resources to municipal authorities for improved sanitation should be increased considerably. This should not be done without a corresponding reduction in other public expenditure, in order to avoid inflating the currency. Perhaps it would be wise to reduce public expenditure in public sector economic development in fields open to private enterprise. Such a policy, whatever the period of its application, could be not only a check on inflation of the money supply, but have the valuable effect of preparing the towns to receive more industrial workers in the remoter future and contributing usefully to the efficiency and welfare of the urban population *then*. Second, even if elective principles are not abandoned in municipal government, there seems to be scope for more authoritarian, directly administered township government, in the light of the experience of the Tata company itself.

When I mentioned such notions tentatively to a highly intelligent man from Bihar whom I met in London recently, he said wanly: 'But we already have a grant-in-aid system in Bihar. The trouble is that most of the money just goes in bribery.' He seemed entirely without hope.

We reached the station shortly before 6 p.m. From my diary:

. . . There followed about half an hour of anxiety about a reservation for me on the Bombay train. In a crowded office on the platform I was told by a senior-looking official that I would be allowed to travel second class but be given a first class berth should any such berth be vacated at any stage of the journey. We moved to the platform itself just near the two first-class coaches, where stood a large crowd of other passengers, all uncertain whether or not they would be allotted seats. We joined the crowd which swarmed round a group of officials with sheets of paper in their hands containing long lists of names. After a long, anxious wait I heard my own name called. Yes, I had been granted a first-class seat.

The train left in darkness – a small, very dirty compartment with three other men – cramped, gritty, dusty. In this grubby cell I was to spend two nights and a day, and it was, I think, the most unpleasant railway journey I ever experienced. At night I could lie at full length on a dusty seat of synthetic textile upholstery, sprung and not uncomfortable. But as the night went on the air became cold and very draughty. I had no blanket or pillow. I made a pillow of a towel, a dirty shirt and a pair of pyjama trousers, and put my feet into an old pullover. Every few hours I went to the lavatory. It was dark green and smothered in dust, the basin extremely grimy and the push-tap yielding only a few drops of water. Food was served at very long intervals after the train had halted at main stations, and one could choose 'western', 'vegetarian' and 'non-vegetarian' food. I had two 'western' meals. The first consisted of two greasy minced vegetable 'cutlets', stodgy and peppery, with chopped beans, cauliflower and potato, all cooked somehow in a repulsive oil, with some square portions of sweetish bread – the whole business so unappetising that I could eat only a few mouthfuls. The other 'western' meal consisted of a greasy omelette with sweet bread and water to drink – also a cup of hot soup. The soup was acceptable and I forced myself to eat a little of the omelette. I noticed that the Indian food taken by my companions was the usual tepid rice, watery dahl and curried cauliflower that I knew so well. It produced no evident satisfaction in the features of the consumers. I had brought a few bananas from Jamshedpur and these were most helpful. My fellow travellers were middle-class men who all had blankets and pillows. I suppose I had always been too preoccupied by thoughts about India to give attention to such amenities.

During most of the daylight hours on 25 November I gazed at the landscape of the Deccan with deep interest. In India it is the immensity of the rural scene that moves me most. Why is this? The people so clearly belong to and emerge from the land, and people acting within a physical environment that they accept as their own always have an aspect that appeals to the heart, however alien the heart. The Deccan, a vast undulating tableland of red soil, rocky ridges of hills burning in the sun, contains millions of small fields cultivated with millet, rice, pulses and many minor crops. Occasionally there is a sandy river bed and a little water – sometimes a larger river. Deeper bunds between the fields are built here than in the northern plain because the land undulates and the levels of rice must be flat. I saw several large industrial areas with new metal chimneys heaving smoke into the sky.

In the afternoon a large Hindu in a dhoti entered the compartment – garrulous, pan-chewing with heavily stained teeth and lips, untidy, sixtyish. His features were big, handsome and fleshy, with a loose mouth. He wore a big fawn overcoat which must, thirty years before, have belonged to some British officer. It lacked two buttons and was pinned together with a safety pin. Ball-point pens projected from an upper pocket, old newspapers bulged from a lower one. He sat down opposite to me, gazed fixedly at my face and began to question me, chewing pan loosely and disgustingly. In a few seconds his identity emerged – an old political leftist, probably professional. The vast woolly arguments of the kind I had embraced in my early twenties were now thrust again upon me by this pathetic figure, *homo politicus indiensis*, far too talkative and foolish to be importantly corrupt. He was an elected member of the legislative assembly of Maharashtra, on his way to some committee meeting in Bombay. I carefully avoided asking him to which party he belonged, or his name. His appearance and manner of speech seemed to caricature the rank-and-file politician of any state legislature as such figures had often been outlined to me, and as my father had described them over forty years ago. For such a broken-down actor of a man the main business of living for several decades had obviously consisted of interminable intrigue, arranging for factions at local meetings to ensure that this or that resolution should be opposed, supported or amended, this or that strike or go slow or protest be supported or opposed, this or that person be supported or opposed as a candidate for this or that post – in short, the faded activist of unshakeable views and cliché-ridden harangues. He asked me what I thought of a particular British hero of his, Bernard Shaw, and was evidently disturbed when I mentioned that the hero had actually died some time back. As time went on I began to feel sorry for this old victim of the world's delusions. He would, poor man, die in a dark corner, as he had lived, his battered pan-box dropping into a muddy alley of Bombay. Dostoievsky had known him elsewhere.

After listening for a considerable time I told him that I did not wish to argue with him about politics. Some silence ensued, and he later shifted his ground to more general philosophical themes in which I found myself in broad agreement with him – a tottering rationalism clearly derived from Europe, reading plays by Bernard Shaw in a village in India in his youth. He had been a schoolmaster for a few years but had had no other experience or responsibility apart from the politics of following more sophisticated leaders and paymasters.

I had been a bit worried about the prospect of arriving in

Bombay in the early morning (about 6.30) without any assurance as to whether Ananda would be in his flat. It would be helpful if I could telephone him, but I did not know his home telephone number and could only vaguely identify his block of flats in the Pédder Road, not far from Malabar Hill. I mentioned all this to an educated man sitting next to me and asked if he would perhaps be so kind as to assist me with the telephone at the station in Bombay. He said he would have left the train by then and referred my question to the old politician. The latter eagerly insisted on helping me, requesting me to accompany him to the special hostel for members of the legislature. I was grateful and accepted his invitation. At Bombay, therefore I followed him and a porter to an area outside the station where people were supposed to queue for taxis. There was no such queue, however, but a disorderly hailing of taxis by would-be passengers and an arrogant determination by taxi drivers to accept clients only of their own choice. I was dishevelled and smothered in dust and my companion, with his filthy coat and dhoti, red-stained mouth and biscuit crumbs clinging to wet areas of his face, held out no very obvious prospect of being a good fare. He stood at my side holding a very shabby suitcase, trying to appear unconcerned when taxi drivers swept past him to pick up more prosperous-looking clients. It seemed to me unlikely that we should manage to get a taxi at all. I was about to seize my baggage and walk away when a policeman stopped a taxi and sternly ordered the driver to transport the pair of us to whatever destination we chose.

We went at once to the hostel, a biggish new building in the middle of the most prestigious part of the city, near the new parliament. Here we took a lift to the second floor and walked along a passage, a bearer carrying our things, to a numbered room. Inside were two beds, a fan overhead and an adjoining washroom. Two young men were lying on mattresses on the floor. When the politician opened the door and entered, the prostrate figures rose to greet him and two or three other youths, evidently students, also appeared. All were clearly followers of the great man. He at once sat down on one of the beds, cross-legged, and a long period of talk ensued – presumably political gossip. I was invited to lie down on the other bed but declined and sat on the edge of it (it was unmade and evidently much used) waiting for a moment in which to seek the help I wanted with the telephone. For at least half an hour, however, I was completely ignored.

Eventually there was a pause and I asked very quietly if it would perhaps be possible to find Ananda's telephone number in a directory. The politician, startled by the reminder of my existence, ordered one of the acolytes to assist me, and the young man sprang forward. Unfortunately Ananda's number could not be found – it happened to be that of his late father, whose name was spelt in a slightly different way, a fact of which I was not then aware. I decided simply to get a taxi, go to Pedder Road and look for the block, which I should probably recognise once I reached the neighbourhood. I shook hands with my host and was graciously helped by the young man to get a taxi. I found the flat easily and was much relieved to find Ananda and his wife at home. Nita ushered me into my old room.

After breakfast, instead of going to my room to sleep, I joined my hosts in the car on their daily drive to work. We dropped Nita at the airline headquarters where she works and went to Ananda's office more deeply in the old town. I went out into the streets whilst he attended to my air passage.

In Bombay at last, after the long, grim rail journey from the other side of India, I felt an excitement reminiscent of a wartime leave. The small events of my last two days there are remembered not as belonging to the continuum of the visit to India, but to an afterglow. They took me to lunch on the 28th at the Ambassadors, a fine velvety restaurant with red lights, where I was given lobster Thermidor that had been especially ordered the day before. Late that afternoon I walked in the gardens on the Malabar Hill and took some colour transparencies of the bay. Sitting on a bench with one of my Indian novels I was able, with one eye, to watch young adults, students, sitting or reclining on the grass. This was the only place in India where I saw the smallest overt expression of affection between young men and women.

On my way back to the flat a poor man spoke to me in English, asking if I could tell him the address of The Society of Friends in Bombay. I said I was a stranger in the city and suggested that he might look at a telephone directory. He kept close to me, however, and went on to describe how he had arrived from Delhi a few days before. He said he had been working as a driver for some Christian organisation whose name I do not recall. His immediate employer had returned to Europe and paid him off. He was now penniless. I suggested that he might try to find any one of the various Christian organisations in the city, for all would probably know the address of the Quaker organisation. He asked pitifully if I knew of any master who wanted a driver, and all I could do was to give him a few coins. How easily we forget, after a good lunch in such a country as India, that beneath the feet of all its people there is darkness.

Index

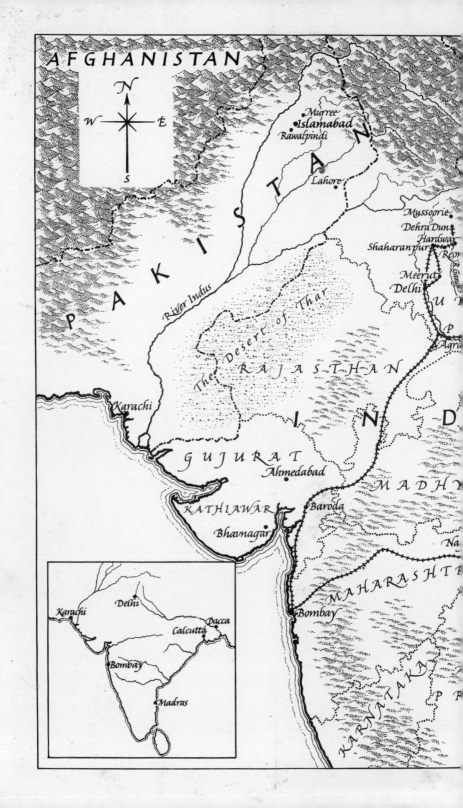